BUMPER BOOK OF
Sewing

BUMPER BOOK OF
Sewing

LONDON, NEW YORK, MELBOURNE,
MUNICH, DELHI

Designers Alison Gardner, Alison Shackleton
Project Editor Elizabeth Yeates
Producer, Pre-Production Andy Hilliard
Senior Producer Charlotte Oliver
Special Sales Creative Project Manager
Alison Donovan

First published in Great Britain in 2014
by Dorling Kindersley Limited,
80 Strand, London WC2R 0RL

Material in this publication preiviously published in:
The Sewing Book (2009), Sew Step by Step (2011),
Dressmaking (2012), and A Little Course in Sewing (2013)

A Penguin Random House Company

Copyright © 2013, 2014 Dorling Kindersley Limited

2 4 6 8 10 9 7 5 3 1
001 – 278248 – Oct/2014

A CIP catalogue record for this book
is available from the British Library.

ISBN 978-0-2411-8504-9

Printed and bound in China by
Hung Hing Printing Co. Ltd

Discover more at
www.dk.com/crafts

Contents

Introduction

If you are new to sewing and eager to master the key techniques, the *Bumper Book of Sewing* is the book for you. These clearly laid out pages cover the essential tools and equipment, plus the basic techniques to help you make and restyle simple soft furnishings, clothes, and accessories.

Starting with equipment and haberdashery and moving on through fabrics to the many techniques, the *Bumper book of Sewing* demonstrates all the basic stitches, shows you how to master seams, hems, and edges, teaches you easy ways to add shape to clothing, with gathers, darts, and waistlines, and how to finish your work with buttons, pockets, fasteners, and appliqué stitches.

This book will encourage you to enjoy this satisfying hobby, and inspire you to create beautiful things – for yourself, your family and friends., and your home. Why not use your sewing skills to create a wonderful personal gift?

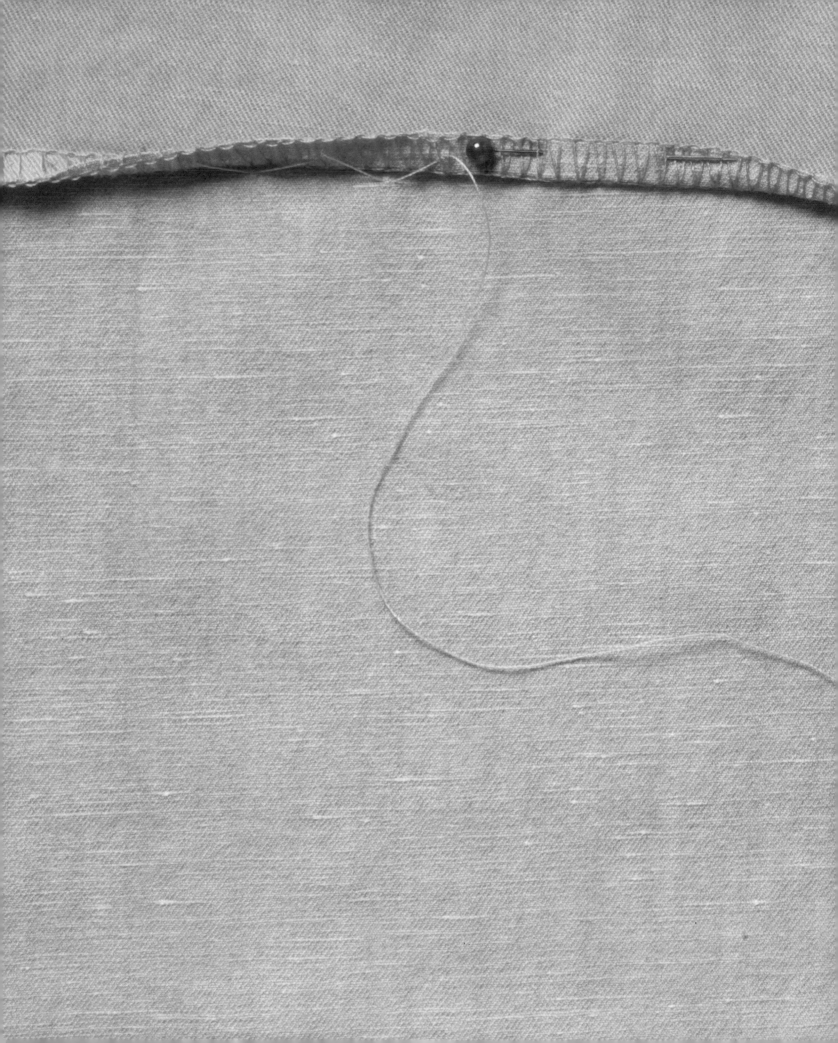

Tools and equipment

Basic sewing kit

A well-equipped sewing kit will include all of the items shown below and many more, depending on the type of sewing that you do regularly. It is important that a suitable container is used to keep your tools together, so that they will be readily to hand, and to keep them tidy.

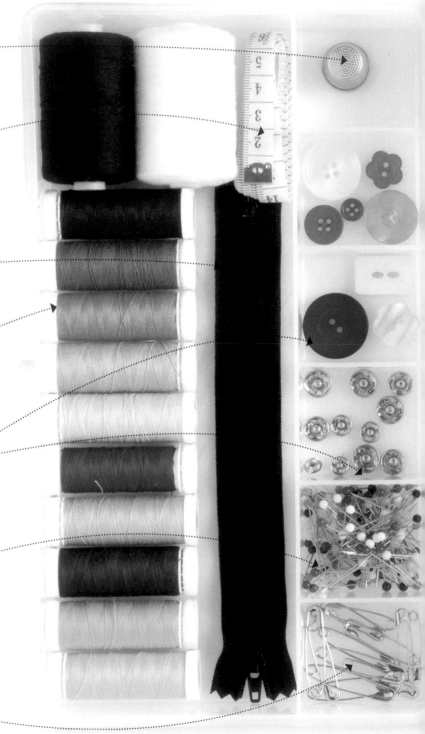

Thimble
This is useful to protect the end of your finger when hand sewing. Thimbles are available in various shapes and sizes. **See page 16.**

Tape measure
Essential, not only to take body measurements, but also to help measure fabric, seams, etc. Choose one that gives both metric and imperial. A tape made of plastic is best as it will not stretch. **See page 14.**

Zips
It is always a good idea to keep a couple of zips in your sewing kit. Black, cream, and navy are the most useful colours.

Threads
A selection of threads for hand sewing and machine/overlocker sewing in a variety of colours. Some threads are made of polyester, while others are cotton or rayon. **See pages 20–21.**

Haberdashery
All the odds and ends a sewer needs, including everything from buttons and snaps to trimmings and elastic. A selection of buttons and snaps in your basic kit is useful for a quick repair. **See pages 22–23.**

Pins
Needed by every sewer to hold the fabric together prior to sewing it permanently. There are different types of pins for different types of work. **See page 19.**

Safety pins
In a variety of sizes and useful for emergency repairs as well as threading elastics. **See page 19.**

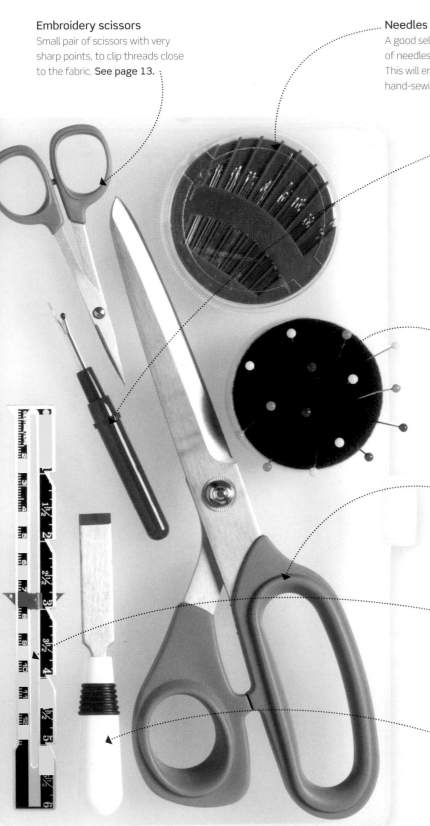

Embroidery scissors
Small pair of scissors with very sharp points, to clip threads close to the fabric. **See page 13.**

Needles
A good selection of different types of needles for sewing by hand. This will enable you to tackle any hand-sewing project. **See page 18.**

Seam ripper
Also called a stitch ripper, to remove any stitches that have been sewn in the wrong place. Various sizes of seam rippers are available. Keep the cover on when not in use to protect the sharp point. **See page 12.**

Pin cushion
To keep your needles and pins safe and clean. Choose one that has a fabric cover and is firm. **See page 19.**

Cutting shears
Required for cutting fabric. When buying, select a pair that feels comfortable in your hand and that is not too heavy. **See page 13.**

Sewing gauge
A handy gadget for small measurements. The slide can be set to measure hem depths, buttonhole diameters, and much more. **See page 14.**

Buttonhole chisel
An exceedingly sharp mini-chisel that gives a clean cut through machine buttonholes. Place a cutting mat underneath when using this tool, or you might damage the blade. **See page 12.**

Cutting tools

There are many types of cutting tools, but one rule applies to all: buy good-quality products that can be re-sharpened. When choosing cutting shears, make sure that they fit the span of your hand – this means that you can comfortably open the whole of the blade with one action, which is very important to allow clean and accurate cutting lines. Shears and scissors of various types are not the only cutting tools that are required, as everyone will at some time need a seam ripper to remove misplaced stitches or to unpick seams for mending. Rotary cutters that are used in conjunction with a special cutting mat and ruler are invaluable for cutting multiple straight edges

Snips ▶

A very useful, small, spring-loaded tool that easily cuts the ends of thread. Not suitable for fabrics.

▼ Rotary cutter

Available with different sizes of retractable blades. It must be used in conjunction with a special cutting mat to protect the blade and cutting surface.

▼ Buttonhole chisel

A smaller version of a carpenter's chisel, to cut cleanly and accurately through buttonholes. As this is so sharp it must be used with a self-healing cutting mat.

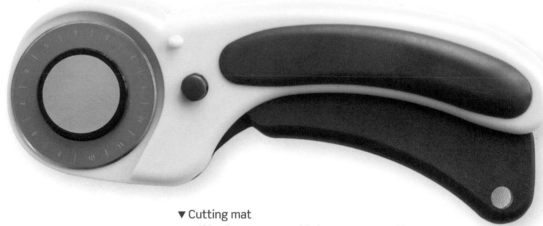

▼ Cutting mat

A self-healing mat to use with the rotary cutter. This mat can also be used under the buttonhole chisel.

◀ Seam ripper

A sharp, pointed hook to slide under a stitch, with a small cutting blade at the base to cut the thread. Various sizes of seam ripper are available, to cut through light to heavyweight fabric seams.

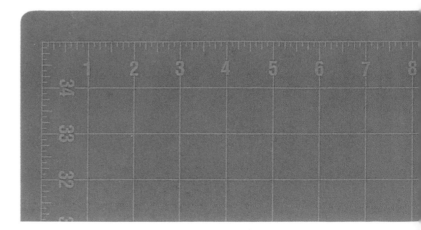

◄ Bent-handled shears
This type of shear has a blade that can sit flat against the table when cutting out, due to the angle between the blade and handle. Popular for cutting long, straight edges.

Pinking shears ►
Similar in size to cutting shears but with a blade that cuts with a zigzag pattern. Used for neatening seams and decorative edges.

▼ Cutting shears
The most popular type of shear, used for cutting large pieces of fabric. The length of the blade can vary from 20–30cm (8–12in) in length.

▼ Embroidery scissors
A small and very sharp scissor used to get into corners and clip threads close to the fabric.

▲ Trimming Scissors
These scissors have a 10cm (4in) blade and are used to trim away surplus fabric and neaten ends of machining.

◄ Paper scissors
Use these to cut around pattern pieces – cutting paper will dull blades of fabric scissors and shears.

Measuring tools and marking aids

A huge range of tools enables a sewer to measure accurately. Choosing the correct tool for the task in hand is important, so that your measurements are precise. The next step is to mark your work using the appropriate marking technique or tool. Some tools are very specific to one job while others are specific to types of sewing.

Measuring tools

There are many tools available to help you measure everything from the width of a seam or hem, to body dimensions, to the area of a window. One of the most basic yet invaluable measuring tools is the tape measure. Be sure to keep yours in good condition – once it stretches or gets snipped on the edges, it will no longer be accurate and should be replaced.

Metal tape for windows ▲
A metal tape that can be secured when extended is used to measure windows and soft furnishings.

Extra-long tape ▲
This is usually twice the length of a normal tape measure, at 300cm (10ft) long. Use it when making soft furnishings. It's also useful to help measure the length of bridal trains.

Sewing gauge ▲
A handy small tool about 15cm (6in) long, marked in centimetres and inches, with a sliding tab. Use as an accurate measure for small measurements such as hems.

Retractable tape ▶
Very useful to have in your handbag when shopping as you never know when you may need to measure something!

Tape measure ▲
Available in various colours and widths. Try to choose one that is the same width as standard seam allowance (1.5cm/⅝in), because it will prove exceedingly useful.

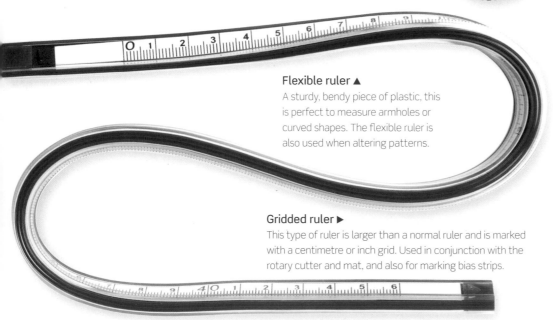

Flexible ruler ▲
A sturdy, bendy piece of plastic, this is perfect to measure armholes or curved shapes. The flexible ruler is also used when altering patterns.

Gridded ruler ▶
This type of ruler is larger than a normal ruler and is marked with a centimetre or inch grid. Used in conjunction with the rotary cutter and mat, and also for marking bias strips.

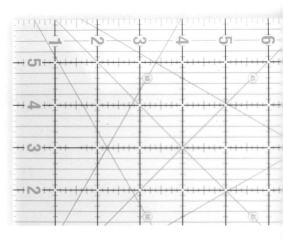

Marking aids

Marking certain parts of your work is essential, to make sure that things like pockets and darts are placed correctly and seamlines are straight as drawn on the pattern. With some marking tools, such as pens and a tracing wheel and carbon paper, it is always a good idea to test on a scrap of fabric first to make sure that the mark made will not be permanent.

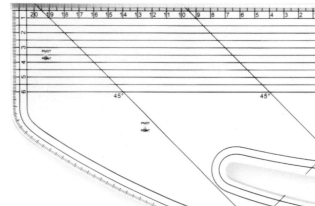

▼ Chalk propelling pencil
Chalk leads of different colours can be inserted into this propelling pencil, making it a very versatile marking tool. The leads can be sharpened.

Drafting ruler ▲
A plastic curved tool, also called a pattern marking ruler, used primarily when drafting or altering patterns.

◄ Water/air-soluble pen
This resembles a felt marker pen. Marks made can be removed from the fabric with either a spray of water or by leaving to air-dry. Be careful – if you press over the marks, they may become permanent.

◄ Tailor's chalk
Also known as French chalk, this solid piece of chalk in either a square or triangular shape is available in a large variety of colours. The chalk easily brushes off fabric.

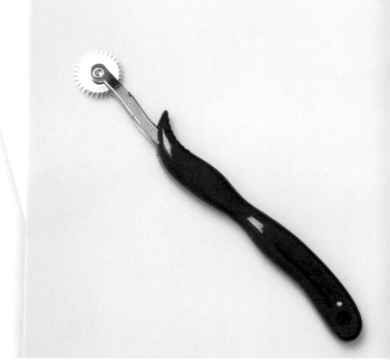

◄ Chalk pencil
Available in blue, pink, andwhite. As it can be sharpened like a normal pencil, it will draw accurate lines on fabric.

Tracing wheel and carbon paper ►
These two items are used together to transfer markings from a paper pattern or a design on to fabric. Not suitable for all types of fabric though, as marks may not be able to be removed easily.

Useful extras

There are many more accessories that can be purchased to help with your sewing, and knowing which products to choose and for which job can be daunting. The tools shown here can be useful aids, although it depends on the type of sewing that you do – dressmaking, craft work, making soft furnishings, or running repairs – as to whether you would need all of them in your sewing kit.

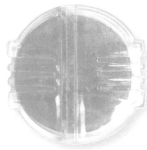

◄ Beeswax

When hand sewing, this will prevent the thread from tangling, and will strengthen it. First draw the thread through the wax, then press the wax into the thread by running your fingers along it.

Collar point turner ▲

This is excellent for pushing out those hard-to-reach corners in collars and cuffs.

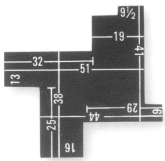

14-in-1 measure ►

A strange-looking tool that has 14 different measurements on it. Use to turn hems or edges accurately. Available in both metric and imperial.

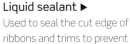

Tape maker ▲

Available in 12, 18, and 25mm ($\frac{1}{2}$, $\frac{3}{4}$, and 1in) widths, this tool evenly folds the edges of a fabric strip, which can then be pressed to make binding.

Thimble ►

An essential item for many sewers, to protect the middle finger from the end of the needle. Choose a thimble that fits your finger comfortably as there are many varieties to choose from.

Tweezers ▲

These can be used for removing stubborn tacking stitches that have become caught in the machine stitching. An essential aid to threading the overlocker.

Liquid sealant ►

Used to seal the cut edge of ribbons and trims to prevent fraying. Also useful to seal the ends of overlock stitching.

Glue pen ►

Similar to a glue pen for paper, this will hold fabric or trims temporarily in place until they can be secured with stitches. It will not damage the fabric or make the sewing needle sticky.

◄ Emergency sewing kit

All the absolute essentials to fix loose buttons or dropped hems while away from your sewing machine. Take it with you when travelling.

Loop turner ►

A thin metal rod with a latch at the end. Use to turn narrow fabric tubes or to thread ribbons through a slotted lace.

Pressing aids

Successful sewing relies on successful pressing. Without the correct pressing equipment, sewing can look too "home-made", whereas if correctly pressed any sewn item will have a neat, professional finish.

Pressing cloth ▶
Choose a cloth made from silk organza or muslin as you can see through it. The cloth will stop the iron marking fabric and prevent burning delicate fabrics.

Iron ▲
A good-quality steam iron is a wonderful asset. Choose a reasonably heavy iron that has steam and a shot of steam facility.

Pressing mitten ▶
Slips on to your hand to enable more control over where you are pressing.

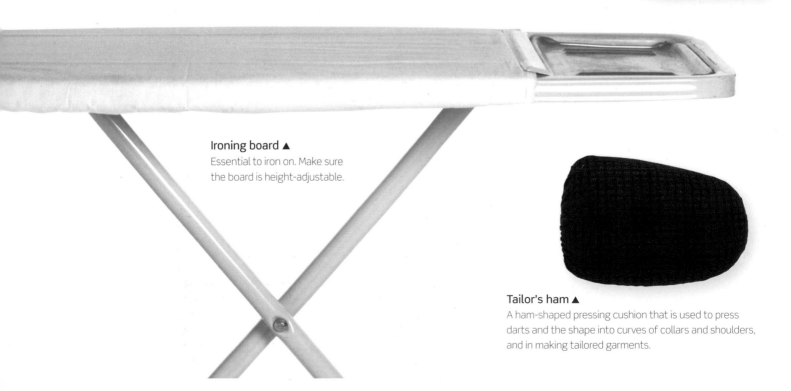

Ironing board ▲
Essential to iron on. Make sure the board is height-adjustable.

Tailor's ham ▲
A ham-shaped pressing cushion that is used to press darts and the shape into curves of collars and shoulders, and in making tailored garments.

Needles and pins

Using the correct pin or needle for your work is so important, as the wrong choice can damage fabric or leave small holes. Needles are made from steel and pins from steel or occasionally brass. Look after them by keeping pins in a pin cushion and needles in a needle case – if kept together in a small container they could become scratched and blunt.

Needles and threaders

Needles are available for all types of fabrics and projects. A good selection of needles should be to hand at all times, whether it be for emergency mending of tears, or sewing on buttons, or adding trimmings to special-occasion wear. With a special needle threader, inserting the thread through the eye of the needle is simplicity itself.

Sharps A general-purpose hand-sewing needle, with a small, round eye. Available in sizes 1 to 12. For most hand sewing use a size 6 to 9.	
Crewel Also known as an embroidery needle, a long needle with a long, oval eye that is designed to take multiple strands of embroidery thread.	
Milliner's or Straw A very long, thin needle with a small, round eye. Good for hand sewing and tacking as it doesn't damage fabric. A size 8 or 9 is most popular.	
Betweens or Quilting Similar to a milliner's needle but very short, with a small, round eye. Perfect for fine hand stitches and favoured by quilters.	
Beading Long and exceedingly fine, to sew beads and sequins to fabric. As it is prone to bending, keep it wrapped in tissue when not in use.	
Darner's A long, thick needle that is designed to be used with wool or thick yarns and to sew through multiple layers.	
Tapestry A medium-length, thick needle with a blunt end and a long eye. For use with wool yarn in tapestry. Also for darning in overlock threads.	
Chenille This looks like a tapestry needle but it has a sharp point. Use with thick or wool yarns for darning or heavy embroidery.	
Bodkin A strange-looking needle with a blunt end and a large, fat eye. Use to thread elastic or cord. There are larger eyes for thicker yarns.	
Self-Threading Needle A needle that has a double eye. The thread is placed in the upper eye through the gap, then pulled into the eye below for sewing.	
Wire Needle Threader A handy gadget, especially useful for needles with small eyes. Also helpful in threading sewing-machine needles.	**Automatic Needle Threader** This threader is operated with a small lever. The needle, eye down, is inserted and the thread is wrapped around.

Pins

There is a wide variety of pins available, in differing lengths and thicknesses, and ranging from plain household pins to those with coloured balls or flower shapes on their ends.

Household
General-purpose pins of a medium length and thickness. Can be used for all types of sewing.

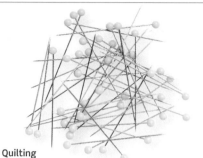

Quilting
A long pin of medium thickness, designed to hold multiple layers of fabric together.

Pearl-headed
Longer than household pins, with a coloured pearl head. They are easy to pick up and use.

Lace or Bridal
A fine, short pin designed to be used with fine fabrics, such as those for bridal gowns, because the pin will not damage the fabric.

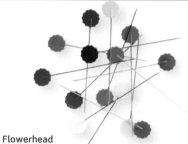

Flowerhead
A long pin of medium thickness with a flat, flower-shaped head. It is designed to be pressed over, as the head lays flat on the fabric.

Extra Fine
Extra long and extra fine, this pin is favoured by many professional dressmakers, because it is easy to use and doesn't damage finer fabrics.

Glass-headed
Similar to pearl-headed pins but shorter. They have the advantage that they can be pressed over without melting.

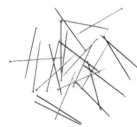

Dressmaker's
Similar to a household pin in shape and thickness, but slightly longer. These are the pins for beginners to choose.

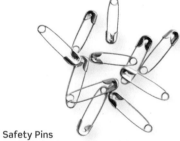

Safety Pins
Available in a huge variety of sizes and made either of brass or stainless steel. Used for holding two or more layers together.

Staple
A strong pin that looks like a very large staple, used for pinning loose covers to furniture. Take care as staple pins are very sharp.

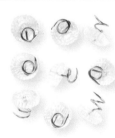

Spiral
Shaped like a spiral with a very sharp point at one end to enable it to be twisted in and out easily. Used to secure loose covers to furniture.

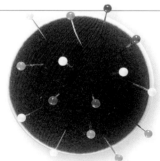

Pin Cushion
To keep pins clean and sharp. Choose a fabric cover: a foam cushion may blunt pins.

Threads

There are so many threads available and knowing which ones to choose can be confusing. There are specialist threads designed for special tasks, such as machine embroidery or quilting. Threads also vary in fibre content, from pure cotton to rayon to polyester. Some threads are very fine while others are thick and coarse. Failure to choose the correct thread can spoil your project and lead to problems with the stitch quality of the sewing machine or overlocker.

Cotton thread
A 100% cotton thread. Smooth and firm, this is designed to be used with cotton fabrics and is much favoured by quilters.

Polyester all-purpose thread
A good-quality polyester thread that has a very slight "give", making it suitable to sew all types of fabrics and garments, as well as soft furnishings. The most popular type of thread.

Silk thread
A sewing thread made from 100% silk. Used for machining delicate silk garments. It is also used for tacking or temporary stitching in areas that are to be pressed, such as jacket collars, because it can be removed without leaving an imprint.

Top-stitching thread
A thicker polyester thread used for decorative top-stitching and buttonholes. Also for hand sewing buttons on thicker fabrics and some soft furnishings.

Elastic thread
A thin, round elastic thread normally used on the bobbin of the sewing machine for stretch effects such as shirring.

Overlocker thread

A dull yarn on a larger reel designed to be used on the overlocker. This type of yarn is normally not strong enough to use on the sewing machine.

Metallic thread

A rayon and metal thread for decorative machining and machine embroidery. This thread usually requires a specialist sewing-machine needle.

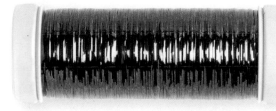

Embroidery thread

Often made from a rayon yarn for shine. This is a finer thread designed for machine embroidery. Available on much larger reels for economy.

Haberdashery

The term haberdashery covers all of the bits and pieces that a sewer tends to need, for example fasteners such as buttons, snaps, hooks and eyes, and Velcro™. But haberdashery also includes elastics, ribbons, trimmings of all types, and boning.

Buttons

Buttons can be made from almost anything – shell, bone, coconut, nylon, plastic, brass, silver. They can be any shape, from geometric to abstract to animal shapes. A button may have a shank or have holes on the surface to enable it to be attached to fabric.

Other fasteners

Hooks and eyes (below left), snaps (below centre), and Velcro™ (below right) all come in a wide variety of forms, differing in size, shape, and colour. Some hooks and eyes are designed to be seen, while snaps and Velcro™ are intended to be hidden fasteners.

Trimmings, decorations, fringes, and braids

Decorative finishing touches – fringes, strips of sequins, ric-rac braids, feathers, pearls, bows, flowers, and beads – can dress up a garment, embellish a bag, or personalize soft furnishings. Some are designed to be inserted into seams while others are surface-mounted.

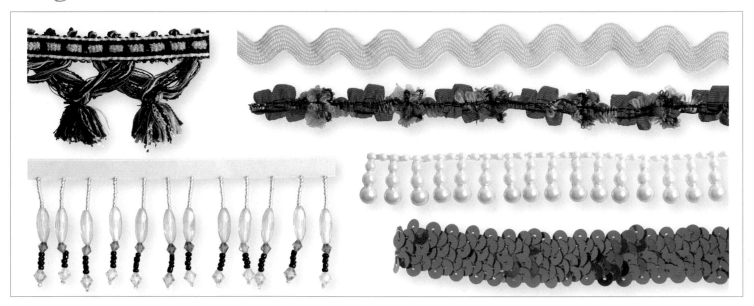

Ribbons

From the narrowest strips to wide swathes, ribbons are made from a variety of yarns, such as nylon, polyester, and cotton. They can be printed or plain and may feature metallic threads or wired edges.

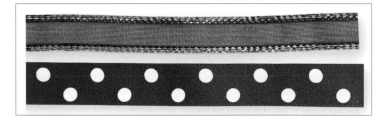

Elastic

Elastic is available in many forms, from very narrow, round cord to wide strips (below left). It may have buttonhole slots in it (below right) or even have a decorative edge.

Boning

You can buy various types of boning in varying widths. Polyester boning (bottom left), used in boned bodices, can be sewn through, while nylon boning (bottom right), also used on boned bodices, has to be inserted into a casing. Specialist metal boning (below left and right), which may be either straight or spiral, is for corsets and bridal wear.

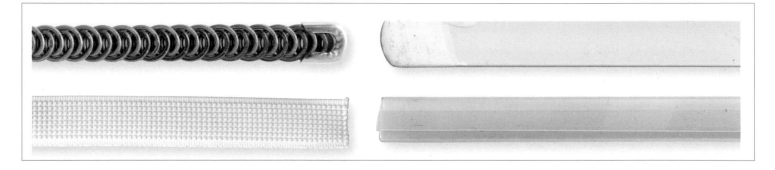

Sewing machine

A sewing machine will quickly speed up any job, whether it be a quick repair or a huge home-sewing project. Most sewing machines today are aided by computer technology, which enhances stitch quality and ease of use. Always spend time trying out a sewing machine before you buy, to really get a feel for it.

Threading guides
Markings to help guide you in threading the machine.

Tension dial
To control the stitch tension on the upper thread, i.e. how fast the thread feeds through the sewing machine.

Automatic needle threader
A pull-down gadget to aid threading the machine needle.

Buttonhole sensor
A pull-down sensor that automatically judges the size of the buttonhole required to fit the button chosen.

Presser foot
To hold the fabric in place while stitching. Various feet can be used here to aid different sewing processes. See pages 26–27.

Dog feeds
These metal teeth grip the fabric and feed it through the machine.

Removable free arm
This section of the machine will pull away to give a narrow work bed that can be used when inserting sleeves. It also contains a useful storage section.

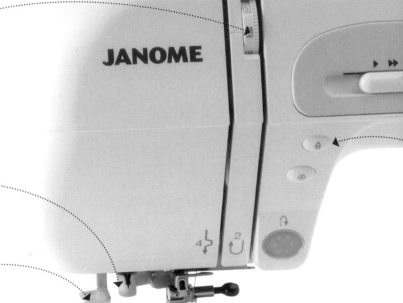

Needle
The machine needle. Replace it regularly to ensure good stitch quality. See page 26.

Shank
To hold the various feet in place.

Needle plate
A transparent removable cover reveals the bobbin. This plate is gridded to help stitch seams of various widths.

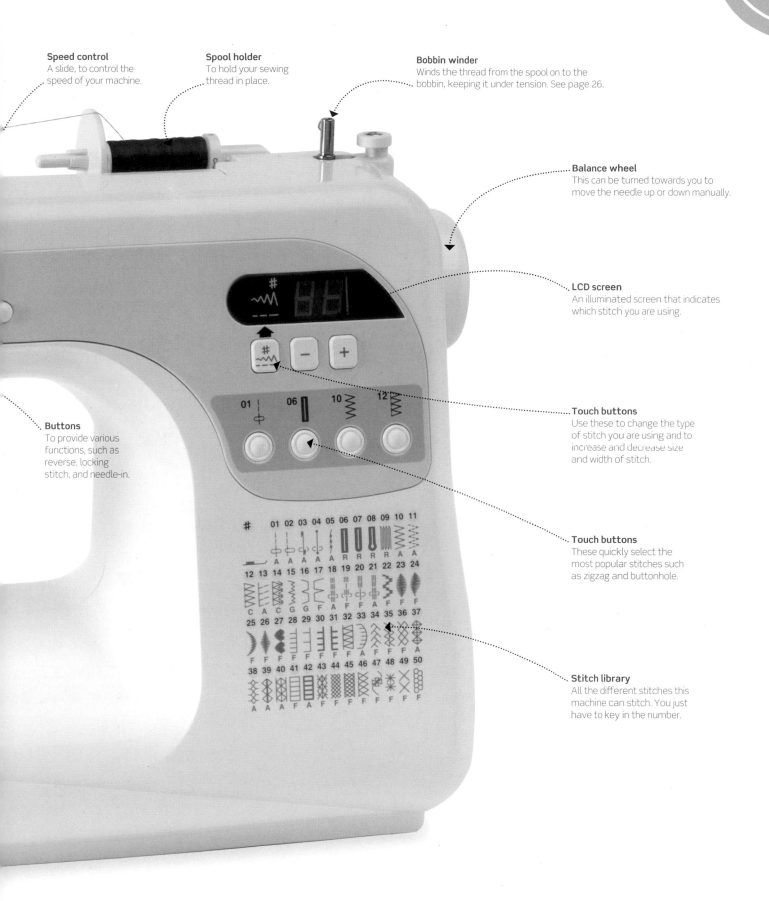

Speed control
A slide, to control the speed of your machine.

Spool holder
To hold your sewing thread in place.

Bobbin winder
Winds the thread from the spool on to the bobbin, keeping it under tension. See page 26.

Balance wheel
This can be turned towards you to move the needle up or down manually.

LCD screen
An illuminated screen that indicates which stitch you are using.

Buttons
To provide various functions, such as reverse, locking stitch, and needle-in.

Touch buttons
Use these to change the type of stitch you are using and to increase and decrease size and width of stitch.

Touch buttons
These quickly select the most popular stitches such as zigzag and buttonhole.

Stitch library
All the different stitches this machine can stitch. You just have to key in the number.

Sewing-machine accessories

Many accessories can be purchased for your sewing machine to make certain sewing processes so much easier. There are different machine needles not only for different fabrics but also for different types of threads. There is also a huge number of sewing-machine feet, and new feet are constantly coming on to the market. Those shown here are some of the most popular.

Plastic bobbin
The bobbin is for the lower thread. Some machines take plastic bobbins, others metal. Always check which sort of bobbin your machine uses as the incorrect choice can cause stitch problems.

Metal bobbin
Also known as a universal bobbin, this is used on many types of sewing machine. Be sure to check that your machine needs a metal bobbin before you buy.

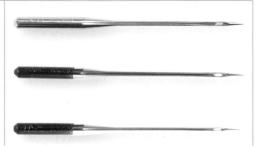

Machine needles
There are different types of sewing machine needle to cope with different fabrics. Machine needles are sized from 60 to 100, a 60 being a very fine needle. There are special needles for machine embroidery and also for metallic threads.

Overedge foot
A foot that runs along the raw edge of the fabric and holds it stable while an overedge stitch is worked.

Embroidery foot
A clear plastic foot with a groove underneath that allows linear machine embroidery stitches to pass under.

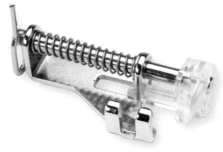

Free embroidery or darning foot
A foot designed to be used when the dog feeds on the machine are lowered. This enables a free motion stitch to be worked.

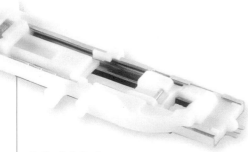

Buttonhole foot
This extends and the button is placed in the back of the foot. The machine will stitch a buttonhole to fit due to the buttonhole sensor.

Blind hem foot
Use this foot in conjunction with the blind hem stitch to create a neat hemming stitch.

Rolled hem foot
This foot rolls the fabric while stitching with a straight stitch or a zigzag stitch.

Walking foot
This strange-looking foot "walks" across the fabric, so that the upper layer of fabric does not push forward. Great for matching checks and stripes and also for difficult fabrics.

Zip foot
This foot fits to either the right or left-hand side of the needle to enable you to stitch close to a zip.

Concealed zip foot
A foot that is used to insert a concealed zip – the foot holds open the coils of the zip, enabling you to stitch behind them.

Pin tuck foot
A foot with grooves underneath to allow multiple pin tucks to be sewn.

Piping foot
A deep groove in this foot allows a piping cord to fit underneath, enabling close stitching to the cord.

Ribbon foot
A foot that will feed either one or two ribbons evenly under the machine needle to ensure accurate stitching.

Beading foot, narrow
This foot has a narrow groove and is used to attach small beads or decorative cords.

Beading foot, wide
Beads on a string will fit under the foot, which has a wide groove, and they can then be zigzag stitched over.

Ultra-glide foot
A foot made from Teflon™ that glides over the fabric. Useful for synthetic leathers.

Wool

A natural fibre, wool comes primarily from sheep – Australian merino sheep's wool is considered to be the best. However, we also get wool fibres from goats (mohair and cashmere), rabbits (angora), camels (camel hair), and llamas (alpaca). A wool fibre is either short and fluffy, when it is known as a woollen yarn, or it is long, strong, and smooth, when it is called worsted. The term virgin (or new) wool denotes wool fibres that are being used for the first time. Wool may be reprocessed or reused and is then often mixed with other fibres.

Properties of wool

- **Comfortable to wear** in all climates as it is available in many weights and weaves
- **Warm in the winter** and cool in the summer, because it will breathe with your body
- **Absorbs moisture** better than other natural fibres – will absorb up to 30 per cent of its weight before it feels wet
- **Flame-resistant**

- **Relatively** crease-resistant
- **Ideal to tailor** as it can be easily shaped with steam
- **Often blended** with other fibres to reduce the cost of a fabric
- **Felts** if exposed to excessive heat, moisture, and pressure
- **Will be bleached** by sunlight with prolonged exposure
- **Can be damaged** by moths

CASHMERE

Wool from the Kashmir goat, and the most luxurious of all the wools. A soft yet hard-wearing fabric available in different weights.

Cutting out: As cashmere often has a slight pile, use a nap layout
Seams: Plain, neatened with overlocker stitch or pinking shears (a zigzag stitch would curl the edge of the seam)

Thread: A silk thread is ideal, or a polyester all-purpose thread
Needle: Machine size 12/14, depending on the thickness of the fabric; sharps for hand sewing
Pressing: Steam iron on a steam setting, with a pressing cloth and seam roll
Used for: Jackets, coats, men's wear; knitted cashmere yarn for sweaters, cardigans, underwear

CREPE

A soft fabric made from a twisted yarn that produces an uneven surface. Crepe will have stretched on the bolt and is prone to shrinkage so it is important to preshrink it by steaming prior to use.

Cutting out: A nap layout is not required

Seams: Plain, neatened with overlocker stitch (a zigzag stitch may curl the edge of the seam)
Thread: Polyester all-purpose thread
Needle: Machine size 12; sharps or milliner's for hand sewing
Pressing: Steam iron on a wool setting; a pressing cloth is not always required
Used for: All types of clothing

FLANNEL

A wool with a lightly brushed surface, featuring either a plain or a twill weave. Used in the past for underwear.

Cutting out: Use a nap layout
Seams: Plain, neatened with overlocker or zigzag stitch or a Hong Kong finish
Thread: Polyester all-purpose thread
Needle: Machine size 14; sharps for hand sewing

Pressing: Steam iron on a wool setting with a pressing cloth; use a seam roll as the fabric is prone to marking
Used for: Coats, jackets, skirts, trousers, men's wear

GABARDINE

A hard-wearing suiting fabric with a distinctive weave. Gabardine often has a sheen and is prone to shine. It can be difficult to handle as it is springy and frays badly.

Cutting out: A nap layout is advisable as the fabric has a sheen
Seams: Plain, neatened with overlocker or zigzag stitch
Thread: Polyester all-purpose thread or 100 per cent cotton thread

Needle: Machine size 14; sharps for hand sewing
Pressing: Steam iron on a wool setting; use just the toe of the iron and a silk organza pressing cloth as the fabric will mark and may shine
Used for: Men's wear, jackets, trousers

MOHAIR

From the wool of the Angora goat. A long, straight, and very strong fibre that produces a hairy cloth or yarn for knitting.

Cutting out: Use a nap layout, with the fibres brushing down the pattern pieces in the same direction, from neck to hem
Seams: Plain, neatened with overlocker stitch or pinking shears
Thread: Polyester all-purpose thread

Needle: Machine size 14; sharps for hand sewing
Pressing: Steam iron on a wool setting; "stroke" the iron over the wool, moving in the direction of the nap
Used for: Jackets, coats, men's wear, soft furnishings; knitted mohair yarns for sweaters

TARTAN

An authentic tartan belongs to a Scottish clan, and each has its own unique design that can only be us ed by that clan. The fabric is made using a twill weave from worsted yarns.

Cutting out: Check the design for even/uneven checks as it may need a nap layout or even a single layer layout
Seams: Plain, matching the pattern and neatened with overlocker or zigzag stitch

Thread: Polyester all-purpose thread
Needle: Machine size 14; sharps for hand sewing
Pressing: Steam iron on a wool setting; may require a pressing cloth, so test first
Used for: Traditionally kilts, but these days also skirts, trousers, jackets, soft furnishings

TWEED

A rough fabric with a distinctive warp and weft, often in different colours. Traditional tweed is associated with the English countryside.

Cutting out: A nap layout is not required unless the fabric features a check
Seams: Plain, neatened with overlocker or zigzag stitch; can also be neatened with pinking shears
Thread: Polyester all-purpose thread or 100 per cent cotton thread

Needle: Machine size 14; sharps for hand sewing
Pressing: Steam iron on a steam setting; a pressing cloth may not be required
Used for: Jackets, coats, skirts, men's wear, soft furnishings

WOOL WORSTED

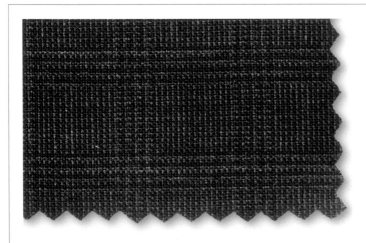

A light and strong cloth, made from good-quality thin, firm filament fibres. Always steam prior to cutting out as the fabric may shrink slightly after having been stretched around a bolt.

Cutting out: Use a nap layout
Seams: Plain, neatened with overlocker or zigzag stitch or a Hong Kong finish
Thread: Polyester all-purpose thread

Needle: Machine size 12/14, depending on fabric; milliner's or sharps for hand sewing
Pressing: Steam iron on a wool setting with a pressing cloth; use a seam roll to prevent the seam from showing through
Used for: Skirts, jackets, coats, trousers

Cotton

A natural fibre, wool comes primarily from sheep – Australian merino sheep's wool is considered to be the best. However, we also get wool fibres from goats (mohair and cashmere), rabbits (angora), camels (camel hair), and llamas (alpaca). A wool fibre is either short and fluffy, when it is known as a woollen yarn, or it is long, strong, and smooth, when it is called worsted. The term virgin (or new) wool denotes wool fibres that are being used for the first time. Wool may be reprocessed or reused and is then often mixed with other fibres.

Properties of cotton

- **Absorbs moisture well** and carries heat away from the body
- **Stronger wet** than dry
- **Does not build up** static electricity
- **Dyes well**

- **Prone to shrinkage** unless it has been treated
- **Will deteriorate** from mildew and prolonged exposure to sunlight
- **Creases easily**
- **Soils easily,** but launders well

BRODERIE ANGLAISE

A fine, plain-weave cotton that has been embroidered in such a way as to make small holes.

Cutting out: May need layout to place embroidery at hem edge
Seams: Plain, neatened with overlocker or zigzag stitch; a French seam can also be used
Thread: Polyester all-purpose thread
Needle: Machine size 12/14; sharps for hand sewing

Pressing: Steam iron on a cotton setting; a pressing cloth is not required
Used for: Baby clothes, summer skirts, blouses

CALICO

A plain-weave fabric that is usually unbleached and quite firm. Available in many different weights, from very fine to extremely heavy.

Cutting out: A nap layout is not required
Seams: Plain, neatened with overlocker or zigzag stitch
Thread: Polyester all-purpose thread

Needle: Machine size 11/14, depending on thickness of thread; sharps for hand sewing
Pressing: Steam iron on a steam setting; a pressing cloth is not required
Used for: Toiles (test garments), soft furnishings

CHAMBRAY

A light cotton that has a coloured warp thread and white weft thread. Chambray can also be found as a check or a striped fabric.

Cutting out: A nap layout should not be required
Seams: Plain, neatened with overlocker or zigzag stitch
Thread: Polyester all-purpose thread
Needle: Machine size 11; sharps for hand sewing

Pressing: Steam iron on a cotton setting; a pressing cloth is not required
Used for: Blouses, men's shirts, children's wear

CORDUROY

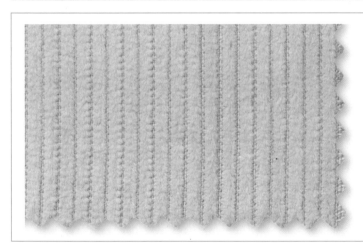

A soft pile fabric with distinctive stripes (known as wales or ribs) woven into it. The name depends on the size of the ribs: baby or pin cord has extremely fine ribs; needle cord has slightly thicker ribs; corduroy has 10–12 ribs per 2.5cm (1in); and elephant or jumbo cord has thick, heavy ribs.

Cutting out: Use a nap layout with the pile on the corduroy brushing up the pattern pieces from hem to neck, to give depth of colour
Seams: Plain, stitched using a walking foot and neatened with overlocker or zigzag stitch
Thread: Polyester all-purpose thread
Needle: Machine size 12/16; sharps or milliner's for hand sewing
Pressing: Steam iron on a cotton setting; use a seam roll under the seams with a pressing cloth
Used for: Trousers, skirts, men's wear

DENIM

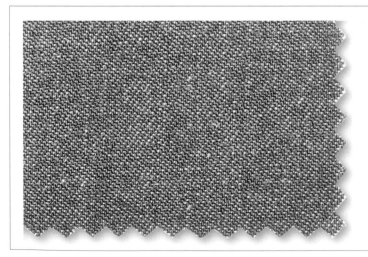

Named after Nîmes in France. A hard-wearing, twill-weave fabric with a coloured warp and white weft, usually made into jeans. Available in various weights and often mixed with an elastic thread for stretch. Denim is usually blue, but is also available in a variety of other colours.

Cutting out: A nap layout is not required
Seams: Run and fell or top-stitched

Thread: Polyester all-purpose thread with top-stitching thread for detail top-stitching
Needle: Machine size 14/16; sharps for hand sewing
Pressing: Steam iron on a cotton setting; a pressing cloth should not be required
Used for: Jeans, jackets, children's wear

GINGHAM

A fresh, two-colour cotton fabric that features a check of various sizes. A plain weave made by having groups of white and coloured warp and weft threads.

Cutting out: Usually an even check, so nap layout is not required but recommended; pattern will need matching
Seams: Plain, neatened with overlocker or zigzag stitch
Thread: Polyester all-purpose thread

Needle: Machine size 11/12; sharps for hand sewing
Pressing: Steam iron on a cotton setting; a pressing cloth should not be required
Used for: Children's wear, dresses, shirts, home furnishings

JERSEY

A fine cotton yarn that has been knitted to give stretch, making the fabric very comfortable to wear. Jersey will also drape well.

Cutting out: A nap layout is recommended
Seams: 4-thread overlock stitch; or plain seam stitched with a small zigzag stitch and then seam allowances stitched together with a zigzag
Thread: Polyester all-purpose thread

Needle: Machine size 12/14; a ballpoint needle may be required for overlocker and a milliner's for hand sewing
Pressing: Steam iron on a wool setting as jersey may shrink on a cotton setting
Used for: Underwear, drapey dresses, leisurewear, bedding

MADRAS

A check fabric made from a fine cotton yarn, usually from India. Often found in bright colours featuring an uneven check. An inexpensive cotton fabric.

Cutting out: Use a nap layout and match the checks
Seams: Plain, neatened with overlocker or zigzag stitch
Thread: Polyester all-purpose thread
Needle: Machine size 12/14; sharps for hand sewing

Pressing: Steam iron on a cotton setting; a pressing cloth is not required
Used for: Shirts, skirts, home furnishings

MUSLIN

A fine, plain, open-weave cotton. Can be found in colours but usually sold as natural/unbleached or white. Makes great pressing cloths and interlinings. Washing prior to use is recommended.

Cutting out: A nap layout is not required
Seams: 4-thread overlock stitch or plain seam, neatened with overlocker or zigzag stitch; a French seam could also be used
Thread: Polyester all-purpose thread

Needle: Machine size 11; milliner's for hand sewing
Pressing: Steam iron on a cotton setting; a cloth is not required
Used for: Curtaining and other household uses

SHIRTING

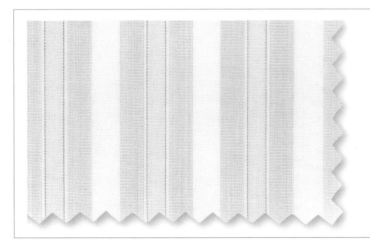

A closely woven, fine cotton with coloured warp and weft yarns making stripes or checks.

Cutting out: Use a nap layout if fabric has uneven stripes
Seams: Plain, neatened with overlocker or zigzag stitch; a run and fell seam can also be used
Thread: Polyester all-purpose thread
Needle: Machine size 12; milliner's for hand sewing

Pressing: Steam iron on a cotton setting; a pressing cloth is not required
Used for: Ladies' and men's shirts

VELVET

A pile-weave fabric, made by using an additional yarn that is then cut to produce the pile. Difficult to handle and can be easily damaged if seams have to be unpicked.

Cutting out: Use a nap layout with the pile brushing up from hem to neck, to give depth of colour

Seams: Plain, stitched using a walking foot (stitch all seams from hem to neck) and neatened with overlocker or zigzag stitch
Thread: Polyester all-purpose thread
Needle: Machine size 14; milliner's for hand sewing
Pressing: Only if you have to; use a velvet board, a little steam, the toe of the iron, and a silk organza cloth
Used for: Jackets, coats

Silk

Often referred to as the queen of fabrics, silk is made from the fibres of the silkworm's cocoon. This strong and luxurious fabric dates back thousands of years to its first development in China, and the secret of silk production was well protected by the Chinese until 300AD. Silk fabrics can be very fine or thick and chunky. They need careful handling as some can be easily damaged.

Properties of silk

- **Keeps you warm** in winter and cool in summer
- **Absorbs moisture** and dries quickly
- **Dyes well,** producing deep, rich colours
- **Static electricity** can build up and fabric may cling
- **Will fade** in prolonged strong sunlight
- **Prone to** shrinkage
- **Best** dry-cleaned
- **Weaker** when wet than dry
- **May** water-mark

CHIFFON

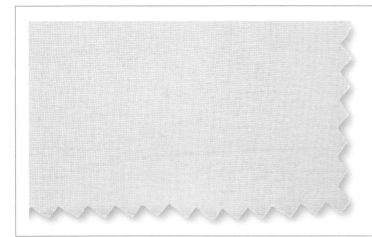

A very strong and very fine, transparent silk with a plain weave. Will gather and ruffle well. Difficult to handle.

Cutting out: Place tissue paper under the fabric and pin the fabric to the tissue, cutting through all layers if necessary; use extra-fine pins
Seams: French

Thread: Polyester all-purpose thread
Needle: Machine size 9/11; fine milliner's for hand sewing
Pressing: Dry iron on a wool setting
Used for: Special-occasion wear, over-blouses

DUCHESSE SATIN

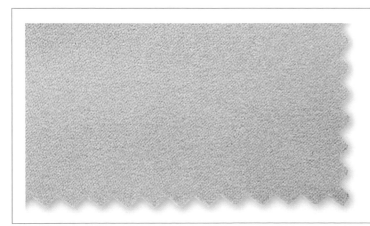

A heavy, expensive satin fabric used almost exclusively for special-occasion wear.

Cutting out: Use a nap layout
Seams: Plain, with pinked edges
Thread: Polyester all-purpose thread
Needle: Machine size 12/14; milliner's for hand sewing

Pressing: Steam iron on a wool setting with a pressing cloth; use a seam roll under the seams to prevent shadowing
Used for: Special-occasion wear

DUPION

Woven using a textured yarn that produces irregularities in the weave.

Cutting out: Use a nap layout to prevent shadowing
Seams: Plain, neatened with overlocker or zigzag stitch
Thread: Polyester all-purpose thread
Needle: Machine size 12; milliner's for hand sewing
Pressing: Steam iron on a wool setting with a pressing cloth as fabric may water-mark

Used for: Dresses, skirts, jackets, special-occasion wear, soft furnishings

HABUTAI

Originally from Japan, a smooth, fine silk that can have a plain or a twill weave. Fabric is often used for silk painting.

Cutting out: A nap layout is not required
Seams: French
Thread: Polyester all-purpose thread

Needle: Machine size 9/11; very fine milliner's or betweens for hand sewing
Pressing: Steam iron on a wool setting
Used for: Lining, shirts, blouses

MATKA

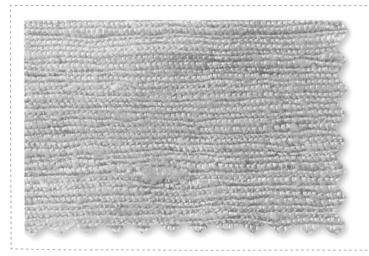

A silk suiting fabric with an uneven-looking yarn. Matka can be mistaken for linen.

Cutting out: Use a nap layout as silk may shadow
Seams: Plain, neatened with overlocker or zigzag stitch or a Hong Kong finish
Thread: Polyester all-purpose thread
Needle: Machine size 12/14; milliner's for hand sewing
Pressing: Steam iron on a wool setting with a pressing cloth; a seam roll is recommended to prevent the seams from showing through
Used for: Dresses, jackets, trousers

ORGANZA

A sheer fabric with a crisp appearance that will crease easily.

Cutting out: A nap layout is not required
Seams: French or use a seam for a difficult fabric
Thread: Polyester all-purpose thread
Needle: Machine size 11; milliner's or betweens for hand sewing
Pressing: Steam iron on a wool setting; a pressing cloth should not be required

Used for: Sheer blouses, shrugs, interlining, interfacing

SATIN

A silk with a satin weave that can be very light to quite heavy in weight.

Cutting out: Use a nap layout in a single layer as fabric is slippery
Seams: French; on thicker satins, use a seam for a difficult fabric
Thread: Polyester all-purpose thread (not silk thread as it becomes weak with wear)

Needle: Machine size 11/12; milliner's or betweens for hand sewing
Pressing: Steam iron on a wool setting with a pressing cloth as fabric may water-mark
Used for: Blouses, dresses, special-occasion wear

TAFFETA

A smooth, plain-weave fabric with a crisp appearance. It makes a rustling sound when worn. Can require special handling and does not wear well.

Cutting out: Use a nap layout, with extra-fine pins in seams to minimize marking the fabric
Seams: Plain; fabric may pucker, so sew from the hem upwards, keeping the fabric taut under the machine; neaten with overlocker or pinking shears

Thread: Polyester all-purpose thread
Needle: Machine size 11; milliner's or betweens for hand sewing
Pressing: Cool iron, with a seam roll under the seams
Used for: Special-occasion wear

Linen

Linen is a natural fibre that is derived from the stem of the flax plant. It is available in a variety of qualities and weights, from very fine linen to heavy suiting weights. Coarser than cotton, it is sometimes woven with cotton as well as being mixed with silk.

Properties of linen

- **Cool and comfortable** to wear
- **Absorbs moisture** well
- **Shrinks** when washed
- **Does not ease** well

- **Has a tendency** to crease
- **Prone to** fraying
- **Resists moths** but is damaged by mildew

COTTON AND LINEN MIX

Two fibres may have been mixed together in the yarn or there may be mixed warp and weft yarns. It has lots of texture in the weave.

Cutting out: A nap layout should not be required
Seams: Plain, neatened with overlocker or zigzag stitch
Thread: Polyester all-purpose thread
Needle: Machine size 14; sharps for hand sewing

Pressing: A steam iron on a steam setting with a silk organza pressing cloth
Used for: Summer-weight jackets, tailored dresses

DRESS-WEIGHT LINEN

A medium-weight linen with a plain weave. The yarn is often uneven, which causes slubs in the weave.

Cutting out: A nap layout is not required
Seams: Plain, neatened with overlocker or zigzag stitch or a Hong Kong finish
Thread: Polyester all-purpose thread with a top-stitching thread for top-stitching

Needle: Machine size 14; sharps for hand sewing
Pressing: Steam iron on a cotton setting (steam is required to remove creases)
Used for: Dresses, trousers, skirts

PRINTED LINENS

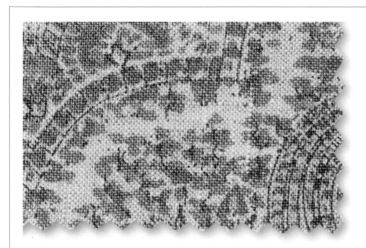

Many linens today feature prints or even embroidery. The fabric may be light to medium weight, with a smooth yarn that has few slubs.

Cutting out: Use a nap layout
Seams: Plain, neatened with overlocker or zigzag stitch
Thread: Polyester all-purpose thread
Needle: Machine size 14; sharps for hand sewing
Pressing: Steam iron on a cotton setting (steam is required to remove creases)
Used for: Dresses, skirts

SUITING LINEN

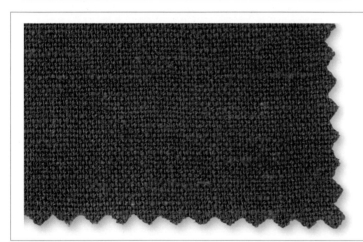

A heavier yarn is used to produce a linen suitable for suits for men and women. Can be a firm, tight weave or a looser weave.

Cutting out: A nap layout is not required
Seams: Plain, neatened with overlocker or a zigzag stitch
Thread: Polyester all-purpose thread with a top-stitch thread for top-stitching
Needle: Machine size 14; sharps for hand sewing
Pressing: Steam iron on a cotton setting (steam is required to remove creases)
Used for: Men's and women's suits, trousers, coats

FANCY WEAVE LINEN

A linen woven with additional decorative yarns such as metallic or lurex.

Cutting out: A nap layout is not required
Seams: Plain, neatened with overlocker or a zigzag stitch
Thread: Polyester all-purpose thread with a top-stitch thread for top-stitching
Needle: Machine size 14; sharps for hand sewing
Pressing: Press carefully as decorative yarns may melt; use a pressing cloth
Used for: Dresses, jackets

Synthetic fabrics

The term synthetic applies to any fabric that is not 100 per cent natural. Many of these fabrics have been developed over the last hundred years, which means they are new compared to natural fibres. Some synthetic fabrics are made from natural elements mixed with chemicals, while others are made entirely from non-natural substances. The properties of synthetic fabrics vary from fabric to fabric.

Properties of synthetic fabrics

- **Durable** and usually launder well
- **Can be prone to static** and "cling" to the body

- **Can dye well** and are often digitally printed
- **Mix well** with natural fibres

ACETATE

Introduced in 1924, acetate is made from cellulose and chemicals. The fabric has a slight shine and is widely used for linings. Acetate can also be woven into fabrics such as acetate taffeta, acetate satin, and acetate jersey.

Properties of acetate:
Dyes well
Can be heat-set into pleats
Washes well

Cutting out: Use a nap layout due to sheen on fabric
Seams: Plain, neatened with overlocker or zigzag stitch, or 4-thread overlock stitch
Thread: Polyester all-purpose thread
Needle: Machine size 11; sharps for hand sewing
Pressing: Steam iron on a cool setting (fabric can melt)
Used for: Special-occasion wear, linings

ACRYLIC

Introduced in 1950, acrylic fibres are made from ethylene and acrylonitrile. The fabric resembles wool and makes a good substitute for machine-washable wool. Often seen as a knitted fabric, the fibres can be mixed with wool.

Properties of acrylic:
Little absorbency
Tends to retain odours
Not very strong
Cutting out: A nap layout may be required

Seams: 4-thread overlock stitch on knitted fabrics; plain seam on woven fabrics
Thread: Polyester all-purpose thread
Needle: Machine size 12/14, but a ballpoint needle may be required on knitted fabrics; sharps for hand sewing
Pressing: Steam iron on a wool setting (fabric can be damaged by heat)
Used for: Knitted yarns for sweaters; wovens for skirts, blouses

POLYESTER

One of the most popular of the man-made fibres, polyester was introduced in 1951 as a man's washable suiting. Polyester fibres are made from petroleum by-products and can take on any form, from a very fine sheer fabric to a thick, heavy suiting.

Properties of polyester:
Non-absorbent
Does not crease
Can build up static
May "pill"

Cutting out: A nap layout is only required if the fabric is printed
Seams: French, plain, or 4-thread overlock, depending on the weight of the fabric
Thread: Polyester all-purpose thread
Needle: Machine size 11/14; sharps for hand sewing
Pressing: Steam iron on a wool setting
Used for: Workwear, school uniforms

RAYON

Also known as viscose and often referred to as artificial silk, this fibre was developed in 1889. It is made from wood pulp or cotton linters mixed with chemicals. Rayon can be knitted or woven and made into a wide range of fabrics. It is often blended with other fibres.

Properties of rayon:
Absorbent
Non-static

Dyes well
Frays badly
Cutting out: A nap layout is only required if the fabric is printed
Seams: Plain, neatened with overlocker or zigzag stitch
Thread: Polyester all-purpose thread
Needle: Machine size 12/14; sharps for hand sewing
Pressing: Steam iron on a silk setting
Used for: Dresses, blouses, jackets

SYNTHETIC FURS

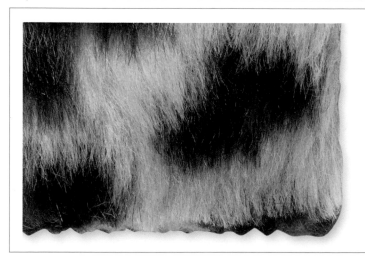

Created using a looped yarn that is then cut on a knitted or a woven base, synthetic fur can be made from nylon or acrylic fibres. The furs vary tremendously in quality and some are very difficult to tell from the real thing.

Properties of synthetic furs:
Require careful sewing
Can be heat-damaged by pressing
Not as warm as real fur

Cutting out: Use a nap layout, with the fur pile brushed from the neck to the hem; cut just the backing carefully and not through the fur pile
Seams: Plain, with a longer stitch and a walking foot; no neatening is required
Thread: Polyester all-purpose thread
Needle: Machine size 14; sharps for hand sewing
Pressing: If required, use a cool iron (synthetic fur can melt under a hot iron)

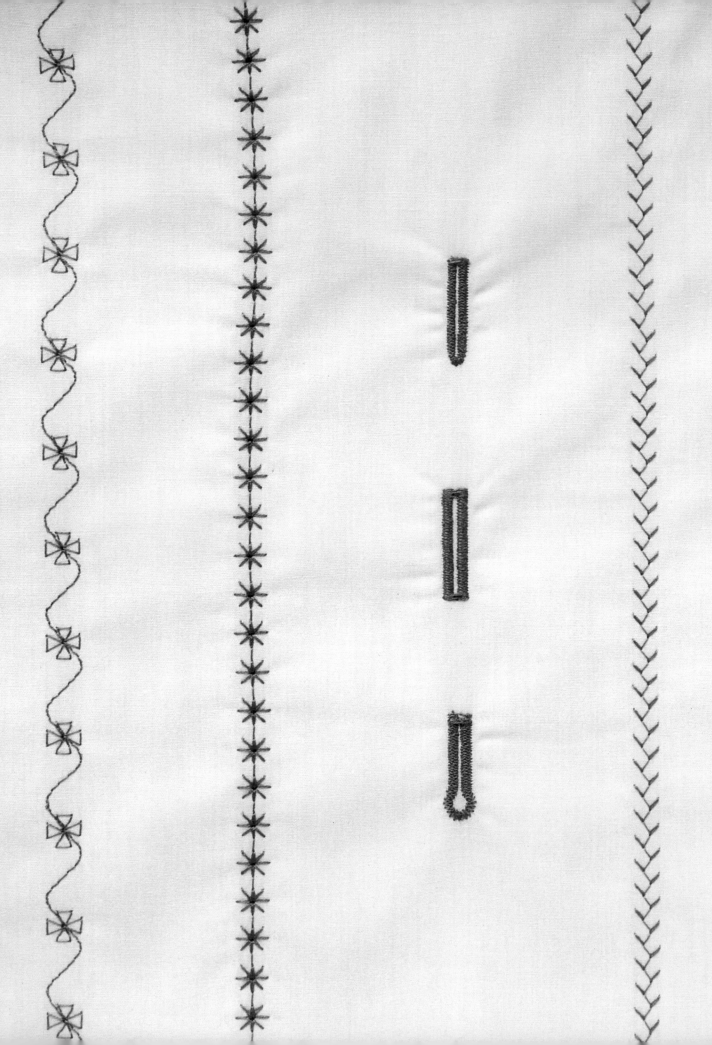

Techniques

Cutting out accurately

Careful, smooth cutting around the pattern pieces will ensure that they join together accurately. Always cut out on a smooth, flat surface such as a table – the floor is not ideal – and be sure your scissors are sharp. Use the full blade of the scissors on long, straight edges, sliding the blades along the fabric; use smaller cuts around curves. Do not nibble or snip at the fabric.

How to cut

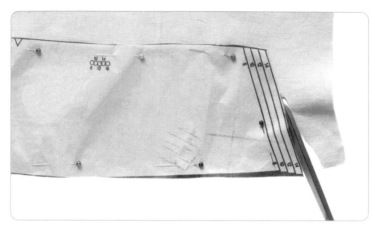

If you are right-handed, place your left hand on the pattern and fabric to hold them in place, and cut cleanly with the scissor blades at a right angle to the fabric.

Marking dots

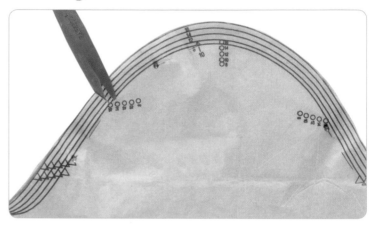

You can cut a small clip into the fabric to mark the dots that indicate the top of the shoulder on a sleeve. Alternatively, these can be marked with tailor's tacks (see page 68).

Marking notches

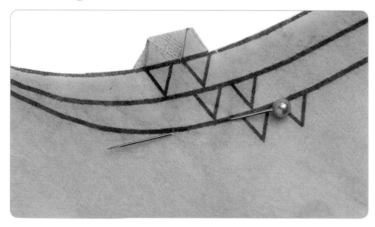

These symbols need to be marked on to the fabric as they are matching points. One of the easiest ways to do this is to cut the mirror image of the notches out into the fabric. Rather than cutting out each notch separately, cut straight across from point to point.

Clipping lines

A small clip or snip into the fabric is a useful way to mark some of the lines that appear on a pattern, such as the centre front line and foldlines.

Pattern marking

Once the pattern pieces have been cut out, you will need to mark the symbols shown on the tissue through to the fabric. There are various methods to do this. Tailor's tacks are good for circles and dots, or mark these with a water or air-soluble pen (when using a pen, it's a good idea to test it on a piece of scrap fabric first). For lines, you can use trace tacking or a tracing wheel with dressmaker's carbon paper.

Tailor's tacks

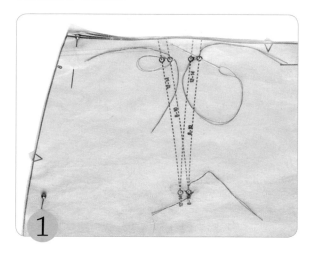

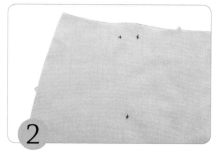

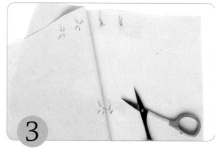

1 As there are often dots of different sizes, it is a good idea to choose a different colour thread for each dot size. It is then easy to match the colours as well as the dots. Have double thread in your needle, unknotted. Insert the needle through the dot from right to left, leaving a tail of thread. Be sure to go through the tissue and both layers of fabric. Now stitch through the dot again, this time from top to bottom to make a loop. Cut through the loop, then snip off excess thread to leave a tail.

2 Carefully pull the pattern tissue away. On the top side you will have four threads marking each dot. When you turn the fabric over, the dot positions will be marked with an X.

3 Gently turn back the two layers of fabric to separate them, then cut through the threads so that thread tails are left in both pieces of fabric.

Tracing paper and wheel

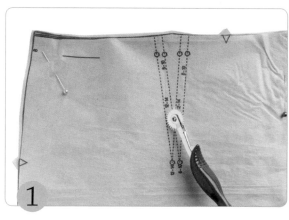

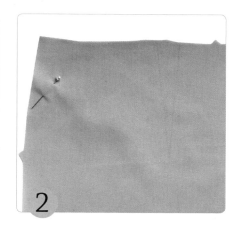

1 This method is not suitable for all fabrics as the marks may not be able to be removed easily. Slide dressmaker's carbon paper against the wrong side of the fabric. Run a tracing wheel along the pattern lines (a ruler will help you make straight lines).

2 Remove the carbon paper and carefully pull off the pattern tissue. You will have dotted lines marked on your fabric.

Marker pens

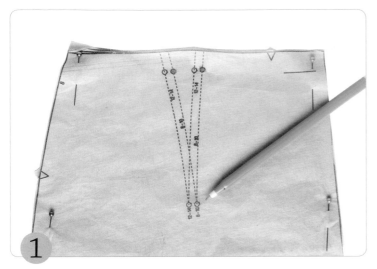

1 This method can only be used with a single layer of fabric. Press the point of the pen into the centre of the dot marked on the pattern piece.

2 Carefully remove the pattern. The pen marks will have gone through the tissue on to the fabric. Be sure not to press the fabric before the pen marks are removed or they may become permanent.

Trace tacking

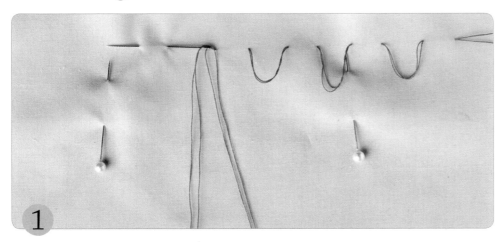

1 This is a really useful technique to mark centre front lines, foldlines, and placement lines. With double thread in your needle, stitch a row of loopy stitches, sewing along the line marked on the pattern.

2 Carefully pull away the tissue. Cut through the loops, then gently separate the layers of fabric to show the threads. Snip apart to leave thread tails in both of the fabric layers.

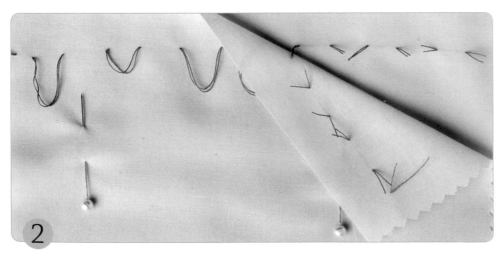

How to apply fusible interfacing

An interfacing is a layer that is applied to fabric to reinforce it and give it extra strength, for example when adding structure to a tote bag, see pp.156–159. There are two types of interfacing: fusible and non-fusible. Fusible interfacings, which are backed with an adhesive activated by heat, are the easiest to use.

Iron-on interfacing

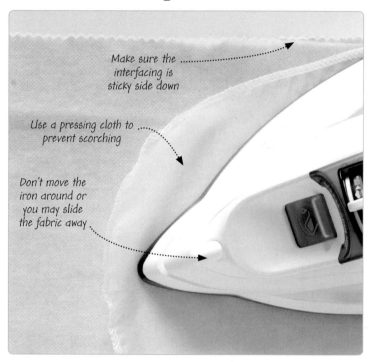

Make sure the interfacing is sticky side down

Use a pressing cloth to prevent scorching

Don't move the iron around or you may slide the fabric away

Using a steam iron set to the correct temperature, lay the fabric on the ironing board, wrong side up. Make sure there are no wrinkles in it. Place the interfacing sticky side down on the fabric and cover with a damp pressing cloth. Hold the iron in place for about 10 seconds for lightweight fabric and 15 seconds for heavier fabric.

Fusible interfacings

Woven fusible interfacings are designed for use with woven fabric

Woven
Like woven fabric, woven fusible interfacing has a lengthwise and a crosswise grain. Always use a woven interfacing if you are working with a woven fabric and make sure you cut the interfacing on the same grain as the fabric.

Lightweight woven fusible interfacings are designed for use with lighter woven fabrics

Lightweight woven
This delicate, almost sheer, woven fusible interfacing is suitable for all light to medium-weight fabrics. It can be difficult to cut out as it has a tendency to stick to the scissors.

Choose the appropriate weight of non-woven fusible interfacing for your project

Non-woven
Made by bonding fibres together, non-woven fusible interfacing doesn't have a grain so it's easier to cut out than a woven interfacing. Another plus is the fact that it does not fray. It is a good, all-purpose interfacing.

Non-fusible interfacing

This interfacing comes in various types and weights. The most commonly used is non-woven, shown here. Hold all non-fusible interfacings in place by pinning them, then tacking to the wrong side of the fabric, before machine stitching. Remove the tacking stitches after you've sewn.

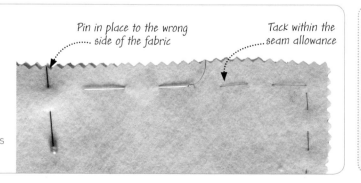

Pin in place to the wrong side of the fabric

Tack within the seam allowance

Tip When you have finished, lift a tiny corner of the interfacing to make sure it has adhered properly to the fabric. If it hasn't, repeat the whole process. Leave to cool and dry before moving.

Sewing preparation

It is necessary to use hand stitching to prepare the fabric prior to permanent stitching – these temporary tacking stitches will eventually be removed. Permanent hand stitching is used to finish a garment and to attach fasteners, as well as to help out with a quick repair.

Threading a needle

When sewing by hand, cut your piece of thread to be no longer than the distance from your fingertips to your elbow. If the thread is much longer than this, it will knot as you sew.

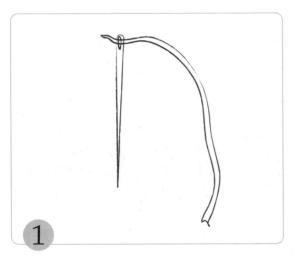

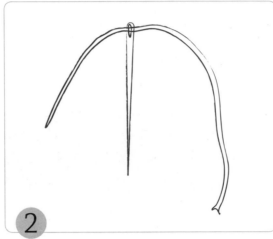

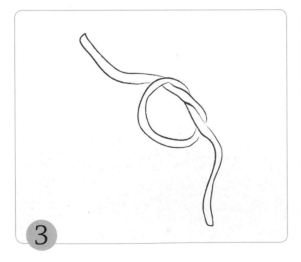

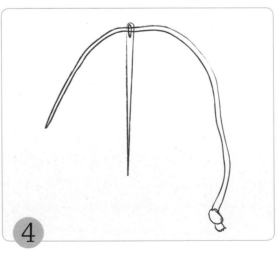

1 Hold your needle in your right hand and the end of the thread in your left. Keeping the thread still, place the eye of the needle over the thread.

2 If the needle will not slip over the thread, dampen your fingers and run the moisture across the eye of the needle. Pull the thread through.

3 At the other end of the thread, tie a knot as shown or secure the thread as shown opposite.

4 You are now ready to start your sewing.

Securing the thread

The ends of the thread must be secured firmly, especially if the hand stitching is to be permanent. A knot (see opposite page) is frequently used and is the preferred choice for temporary stitches. For permanent stitching a double stitch is a better option.

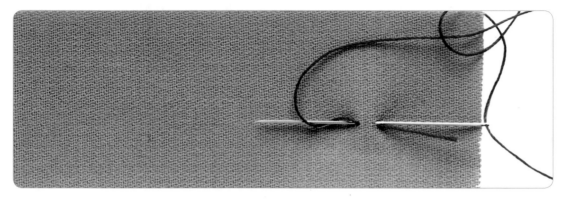

Double stitch

Take a stitch. Go back through the stitch with the thread wrapped under the needle Pull through to make a knot..

Back stitch

········· Make two small stitches in the same place.

Locking stitch

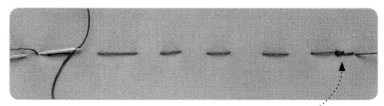

········· Start the stitching with a knot and finish by working a knot at the end.

Tacking stitches

Each of the many types of tacking stitches has its own individual use. Basic tacks hold two or more pieces of fabric together. Long and short tacks are an alternative version of the basic tacking stitch, often used when the tacking will stay in the work for some time. Diagonal tacks hold folds or overlaid fabrics together, while slip tacks are used to hold a fold in fabric to another piece of fabric.

Basic tacks

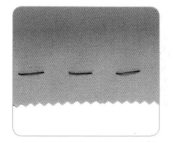

Starting with a knot and, using single thread, make straight stitches, evenly spaced.

Long and short

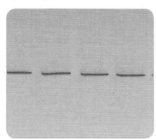

Make long stitches with a short space between each one.

Diagonal tacks

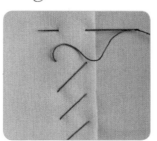

Work vertically, taking horizontal stitches.

Slip tacks

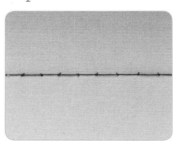

Take a stitch into the fold and then a stitch into the base fabric.

Stitches for hand sewing

There are a number of hand stitches that can be used during construction of a garment or other item. Some are for decorative purposes while others are more functional.

Back stitch

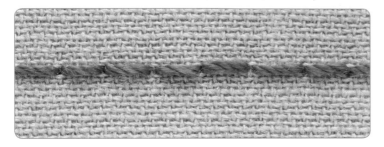

A strong stitch that could be used to construct a piece of work. Work from right to left. Bring the needle up, leaving a space, and then take the thread back to the end of the last stitch.

Running stitch

Very similar to tacking (see page 49), but used more for decorative purposes. Work from right to left. Run the needle in and out of the fabric to create even stitches and spaces.

Whip stitch

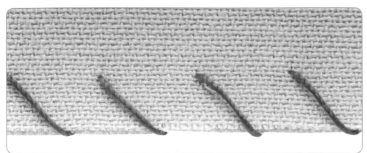

A diagonal stitch sewn with a single thread along a raw edge to prevent fraying. Work from right to left. Take a stitch through the edge of the fabric. The depth of the stitch depends on the thickness of the fabric – for a thin fabric take a shallow stitch.

Buttonhole stitch

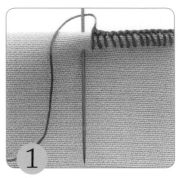

1 Used to make hand-worked buttonholes and also to secure fastenings. It is always stitched on an edge with no spaces between the stitches. Work from right to left. Push the needle from the top edge into the fabric.

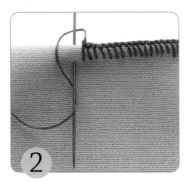

2 Wrap the thread behind the needle as the needle goes in and again as the needle leaves the fabric. Pull through and a knot will appear at the edge. This is an essential stitch for all sewers and is not difficult to master.

Slip stitch

This is an almost invisible stitch that is used to join two folded edges together, such as the opening in a cushion. You can also use it to attach a folded edge to an unfolded piece of fabric. To do this simply pick up one or two threads of the unfolded fabric on your needle as you make your second stitch back through the folded fabric edge.

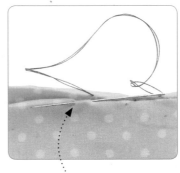

Slide the needle through the fold in one edge and bring it out one stitch ahead

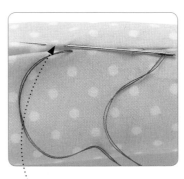

Slide the needle into the fold on the other side to draw the two folds together. Repeat along the length of the seam

Herringbone stitch

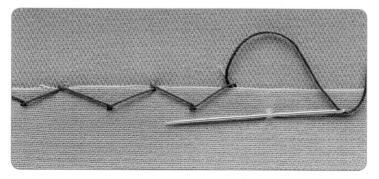

A very useful stitch as it is secure yet has some movement in it. It is used to secure hems and interlinings. Work from left to right. Take a small horizontal stitch into one layer and then the other, so the thread crosses itself.

Flat fell stitch

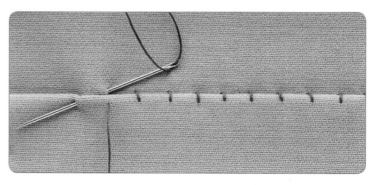

A strong, secure stitch to hold two layers permanently together. This stitch is often used to secure bias bindings and linings. Work from right to left. Make a short, straight stitch at the edge of the fabric.

Slip hem stitch

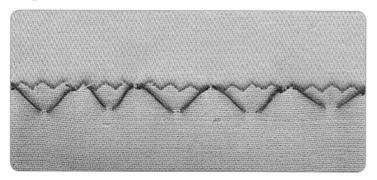

Also called a catch stitch, this is used primarily for securing hems. It looks similar to herringbone (above). Work from right to left. Take a short horizontal stitch into one layer and then the other.

Blind hem stitch

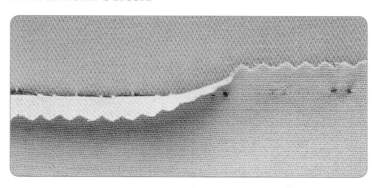

As the name suggests this is for hemming a garment. As the stitch is under the edge of the fabric it should be discreet. Work from right to left and use a slip hem stitch (left).

Blanket stitch

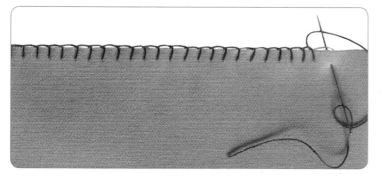

Similar to buttonhole stitch but without the knot. Blanket stitch is useful to neaten edges and for decorative purposes. Always leave a space between the stitches. Push the needle into the fabric and, as it appears at the edge, wrap the thread under the needle.

Cross stitch

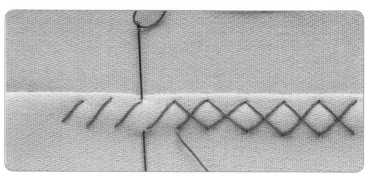

A temporary securing stitch used to hold pleats in place after construction. It can also be used to secure linings. Work a row of even diagonal stitches in one direction and then a row back over them to make crosses.

Machine stitches and seams

Fabric is joined together using seams – whether it be for an item of clothing, craft work, or soft furnishings. The most common seam is a plain seam, which is suitable for a wide variety of fabrics and items. However, there are many other seams to be used as appropriate, depending on the fabric and item being constructed. Some seams are decorative and can add detail to structured garments.

Securing the thread

Machine stitches need to be secured at the end of a seam to prevent them from coming undone. This can be done by hand, tying the ends of the thread, or using the machine with a reverse stitch or a locking stitch, which stitches three or four stitches in the same place.

Reverse stitch

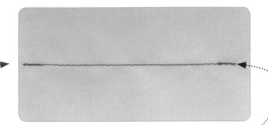

1 When starting, stitch a couple of stitches forward, then hold in the reverse button and reverse over them. Continue forward again.

2 At the end of the seam, reverse again to secure the stitches.

Tie the ends

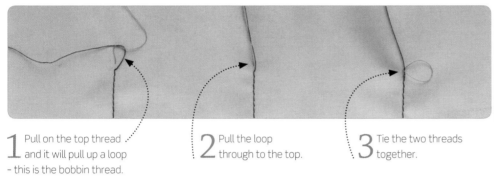

1 Pull on the top thread and it will pull up a loop – this is the bobbin thread.

2 Pull the loop through to the top.

3 Tie the two threads together.

Locking stitch

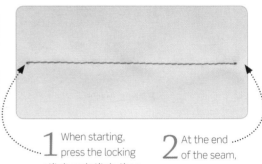

1 When starting, press the locking stitch and stitch, then continue forward.

2 At the end of the seam, press the locking stitch again.

Stitches made with a machine

The sewing machine will stitch plain seams and decorative seams as well as buttonholes of various styles. The length and width of all buttonholes can be altered to suit the garment or craft item.

Straight stitch

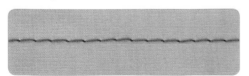

Used for most applications. The length of the stitch can be altered from 0.5 to 5.0 on most sewing machines.

Zigzag stitch

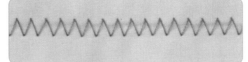

To neaten seam edges and for securing and decorative purposes. Both the width and the length of this stitch can be altered.

3-step zigzag stitch

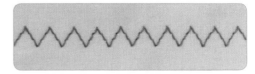

Made up of small, straight stitches. This stitch is decorative as well as functional, and is often found in lingerie. The stitch length and width can be altered.

Blind hem stitch

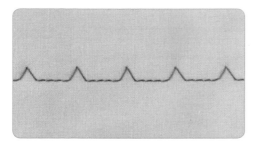

Made in conjunction with the blind hem foot. A combination of straight stitches and a zigzag stitch (see opposite page). Used to secure hems.

Overedge stitch

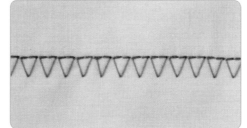

Made in conjunction with the overedge foot. The stitch is used for neatening the edge of fabric. The width and length of the stitch can be altered.

Stretch stitch

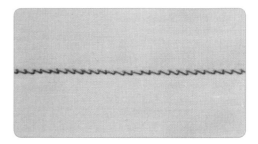

Also known as a lightening stitch. This stitch is recommended for stretch knits but is better used to help control difficult fabrics.

Basic buttonhole stitch

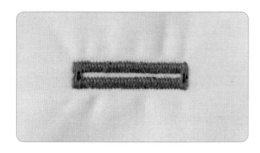

Square on both ends. Used on all styles of garment.

Round-end buttonhole stitch

One square end and one round end. Used on jackets.

Keyhole buttonhole stitch

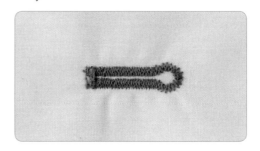

One square end and one end shaped like a loop. Used on jackets.

Decorative stitches

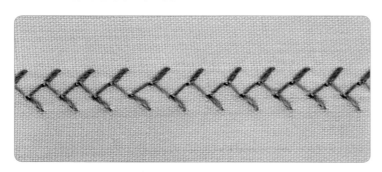

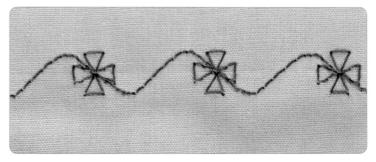

Sewing machines are capable of producing decorative linear stitches. These can be used to enhance the surface of work or a seam as they add interest to edges. Or, when worked as many rows together, they can be used to create a piece of embroidered fabric.

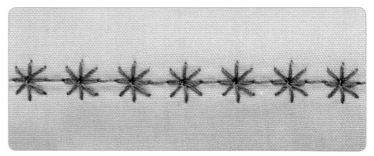

How to make a plain seam

A plain seam is 1.5cm (⅝in) wide. It is important that the seam is stitched accurately at this measurement, otherwise the item being made will come out the wrong size and shape. There are guides on the plate of the sewing machine that can be used to help align the fabric.

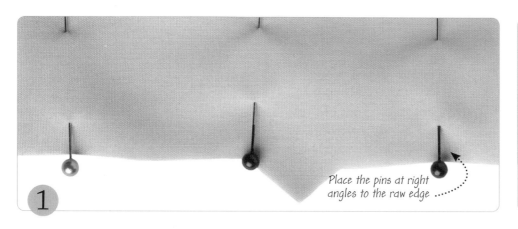

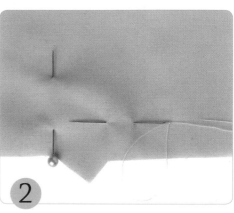

Place the pins at right angles to the raw edge

1

2

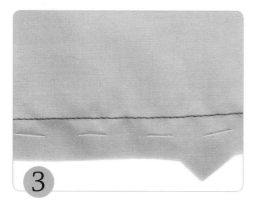

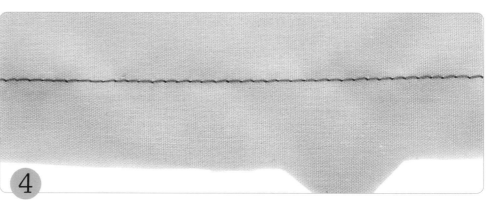

3

4

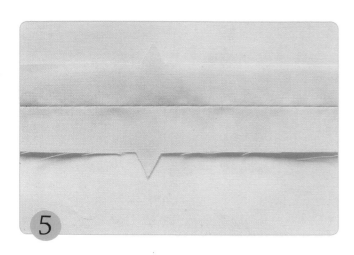

5

1 Pin the two pieces of fabric together, right side to right side, matching notches. Place the pins at right angles to the raw edge at approx 5–8cm (2–3in) intervals

2 Tack the two pieces of fabric together about 1cm (⅜in) from the raw edge, removing the pins as you get to them.

3 Using the seam guide on the machine plate to help you, place the fabric under the machine foot. Turn the balance wheel to place the needle into the fabric, then lower the presser foot on the sewing machine.

4 Machine the seam at 1.5cm (⅝in), securing it at either end by your chosen technique. Carefully remove the tacking stitches.

5 Press the seam flat as it was stitched, then press the seam open.

Seam neatening

It is important that the raw edges of the seam are neatened or finished – this will make the seam hard-wearing and prevent fraying. The method of neatening will depend on the style of item that is being made and the fabric you are using.

Pinked

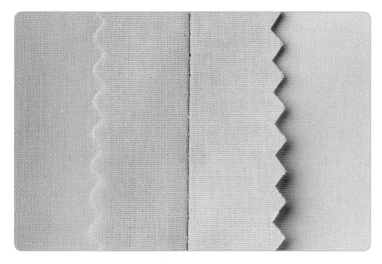

This method of neatening is ideal to use on fabrics that do not fray badly. Using pinking shears, trim as little as possible off the raw edge.

Zigzagged

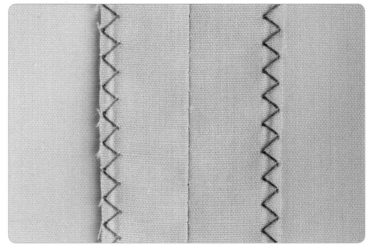

All sewing machines will make a zigzag stitch. It is an ideal stitch to use to stop the edges fraying and is suitable for all types of fabric. Stitch in from the raw edge, then trim back to the zigzag stitch. On most fabrics, use a stitch width of 2.0 and a stitch length of 1.5.

Overedge stitched

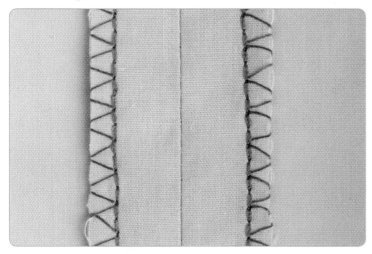

This is found on most sewing machines. Select the overedge stitch on your machine. Using the overedge machine foot and the pre-set stitch length and width, machine along the raw edge of the seam.

Clean finish

This is a very hard-wearing finish and is ideal for cottons and fine fabrics. Using a straight stitch, turn under the raw edge of the seam allowance by 3mm (1/8in) and straight stitch along the fold.

Hong Kong finish

This is a great finish to use on wools and linens, to neaten the seams on unlined jackets. It is made by wrapping the raw edge with bias-cut strips.

Raw edge

Wrap the raw edge,

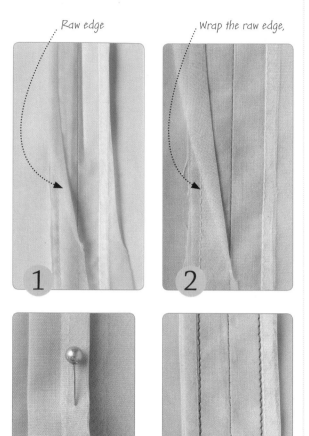

1 Cut bias strips of silk organza 2cm (³⁄₄in) wide. Good-quality lining fabric can also be used. Stitch the raw edge of the bias strip to the raw edge of the seam allowance. Press over the raw edge.

2 Wrap to the wrong side of the raw edge, with the raw edge of the bias strip against the stitching of the seam.

3 Pin the wrapped bias strip to the fabric, then press the folded edge.

4 Machine the wrapped bias strip to the seam, from the upper side of the seam, stitching alongside the edge of the bias.

Stitching corners and curves

Not all sewing is straight lines. The work will have curves and corners that require negotiation, to produce sharp clean angles and curves on the right side. The technique for stitching a corner shown below applies to corners of all angles. On a thick fabric, the technique is slightly different, with a stitch taken across the corner, and on a fabric that frays badly the corner is reinforced with a second row of stitches.

Stitching a corner

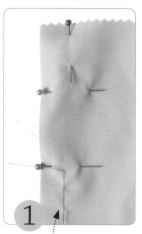 

Stitch a seam at 1.5cm (⁵⁄₈in)

 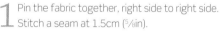

1 Pin the fabric together, right side to right side. Stitch a seam at 1.5cm (⁵⁄₈in).

2 On reaching the corner, insert the machine needle into the fabric. Raise the presser foot and turn the fabric through 90 degrees (this is pivoting at the corner). Lower the presser foot and continue stitching in the other direction.

3 The stitching lines are at right angles to each other, which means the finished corner will have a sharp point when turned through to the right side.

Stitching a corner on heavy fabric

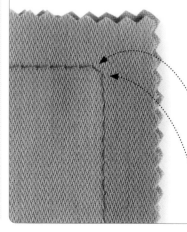

On thick fabric it is difficult to achieve a sharp point, so instead a single stitch is taken across the corner. Stitch to the corner.

1 Insert the needle into the fabric, then lift the presser foot. Turn the fabric 45 degrees. Put the foot down again and make one stitch.

2 With the needle in the fabric, lift the foot and turn the fabric 45 degrees again. Lower the foot and continue stitching along the other side.

Stitching a reinforced corner

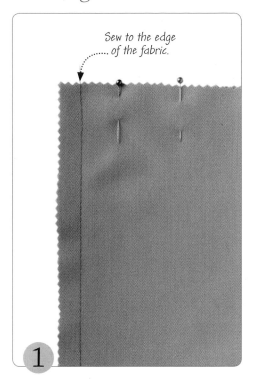

Sew to the edge of the fabric.

1

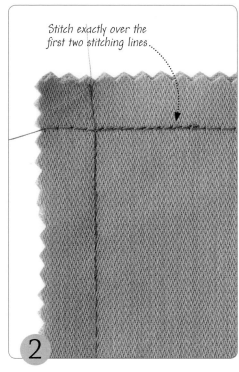

Stitch exactly over the first two stitching lines.

2

1 On the wrong side of the fabric, stitch along one side of the corner to make a 1.5cm (⅝in) seam. Take the machining through to the edge of the fabric.

2 Stitch the other side of the corner at a 1.5cm (⅝in) seam allowance, again machining through the edge of the fabric. The two stitching lines will overlap at the corner. Stitch exactly over the first two stitching lines, this time pivoting at the corner (see Stitching a corner, steps 2–3, page 56). Remove the surplus stitches in the seam allowance by unpicking.

Stitching an inner corner

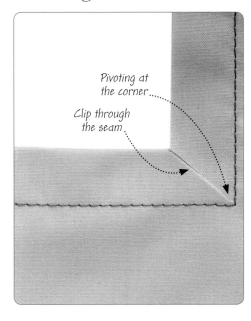

Pivoting at the corner.

Clip through the seam.

Machine accurately at 1.5cm (⅝in) from the edge, pivoting at the corner (see Stitching a corner, steps 2–3, page 56). Clip through the seam allowance into the corner.

Stitching an inner curve

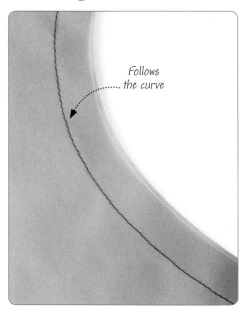

Follows the curve.

Place the right sides of the fabric together. Stitch a seam at 1.5cm (⅝in) from the edge. Be sure the stitching line follows the curve (use the stitching guides on the plate of the machine to help).

Stitching an outer curve

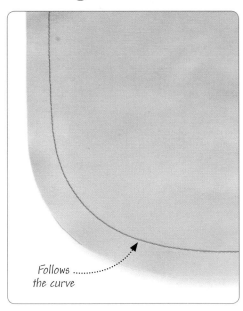

Follows the curve.

Put the right sides of the fabric together and stitch a 1.5cm (⅝in) seam. Follow the curve and keep the stitching line at a uniform distance from the edge.

Reducing seam bulk

It is important that the seams used for construction do not cause bulk on the right side. To make sure this does not happen, the seam allowances need to be reduced in size by a technique known as layering a seam. They may also require V shapes to be removed, which is known as notching, or the seam allowance may be clipped.

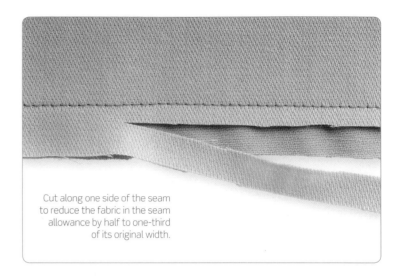

Cut along one side of the seam to reduce the fabric in the seam allowance by half to one-third of its original width.

Layering a seam

On the majority of fabrics, if the seam is on the edge of the work, the fabric in the seam needs reducing. The seam allowance closest to the outside of the garment or item stays full width, while the seam allowance closest to the body or inside is reduced.

Reducing seam bulk on an inner curve

For an inner curve to lie flat, the seam will need to be layered and notched, then understitched to hold it in place (see page 59).

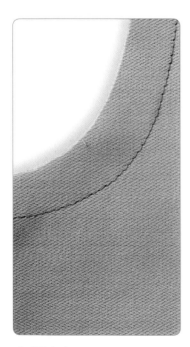

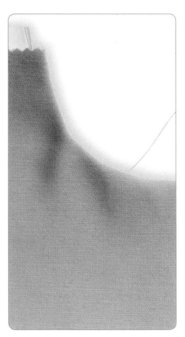

1 Stitch the seam on the inner curve.

2 Layer the seam (see above), then cut out V notches to reduce the bulk.

3 Turn to the right side and press.

4 Understitch the seam allowances on to the wrong side.

Reducing seam bulk on an outer curve

An outer curve also needs layering and notching or clipping to allow the fabric to turn to the right side, after which it is understitched.

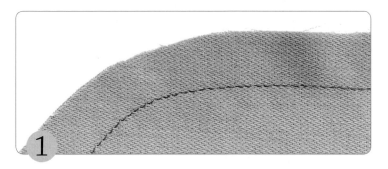

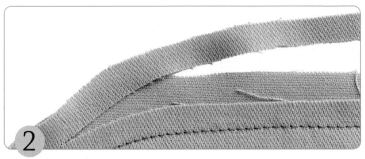

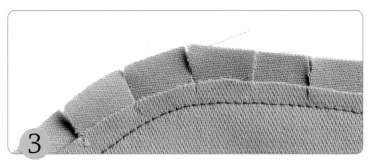

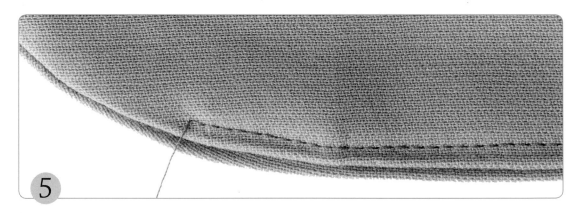

1 Make the seam, stitching along the outer curve.

2 Layer the seam (see page 58).

3 Clip through the seam allowances to reduce bulk.

4 Turn through to the right side and press.

5 Understitch the seam (see below) to finish.

Stitch finishes

Top-stitching and understitching are two methods to finish edges. Top-stitching is meant to be seen on the right side of the work, whereas understitching is not visible from the right side.

Top-stitching

A top-stitch is a decorative, sharp finish to an edge. Use a longer stitch length, of 3.0 or 3.5, and machine on the right side of the work, using the edge of the machine foot as a guide.

Understitching

Used to secure a seam that is on the edge of a piece of fabric. It helps to stop the seam from rolling to the right side. First make the seam, then layer, turn, and press on to the right side. Open the seam again and push the seam allowance over the layered seam allowance. Machine the seam allowance down.

French seam

A French seam is a seam that is stitched twice, first on the right side of the work and then on the wrong side, enclosing the first seam. The French seam has traditionally been used on delicate garments such as lingerie and on sheer and silk fabrics.

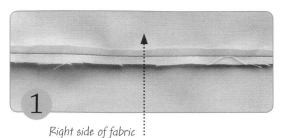

1

Right side of fabric

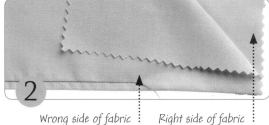

2

Wrong side of fabric   *Right side of fabric*

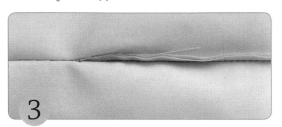

3

4

1 Stitch a seam 5mm (3/16in) from the edge of the fabric, with the fabric wrong side to wrong side so the seam is on the right side of the garment. Trim the seam slightly, then press open.

2 Fold the fabric right side to right side. Machine the joined edge using a 1cm (³⁄₈in) seam allowance.

3 The first seam will be enclosed by the second seam.

4 Press the completed seam flat on the right side.

Run and fell seam

Some garments require a strong seam that will withstand frequent washing and wear and tear. A run and fell seam, also known as a flat fell seam, is very strong. It is made on the right side of a garment and is used on the inside leg seam of jeans, and on men's tailored shirts.

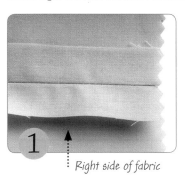

1

Right side of fabric

2

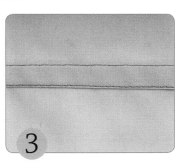

3

1 Stitch a 1.5cm (⁵⁄₈in) seam on the right side of the fabric. Press open.

2 Trim the side of the seam allowance that is towards the back of the garment down to one-third of its width. Wrap the other side of the seam allowance around the trimmed side and pin in position.

3 Machine along the folded pinned edge through all layers. Press. When you turn to the right side, there will be two rows of parallel stitching.

Top-stitched seam

A top-stitched seam is very useful as it is both decorative and practical. This seam is often used on crafts and soft furnishings as well as garments.

1 Make a 1.5cm (⁵⁄₈in) seam on the wrong side of the fabric. Press the seam open.

2 Working from the right side of the work, stitch down either side of the seam. Press.

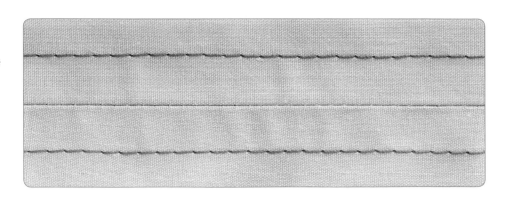

Lapped seam

Also called an overlaid seam, a lapped seam is constructed on the right side of the garment. It is a very flat seam when it is finished.

1 Press under 1.5cm (⅝in) on one side of the seamline to the wrong side. Place the folded edge of the fabric to the other half of the seamline on the right side. Pin in place.

2 Machine close to the fold. Machine again 1cm (⅜in) from the fold. Press.

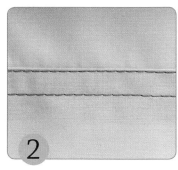

Seams on difficult fabrics

Some fabrics require specialist care for seam construction because they are very bulky, as you find with a fur fabric, or so soft and delicate that they appear too soft to sew. On a sheer fabric, the seam used is an alternative to a French seam; it is very narrow when finished and presses very flat. Making a seam on suede is done by means of a lapped seam. As some suede-effect fabric has a fake fur on the other side, the seam is reversible.

A seam on sheer fabric

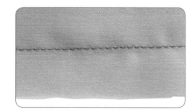

1 On the wrong side of the work, make a 1.5cm (⅝in) seam.

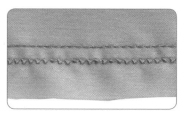

2 Machine again 5mm (³⁄₁₆in) from the first stitching, using either a very narrow zigzag stitch or a stretch stitch. Press.

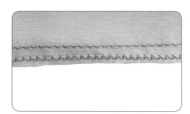

3 Trim the raw edge of the fabric close to the second row of stitching.

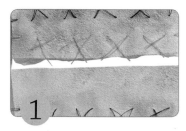

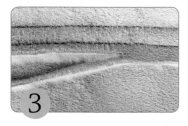

A seam on suede or suede-effect fabric

1 On all seams, trace tack the stitching line 1.5cm (⅝in) from the edge. Trace tack again 1.5cm (⅝in) away from the first row of stitching.

2 Overlap one side of the seam over the other, matching the 1.5cm (⅝in) tack lines. The raw edge should touch the second row of tacks. Using a walking foot and a longer than normal stitch length of 3.5, machine the two layers together along the tacks marking the 1.5cm (⅝in) seam allowance.

3 Stitch again 1cm (⅜in) from the first stitching line. Trim the raw edge by about 3mm (⅛in).

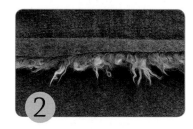

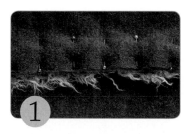

A seam on fur fabric

1 Pin the fabric together right side to right side, placing the pins in alternate directions to stop the fur moving.

2 Using a walking foot and a longer than normal stitch length, machine the seam.

3 Finger press the seam open. Trim the surplus fur fabric off the seam allowances.

How to sew embroidery stitches

Now it's time to move on and learn how to do some simple embroidery stitches. Master these and you'll be able to use them to decorate the felt flower brooches on pp.139–141, as well as in various other projects. But first, you'll need to invest in a crewel needle and some embroidery thread (see p.18 and p.24).

Cross stitch

This simple X-shaped stitch has been used for centuries all over the world. You may have seen it decorating household linens. Work the cross stitches on their own or next to each other to form a row, as shown here. Always start by working from left to right.

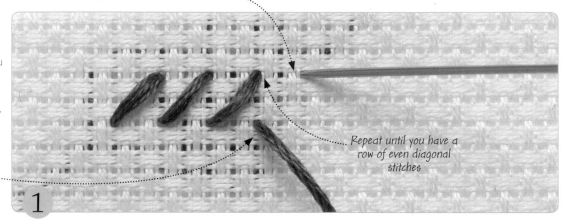

Take the needle diagonally across to the right for the top of the stitch

Bring the needle through to the front of the fabric for the bottom of the stitch

Repeat until you have a row of even diagonal stitches

1

Complete the X by taking the thread over the diagonal stitch to the left and down through the fabric at the top of the next diagonal stitch along

Working from right to left, bring the needle to the front of the fabric, at the bottom of the last diagonal stitch

2

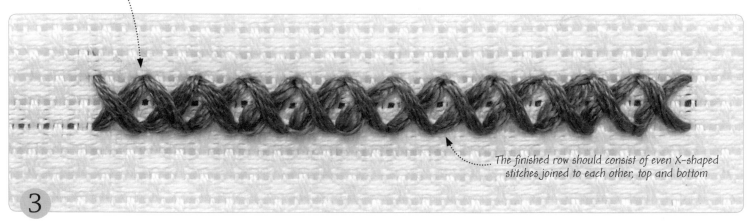

Repeat to complete the row

The finished row should consist of even X-shaped stitches joined to each other, top and bottom

3

Blanket stitch

You can use blanket stitch for finishing any sort of an edge or simply for decoration.
It can also be used for appliqué – attaching a fabric shape to another piece of fabric.
Work from left to right. Start by bringing the needle from the back of the fabric to the front.

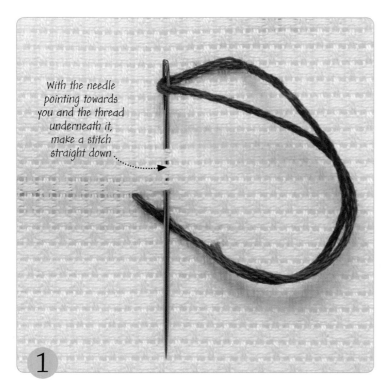

With the needle pointing towards you and the thread underneath it, make a stitch straight down

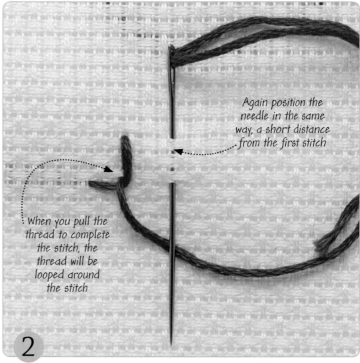

Again position the needle in the same way, a short distance from the first stitch

When you pull the thread to complete the stitch, the thread will be looped around the stitch

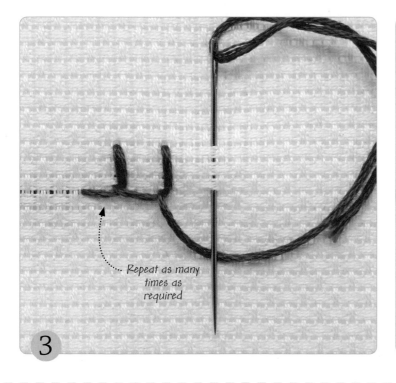

Repeat as many times as required

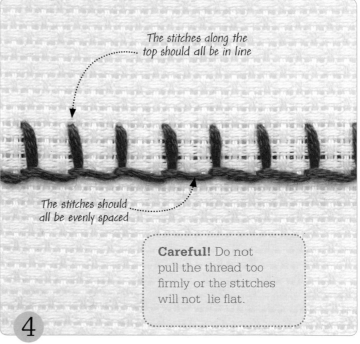

The stitches along the top should all be in line

The stitches should all be evenly spaced

Careful! Do not pull the thread too firmly or the stitches will not lie flat.

Chain stitch

When worked in a continuous row, as shown above, chain stitch creates a chain-like effect. Alternatively, after Step 3, take your needle over the loop and through to the back of the fabric. This will hold the loop in place and produce a stitch that looks like a leaf or petal.

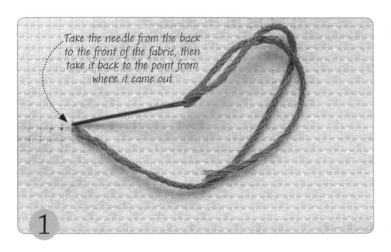

Take the needle from the back to the front of the fabric, then take it back to the point from where it came out

1

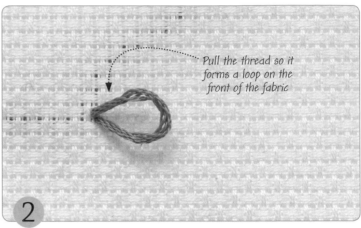

Pull the thread so it forms a loop on the front of the fabric

2

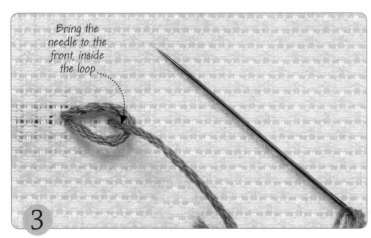

Bring the needle to the front, inside the loop

3

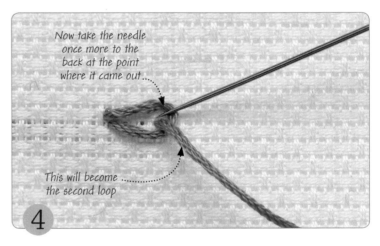

Now take the needle once more to the back at the point where it came out

This will become the second loop

4

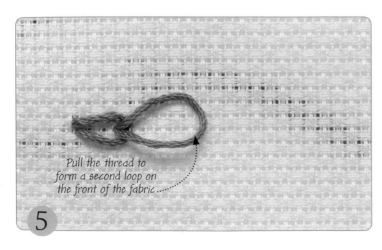

Pull the thread to form a second loop on the front of the fabric

5

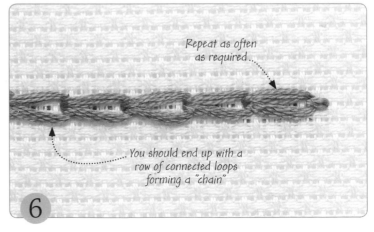

Repeat as often as required

You should end up with a row of connected loops forming a "chain"

6

French knot

This classic stitch adds a welcome element of texture to your work. You can use these little knots for lots of decorative effects, either on their own or in groups. A single knot can be a flower centre, an eye, or a nose, while a group of knots works well as a flower head.

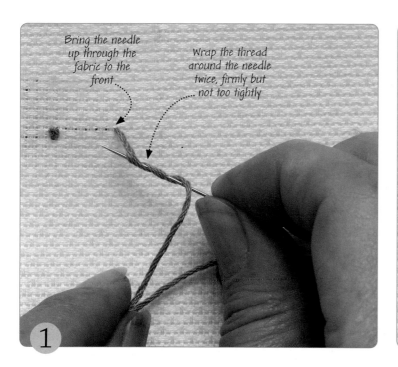

Bring the needle up through the fabric to the front

Wrap the thread around the needle twice, firmly but not too tightly

1

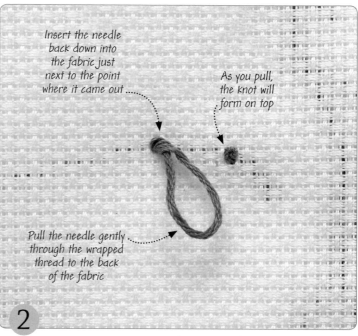

Insert the needle back down into the fabric just next to the point where it came out

As you pull, the knot will form on top

Pull the needle gently through the wrapped thread to the back of the fabric

2

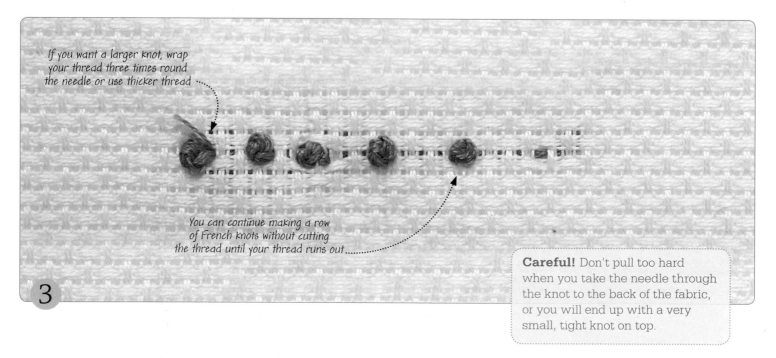

If you want a larger knot, wrap your thread three times round the needle or use thicker thread

You can continue making a row of French knots without cutting the thread until your thread runs out

3

Careful! Don't pull too hard when you take the needle through the knot to the back of the fabric, or you will end up with a very small, tight knot on top.

Gathers

Gathers are an easy way to draw up a piece of larger fabric so that it will fit on to a smaller piece of fabric. The gather stitch is inserted after the major seams have been constructed, and it is best worked on the sewing machine using the longest stitch length that is available. On the majority of fabrics two rows of gather stitches are required, but for very heavy fabrics it is advisable to make three rows. Try to stitch the rows so that the stitches line up under one another.

How to make and fit gathers

Once all the main seams have been sewn, stitch the two rows of gathers so that the stitches are inside the seam allowance. This should avoid the need to remove them because removing gathers after they have been pulled up can damage the fabric.

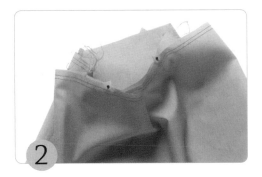

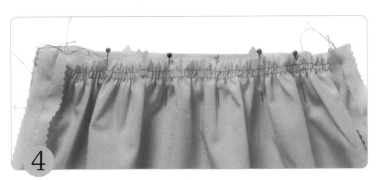

1 Stitch one row of gathers at 1cm (³⁄₈in) and the second row at 1.2cm (¹⁄₂in). Leave long tails of thread for gathering. Break the stitching lines at the seams.

2 Place the piece to be gathered to the other garment section, right side to right side. Match the notches and seams, and pin these first.

3 Gently pull on the two ends of the thread on the wrong side – the fabric will gather along the thread.

4 Secure the threads at the one end to prevent the stitches from pulling out. Even out the gathers and pin.

5 When all the gathers are in place, use a standard machine stitch to stitch a 1.5cm (⁵⁄₈in) wide seam. Stitch with the gathers uppermost and keep pulling them to the side to stop them creasing up.

6 Turn the bodice of the garment inside. Using a mini iron, press the seam very carefully to avoid creasing the gathers.

7 Neaten the seam by stitching both edges together. Use either a zigzag stitch or a 3-thread overlock stitch. Press the seam up towards the bodice.

8 Press the gathers using the mini iron.

Staying a gathered seam

A gathered seam is often stayed by stitching on cotton stay tape, to ensure the gathers remain in place and also to help strengthen the seam.

1 Machine the stay tape in place adjacent to the seam stitching line.

2 Using a zigzag stitch, machine the top of the stay tape to the raw edge of the seam.

Joining two gathered edges together

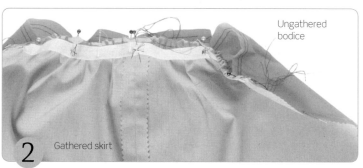

On some garments it may be necessary to join together two gathered edges. This usually happens when gathering a skirt on to a gathered bodice. The one side, usually the skirt, is gathered first on to a stay tape and the second side is gathered to fit, then stitched in place.

1 Stitch two rows of gathers at the waist edge. Pull up the gathers to fit a stay tape that fits the waist. Pin and tack the gathers to the tape.

2 Stitch two rows of gathers at the waist edge of the bodice. Place the bodice waist, right side to right side, to the skirt waist, matching seams and notches. Pull up the bodice gathers to fit the skirt. Pin the two layers together.

3 Machine the two sets of gathers together through the tape. Make a second row of stitching for strength.

4 The waist of the bodice is now gathered to fit the skirt waist.

Tucks

A tuck is a decorative addition to any piece of fabric, and can be big and bold or very delicate. Tucks are made by stitching evenly spaced folds into the fabric on the right side, normally on the straight grain of the fabric. As the tucks take up additional fabric, it is advisable to make them prior to cutting out.

Plain tucks

A plain tuck is made by marking and creasing the fabric at regular intervals. A row of machine stitches are then worked adjacent to the fold.

1 Mark the position of the tucks lightly with chalk on the right side of the fabric. Make sure the lines are parallel.

2 Fold along the chalk lines, making sure the folds are straight, and press in place.

3 Machine close to the foldline, using the edge of the machine foot as a guide Repeat along the next fold, and continue until all the folds are stitched.

4 Press the tucks all in the same direction.

Other simple tucks

These tucks are also made by marking and creasing the fabric. The positioning of the machine stitching determines the type of tuck.

Spaced tucks

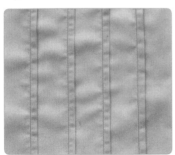

These are similar to a plain tuck but with wider regular spacing. Press the tucks in place along the foldlines and pin. Machine 1cm (3/8in) from the foldline. Press all the tucks in one direction.

Pin tucks

These narrow, regularly spaced tucks are stitched very close to the foldline, which may require moving the machine needle closer to the fold. Use the pintuck foot on the sewing machine.

Twin needle tucks

For these regularly spaced tucks, stitch along the foldlines using the twin needle on the sewing machine. The twin needle produces a shallow tuck that looks very effective when multiple rows are stitched.

Blind tucks

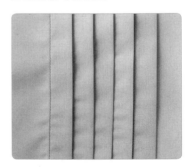

These are stitched so that they touch. Fold back all but one tuck and stitch it in place. Continue stitching the tucks in this way so that the folded edge of each covers the machine line of the previous tuck.

Darted tucks

A tuck that stops to release the fullness is known as a darted tuck. It can be used to give fullness at the bust or hip. The shaped darted tuck is stitched at an angle to release less fabric, while the plain darted tuck is stitched straight on the grainline.

Shaped darted tucks

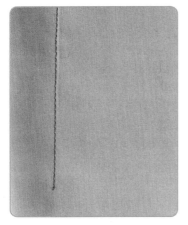

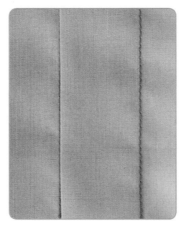

1 Transfer any pattern markings to the fabric. Fold the fabric right side to right side. On the wrong side of the fabric, stitch at an angle to the folded edge.

2 Stop at the point indicated on your pattern. Secure machining.

Plain darted Tucks

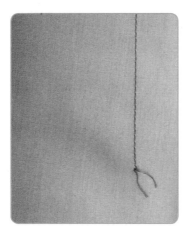

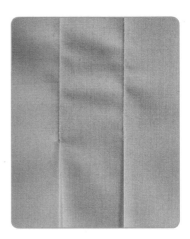

1 Make similar to the shaped darted tuck (see left), but stitch parallel to the folded edge. Stop as indicated on the pattern.

2 The tuck as seen from the right side.

Cross tucks

These are tucks that cross over each other by being stitched in opposite directions.

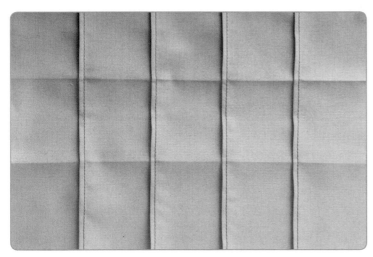

1 Press the crease lines into the fabric, both vertically and horizontally. Stitch all the vertical tucks first: fold the fabric wrong side to wrong side along the crease lines. Stitch 5mm (³⁄₁₆in) from the folded edge

2 Stitch all the horizontal tucks in the same way. Press all the vertical or horizontal tucks in the same direction.

Darts

A dart is used to give shape to a piece of fabric so that it can fit around the contours of the body. Some darts are stitched using straight stitching lines and other darts are stitched using a slightly curved line. Always stitch a dart from the point to the wide end because you are able to sink the machine needle into the point accurately and securely.

Plain dart

This is the most common type of dart and is used to give shaping to the bust in the bodice. It is also found at the waist in skirts and trousers to give shape from the waist to the hip.

Point of dart

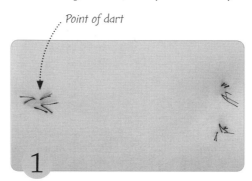

1

1 Tailor tack the points of the dart as marked on the pattern, making one tack at the point and two to mark the wide ends.

2 Fold the fabric right side to right side, matching the tailor's tacks. Pin through the tailor's tacks to match them.

3 Tack along the dart line, joining the tailor's tacks. Remove the pins.

4 Machine stitch alongside the tacking line. Remove the tacks.

5 Sew the machine threads back into the stitching line of the dart to secure them.

6 Press the dart to one side (see page 71).

7 The finished dart on the right side.

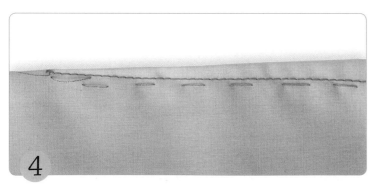

2

3

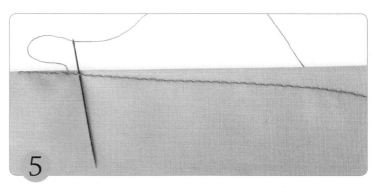

4

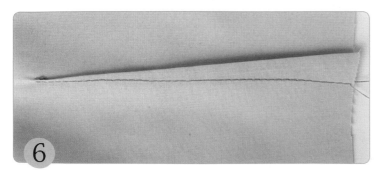

5

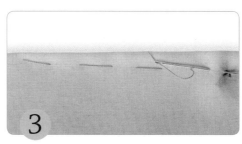

6

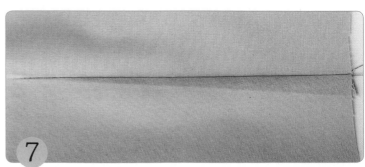

7

Contour or double-pointed dart

This type of dart is like two darts joined together at the fat end. It is used to give shape at the waist of a garment. It will contour the fabric from the bust into the waist and then out again for the hip.

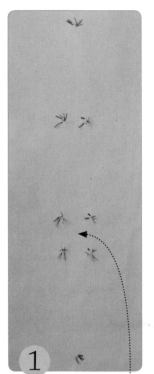

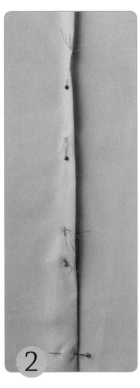

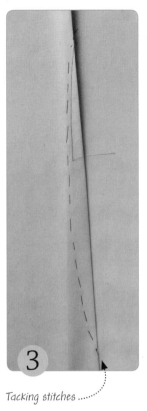

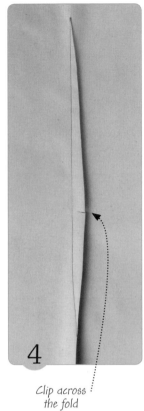

1

Darts closer together at waist.

2

3

Tacking stitches ......

4

Clip across the fold

1 Tailor tack the dots on the pattern piece that mark the dart. Cut through the loops in the tailor's tacks and remove the pattern.

2 Bring the tailor's tacks together, keeping the fabric right side to right side, and pin the tacks together.

3 Make a row of tacking stitches just outside the pin line. Machine stitch following the tailor-tack line, starting at one end and curving out to the widest point, then back to the other point, securing the machine stitching at both ends. Remove the tacking.

4 Clip across the fold in the fabric at the widest point, to allow the dart to be pressed to one side. Press the dart to one side. Contour darts are normally pressed towards the centre front or centre back.

Pressing a dart

If a dart is pressed incorrectly, this can spoil the look of a garment. For successful pressing you will need a tailor's ham and a steam iron on a steam setting. A pressing cloth may be required for delicate fabrics such as silk, satin, and chiffon, and for lining fabrics.

1

2

1 Place the fabric piece, right side down, on the tailor's ham. The point of the dart should be over the end of the ham. Press the fabric around the point of the dart.

2 Move the iron from the point towards the wide end of the dart to press the dart flat, open, or to one side, depending on the type of dart.

Hems and edges

The edge of a piece of fabric can be finished with a hem – which is normally used on garments – or with a decorative edge, which is used for crafts and soft furnishings as well as garments. Sometimes the style of what is being constructed dictates the finish that is used, and sometimes it is the fabric.

Tips for sewing hems by hand

1 Always use a single thread in the needle – a polyester all-purpose thread is ideal for hemming.
2 Once the raw edge of the hem allowance has been neatened by one of the methods below, secure it using a slip hem stitch. For this, take half of the stitch into the neatened edge and the other half into the wrong side of the garment fabric.
3 Start and finish the hand stitching with a double stitch, not a knot, because knots will catch and pull the hem down.
4 It is a good idea to take a small back stitch every 10cm (4in) or so to make sure that if the hem does come loose in one place it will not all unravel.

Turning up a straight hem

Once the crease line for the hem has been marked by the pins, you need to trim the hem allowance to a reasonable amount. Most straight hems are about 4cm (1½in) deep.

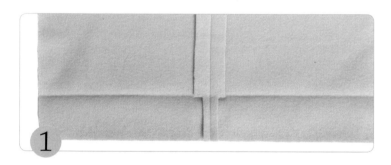

1 Gently press the crease line of the hem with the iron. Don't press too hard as you do not want a sharp crease. Trim the seam allowance back to reduce the bulk. If wished, neaten the raw edge.

2 Turn up the hem at the crease. Match the seams together. Tack the hem into position close to the crease line. The hem is now ready to be stitched in place by hand or machine.

Hand-stitched hems

One of the most popular ways to secure a hem edge is by hand. Hand stitching is discreet and, if a fine hand sewing needle is used, the stitching should not show on the right side of the work.

Clean finish

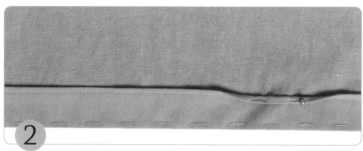

1 This is suitable for fine and lightweight fabrics. Turn the raw edge of the hem allowance to itself, wrong side to wrong side. Tack the edge and then machine. Lightly press the hem into position.

2 Tack the hem in place. Roll the edge stitching back and stitch underneath it. Using a small slip hem stitch, secure the edge of the hem to the wrong side of the fabric. Roll the edge back into place. Remove the tacking and press lightly.

Bias-bound finish

This is a good finish for fabrics that fray or that are bulky. Turn up the hem on to the wrong side of the garment and tack close to the crease line.

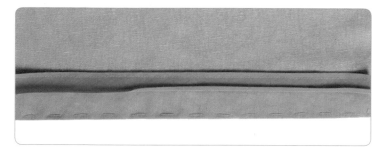

1 Pin the bias binding to the raw edge of the hem allowance. Open out the crease in the bias and stitch along the crease line, keeping the raw edges level. Turn down the bias over the raw edge and press.

2 Using a slip hem stitch, join the edge of the bias to the wrong side of the fabric. Remove the tacking and press lightly.

Zigzag finish

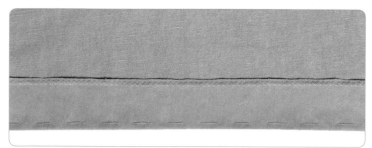

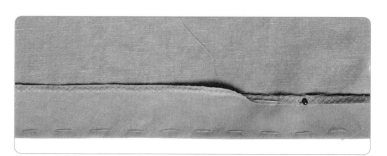

1 Use this to neaten the edge of the hem on fabrics that do not fray too badly. Set the sewing machine to a zigzag stitch, width 4.0 and length 3.0. Machine along the raw edge. Trim the fabric edge back to the zigzag stitch. Turn the hem on to the wrong side of the garment and tack in place close to the crease line.

2 Fold back the zigzag-stitched edge. Using a slip hem stitch, stitch the hem into place. Roll the edge back into position. Remove the tacking and lightly press.

Pinked finish

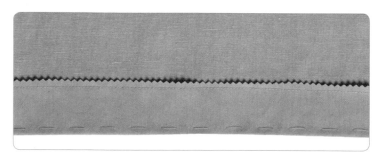

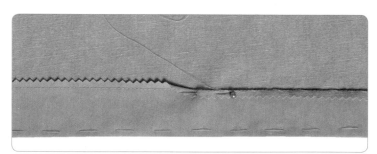

1 Pinking shears can give an excellent hem finish on difficult fabrics. Machine a row of straight stitching along the raw edge, 1cm (³⁄₈in) from the edge. Pink the raw edge. Turn up the hem to the wrong side of the garment and tack in place close to the crease line.

2 Fold back the edge along the machine stitching line and hand stitch the hem in place with a slip hem stitch. Roll the hem edge back into place. Remove the tacking and lightly press.

Turning up a curved hem

When the hem on a shaped skirt is turned up, it will be fuller at the upper edge. This fullness will need to be eased out before the hem is stitched.

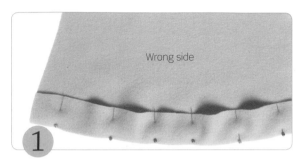

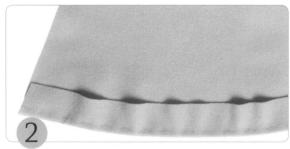

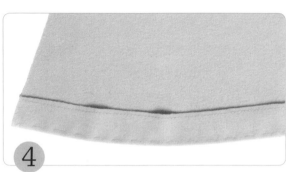

1 Mark the hemline, placing the pins vertically to avoid squashing the fullness out of the upper raw edge.

2 Tack the hem into position close to the crease line. Remove the pins.

3 Make a row of long machine stitches, length 5.0, close to the raw upper edge of the turned-up hem.

4 Pull on one of the threads of the long stitches to tighten the fabric and ease out the fullness. Use the steam iron to shrink out the remainder of the fullness. The hem is now ready to be stitched in place by hand or machine.

Curved hem finish

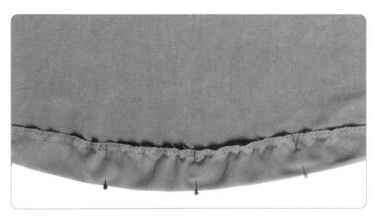

1 With a curved hem on a cotton or firm fabric, it is important that any fullness does not bulge on to the right side. Prior to turning up the hem into position, zigzag the raw edge, using stitch width 4.0 and stitch length 3.0. Machine a row of straight stitching 3mm (1/8in) below the zigzag stitching, using stitch length 5.0. Pin the hem into position, placing the pins vertically.

2 Tack the hem into position close to the crease line. Pull on the straight stitching to tighten the fabric. Roll the zigzagged edge back to the straight stitching line and hand stitch the hem in place using a slip hem stitch. Remove the tacking and press lightly.

Machined hems

On many occasions, the hem or edge of a garment or other item is turned up and secured using the sewing machine. It can be stitched with a straight stitch, a zigzag stitch, or a blind hem stitch.

Single turn hem

This is a popular technique. Turn up the hem to the wrong side of the work. Press in place. Machine with a straight stitch close to the hem edge.

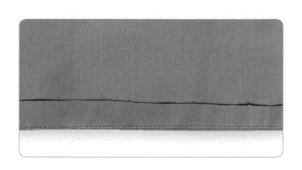

Double turn hem

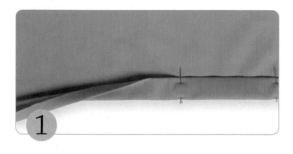

1 This hem will add weight at the edge. Fold up the raw edge of the fabric once and then fold again. Pin in place, then press.

2 Machine using a straight stitch, close to the upper fold.

Blind hem stitch

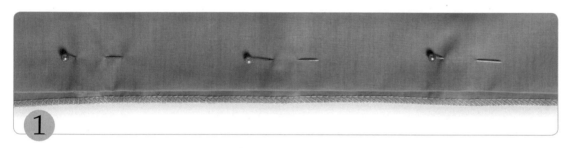

1 This is a single turn hem that is secured using the blind hem stitch on the machine. Neaten the raw edge of the fabric (here an overlock finish has been used). Fold the fabric as indicated for your machine (consult your instruction book). Pin, but not too close to the fold.

2 Using the blind hem foot and the blind hem stitch, secure the hem. The stitch line should be just below the neatened edge.

3 Press lightly on the right side.

Hems on difficult fabrics

Some very fine fabrics or fabrics that fray badly require more thought when a hem is to be made. This technique works very well on delicate fabrics.

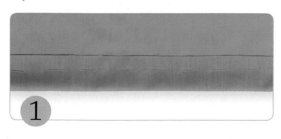

1 Turn up the hem with a single turn. Tack to secure.

2 Set the machine to a zigzag stitch, width 3.5 and length 2.0, and zigzag close to the fold. Trim away surplus hem allowance. Press.

Machined curtain hems

Curtains have hems at the bottom edge as well as at the sides. The hem at the bottom is treated differently from the side hems, using different techniques, although both types of hems are folded twice. The hems can be stitched using either machine or hand methods.

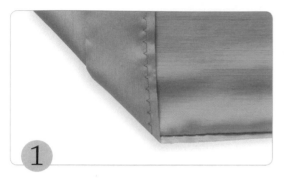
1

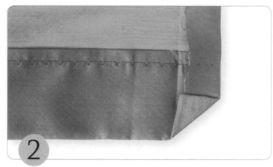
2

3

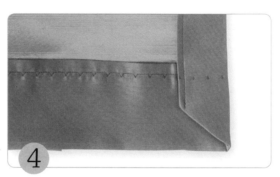
4

1 A curtain bottom hem is turned up twice. Turn the fabric up to the wrong side by 10cm (4in) and press with the iron. Turn up again by the same amount and press again. Machine in place using a blind hem stitch on your sewing machine.

2 At each side, turn under the edge to the wrong side by 4cm (1½in) and press. Turn again by the same amount and press again. Turn the corner in at an angle to mitre it (see opposite page) and press.

3 Open out and remove the fabric from under the mitre to reduce bulk.

4 Fold the doubled side hem back into position and pin in place. Using a straight stitch, machine close to the folded edge.

Hand-stitched curtain hems

Hand stitching is used on heavier curtain fabrics or where you do not want a machine stitch to show on the right side. Everything is pressed in place first.

1

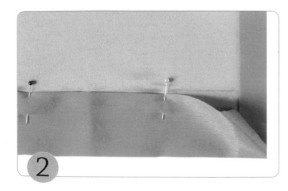
2

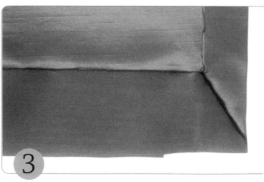
3

1 Turn each side hem in to the wrong side by 4cm (1½in) and press, then turn in again by the same amount and press again.

2 Turn up the bottom hem to the wrong side by 10cm (4in) and press, then turn up again by the same amount and press. Where the bottom hem and side hem meet, press under the hem at an angle to mitre it (see opposite page). Open out all the crease lines and reduce some of the bulk. Fold everything back into place and pin.

3 Use a herringbone stitch to stitch the bottom hem in place. Take shallow stitches that run along the folded edge. Repeat the process down the side hems. Stitch the mitred corner to match.

Mitred corners

At the bottom corners of curtains, where the bottom and side hems meet, the fabric is folded at an angle. This is called a mitre. By pressing the mitre with the iron and then unfolding it, you can use the crease lines that have been formed as a guide for removing surplus fabric to reduce bulk. For lined curtains, where the lining is constructed separately, the side and bottom hems are machined in place. The same mitring technique is used for both curtains and linings.

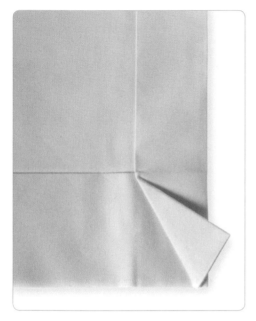

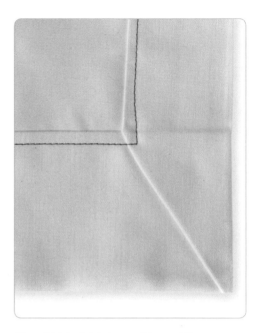

1 After the bottom and side hems have been turned and pressed, fold back the corner at an angle. The angle runs between the outer corner of the curtain and the point where the hems meet, at the inner corner.

2 Unfold the pressed hems and the mitre. Remove the surplus fabric.

3 Refold the fabric into position and, if necessary, press again. Pin into place. For curtain lining, machine the bottom and side hems using one continuous row of stitching, close to the folded edge and pivoting at the corner.

Weighting curtains

A weight is often inserted into the bottom hem of a curtain at the corners, to hold the curtain in place and make it hang properly. Specialist weights can be purchased, although a heavy coin can work just as well.

Measure the diameter of the weight. Cut a strip of curtain lining that is three times as long and twice as wide. Press under the short edges of the lining to the wrong side and press. Fold the strip in half, matching the turned-under edges, to make a rectangle large enough to enclose the weight.

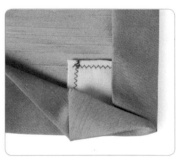

1 Using a zigzag stitch, machine the two long sides. Insert a coin or weight into the pouch.

2 Zigzag stitch across the open side.

3 Insert the weight pouch into the bottom corner of the curtain. When stitching the hems for the side and bottom, place stitches through into the weight pouch to hold it in place.

Hems with banding

Banding is a term applied to a much wider bias strip. Some banding is visible by the same amount at the hem or edge on both sides of the work, while other bandings are surface-mounted to the edge of a fabric, such as for a decorative effect on a blind or a table runner. Dealing with the corners on banding needs accurate marking and stitching. Most of the following techniques are used primarily on craft and home furnishing items.

Banding at inner corners

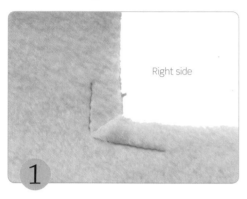

Right side

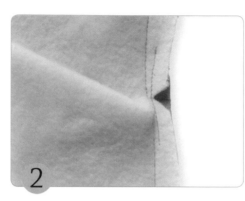

1 For this, the bias banding is machine stitched in place and hand finished. First reinforce the inner corner of the fabric by machine stitching 1cm (³⁄₈in) from the edge. Snip across the corner to the machine stitching.

2 Cut a strip of bias banding 7cm (2³⁄₄in) wide. Press under 1cm (³⁄₈in) on each side of the banding strip to the wrong side. Stitch the strip to the fabric, right side to right side, using a 1cm (³⁄₈in) seam allowance. Open out the clipped corner in the fabric as you stitch. Snip through the banding seam at the corner.

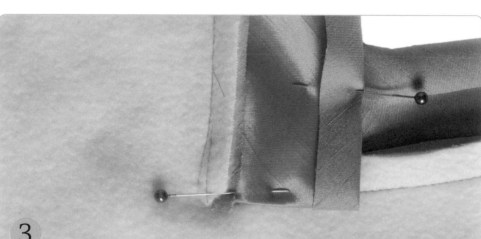

3 Open out the banding. Press the seam towards the banding. Fold the banding as illustrated and pin. Tack a diagonal line as indicated by the dotted red line on the photograph.

4 Fold the banding to the wrong side. Place the folded edge of the banding to the machining. Hand stitch using a flat fell stitch.

5 This is how banding looks on the right side. Press to finish.

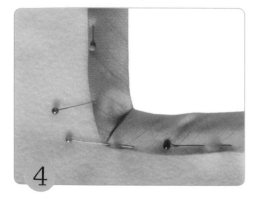

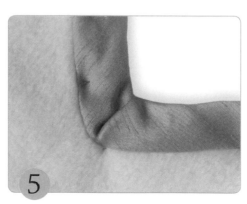

Banding at outer corners

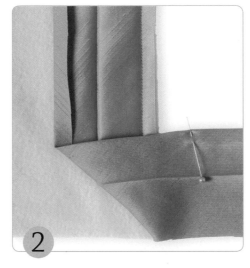

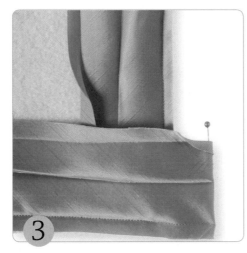

1 Cut a bias banding strip 7cm (2¾in) wide. Press under the long edges to the wrong side by 1cm (⅜in). Press the binding in half lengthways, wrong side to wrong side. Place the banding to the fabric, right side to right side. Stitch along the crease line, stopping the machining 1cm (⅜in) from the corner.

2 Fold the banding on to itself diagonally, wrong side to wrong side. Using a pin or tailor's tack, mark on the banding the centre foldline to the stitching. Then mark the same distance from the stitching line (indicated by the dotted red lines). Mark this point with a vertical pin.

3 Fold the banding at right angles on to itself, right side to right side, aligning edge to edge with the fabric. Make sure the vertical pin is at the fold. Machine along the lower crease in the banding. Extend the machining through the folded part of the banding as well. Stitch in the point for the banding corner as indicated by the dotted red lines. Trim to remove surplus fabric around the point.

4 Open out the banding and press the seams towards the banding. Fold the banding to the wrong side of the fabric along the centre crease line. Fold in the mitred corners on either side. Pin in place. Finish on the wrong side with a flat fell stitch.

5 Turn to the right side and press.

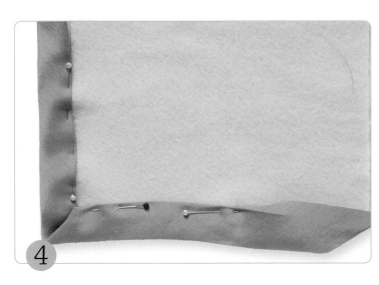

How to make a bias strip

A bias strip is a length of fabric that is cut on the bias, or cross. This gives it some stretch, which makes it perfect for edging and neatening a curve. You can buy bias binding ready-made, but it's useful to know how to make your own as you can then make it to match your fabric exactly if you need to.

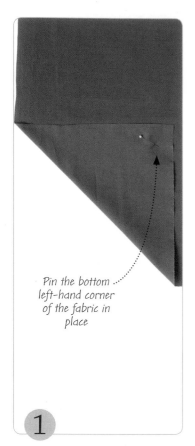

Pin the bottom left-hand corner of the fabric in place

1

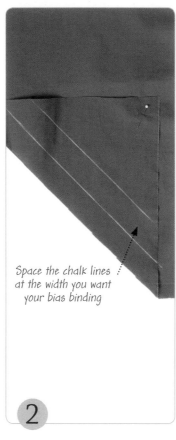

Space the chalk lines at the width you want your bias binding

2

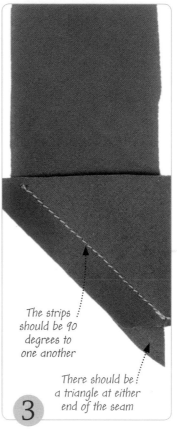

The strips should be 90 degrees to one another

There should be a triangle at either end of the seam

3

1 Place the fabric so the selvedges are on the right and left and the cut edges at the top and bottom. Fold the bottom left-hand corner of the fabric upwards and onto itself at a 45-degree angle. The left-hand selvedge will form a right-angled crease.

2 With the fold pinned in place, use tailor's chalk and a ruler to carefully mark a series of lines parallel with the fold to designate the width of your strips – bias binding is commonly 4cm (1½in) wide. Cut along these lines to make several bias strips of the same width.

3 Place two of the strips right side to right side at 90 degrees to each other so that their angled edges line up. Join the strips together with a line of straight machine stitching. You should end up with a little triangle of overhanging fabric at either end of the seam.

4 Flip the "arm" of the strip over so you have a single straight strip with a diagonal seam running through it. Iron the seam open so that the strip lies completely flat. Trim away the triangles at the seam. Continue to sew strips together until you have the length you need.

The seam will be hard to spot once the bias strip is in place on your project

Unfold this seam then iron flat

Trim away the two excess triangles to create one straight-edged strip of fabric

4

How to apply bias binding

The raw edge of a piece of fabric will require neatening to prevent it from fraying. There are several ways to do this. The edge can simply be finished with a zigzag or overlock stitch or it can be pinked. However, finishing the edge with bias binding makes the project a little more luxurious and can add a designer touch to a garment.

The edge of the fabric and the edge of the binding should align

Machine along the crease line in the bias binding

1

1 Making your own bias strip is easy (see page 80). Alternatively, you can buy bias binding ready made. Open out one folded edge of the bias binding and pin it along the raw edge of the fabric, right side to right side. Sew the two layers together by stitching along the crease in the binding. Make sure the binding edge aligns with the fabric edge.

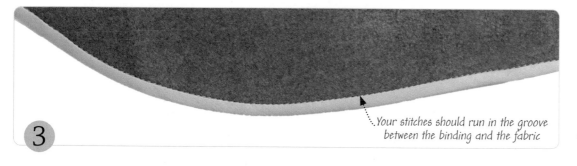

Tack the bias strip in place

The edge of the bias strip is folded under

2

2 Fold the bias binding over the stitching and under the fabric to the wrong side. The folded edge of the bias strip should remain folded under – it will have a neat appearance on the wrong side. Gently ease the binding in place and pin it along the whole length of the fabric. Use a tacking stitch to hold it in place (see p.46) and remove your pins.

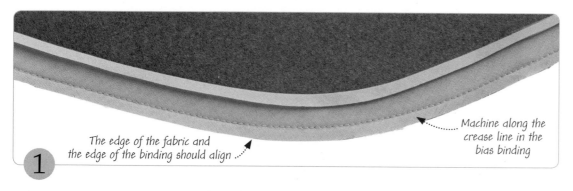

Your stitches should run in the groove between the binding and the fabric

3

3 With the right side of your fabric facing up, machine stitch along the groove made by the bias-binding-to-fabric stitching. Sew very slowly and carefully around any curves to make sure you don't stray off course. Sew through all the layers. If you don't, the bias strip edge will eventually unfold with wear and tear and washing, and will look ragged.

Your stitches should run along the centre of the bias binding

4

4 When you turn your fabric over to the wrong side the bias-bound edge will have a neat finish, with the stitches running along the centre of the binding. As an alternative to machine stitching the second seam you can slip stitch (see p.50) the binding to the back of the fabric using matching thread. No stitches will be visible on the front.

Bias bound hems

A bias-bound hem will give a narrow decorative edge to a garment or an item of home furnishing. It is particularly useful for curved shapes, to finish them neatly and securely. On a bulky or chunky fabric a double bias is used so that it will be more substantial and hold its shape better. A double bias is also used on sheer fabrics as there will be no visible raw edges. The bias strip can be made from purchased bias binding or cut from a matching or contrasting fabric.

Single bias-bound hem

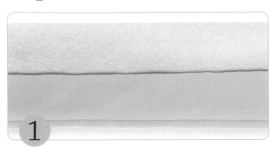

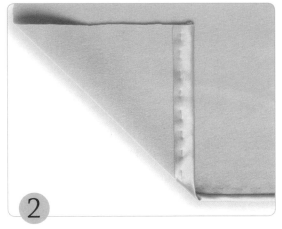

1 Place the bias strip to the hem edge, right side to right side. Machine the bias to the edge using the edge of the machine foot as a guide. Press as sewn. Turn the bias to the wrong side of the fabric and roll the bias around the edge of the fabric.

2 Tack the bias down on to the wrong side of the fabric. Working from the right side, stitch in the ditch formed by the seam. On the wrong side, trim the bias back close to the stitching (bias-cut fabric hardly frays). Remove the tacking and press.

Double bias-bound hem

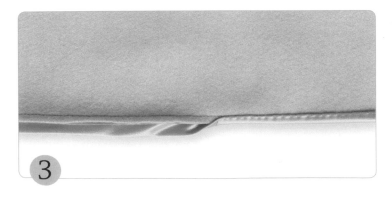

1 Cut bias strips that are 8cm (3¼in) wide. Join them together until the required length is achieved. Fold the bias in half, wrong side to wrong side. Tack along the bias to hold in place.

2 Place the raw edge of the bias to the hem edge of the right side of the fabric. Machine stitch in place, using the edge of the machine foot as a guide.

3 Wrap the folded edge of the bias to the wrong side of the garment. Place the folded edge to the machine stitching. Use a slip hem stitch to secure the folded edge to the machining.

4 If preferred, machine stitch the bias in place using a stitch in the ditch technique.

Interfaced hems

On tailored garments, such as jackets and winter skirts, an interfaced hem can be used. It is only suitable for straight hems as it produces a heavy structured edge. A sew-in woven interfacing cut on the bias grain is used for this technique.

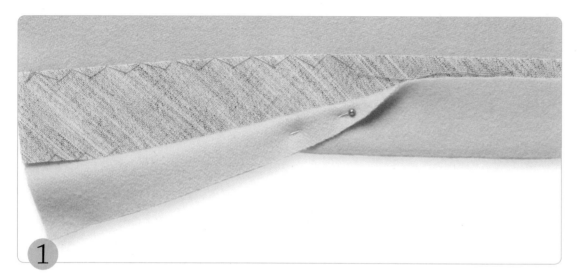

1 Cut a bias strip of sew-in woven interfacing 5cm (2in) wide. If it requires joining, use a lapped seam. Press up a 4cm (1½in) hem on the garment to the wrong side to make a hemline crease. Place the interfacing to the crease line of the hem. Herringbone stitch the interfacing in place, stitching along the upper and lower edges.

2 Pin the hem up over the interfacing. A strip of interfacing should show at the upper edge of the hem. Roll back the top edge of the hem. Herringbone stitch just to the interfacing.

3 Roll back the hem into position. Press. On the right side, no stitching will be visible.

Horsehair braid hems

On special-occasion wear, a horsehair braid is used in the hem edge as it will hold the edge out and give a look of fullness. Although once made from horsehair, the braid is now made from nylon. It is available in various widths. The braid is stretchy so try not to stretch it when applying.

Using a narrow horsehair braid

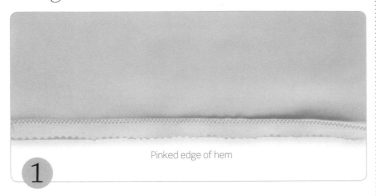

Pinked edge of hem

1

2

1 Place one edge of the braid to the edge of the hem, wrong side to wrong side. Using a narrow zigzag, stitch along the other edge of the braid to secure.

2 Fold the braid on to the wrong side of the fabric along the zigzag stitching. Press into position. Machine stitch with a straight stitch, through the centre of the hem and braid. A row of machining will show on the right side.

Using a wide horsehair braid

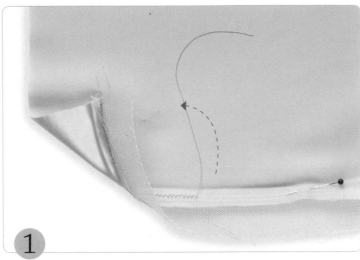

1

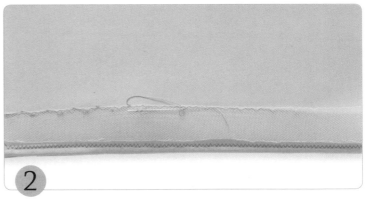

2

1 Overlay by 1cm (³⁄₈in) the edge of the braid to the wrong side of the fabric. Use the edge of the braid that does not have the white stitching inserted. Pin in place. Zigzag stitch in place, 5mm (³⁄₁₆in) from the edge of the braid. On the right side, trim the fabric down to the zigzag stitching.

2 Press the hem and braid up on to the wrong side of the fabric. Use a herringbone stitch to secure. If the hem is curved, pull up the white stitching at the edge of the braid to tighten the braid into shape.

Applying a flat trim

On some items a flat trim braid or ribbon is added for a decorative effect. This may be right on the hem or edge, or placed just above it. To achieve a neat finish, any corners should be mitred.

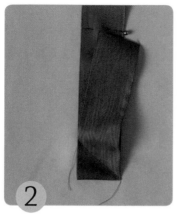

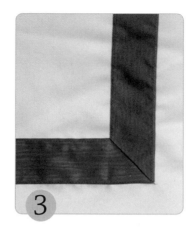

1 Pin the trim to the fabric, wrong side of the trim to right side of the fabric. At the corner point where the trim is to be mitred, fold the trim back on itself and secure with a pin.

2 Stitch across the trim at 45 degrees from the edge of the fold, through all layers.

3 Remove excess trim from the corner. Open the trim out and press. Machine stitch the inner and outer sides of the trim to the fabric, close to the edge. Be sure the stitching at the corners is sharp.

Piped edges

A piped edge can look very effective on a garment, especially if it is made in a contrasting colour or fabric. Piping is also an excellent way of finishing special-occasion wear as well as soft furnishings. The piping may be single, double, or gathered.

Single piping

1 Just one piece of piping is used. Cut a bias strip 4cm (1½in) wide. Wrap the binding, wrong side to wrong side, around the piping cord. Pin in place.

2 Machine along the binding close to the cord, using the zip foot.

3 Pin the raw edge of the piping to the raw edge of the right side of the work. Machine close to the stitching line on the piping, using the zip foot.

4 Place the other side of the fabric over the piping, right side to right side. Machine in place close to the piping, using the zip foot.

5 On the right side of the work, the piping can be seen at the edge. Press to finish.

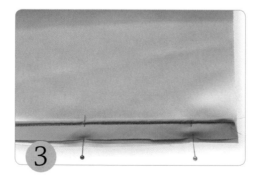

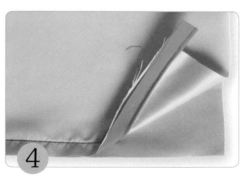

Double piping

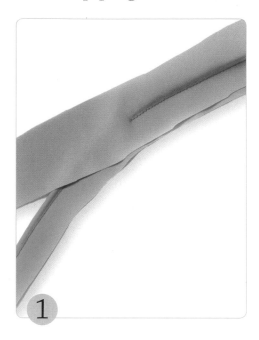

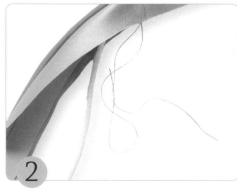

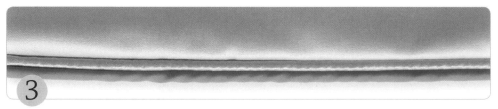

1 Different thicknesses of piping cord can be used for this. Make up single piping (see steps 1–3, page 85). Cut another bias strip, in a contrasting colour if you like. Join the bias strip to the single piping, stitching next to the piping.

2 Place a second piping cord to the wrong side of the contrast strip. Wrap the contrast strip around the cord and stitch.

3 Attach to the edge of the work as for single piping (see steps 4–7 on the opposite page). On the right side, there is a double row of piping at the edge.

Gathered piping

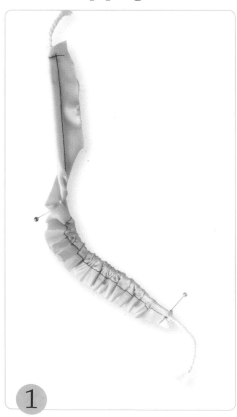

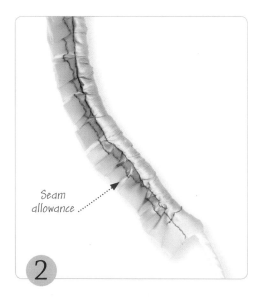

Seam allowance

1 This is a great technique to try on cushions. Cut a bias strip 5cm (2in) wide. Stitch the bias strip loosely around a piece of piping cord. Secure the cord to the bias at one end. Push the bias along the cord to gather.

2 Machine the gathers in place. Secure the gathers at both ends of the cord.

3 Attach to the edge of the work as for single piping (see steps 3–5, page 85).

Buttons

Buttons are one of the oldest forms of fastening. They come in many shapes and sizes, and can be made from a variety of materials including shell, bone, plastic, nylon, and metal. Buttons are sewn to the fabric either through holes on their face, or through a hole in a stalk called a shank, which is on the back. Buttons are normally sewn on by hand, although a two-hole button can be sewn on by machine.

Sewing on a 2-hole button

This is the most popular type of button and requires a thread shank to be made when sewing in place. A cocktail stick will help you to sew on this type of button.

1 Position the button on the fabric. Start with a double stitch and double thread in the needle. Place a cocktail stick on top of the button. Stitch up and down through the holes, going over the stick.

2 Remove the cocktail stick. Wrap the thread around the thread loops under the button to make a shank.

3 Take the thread through to the back of the fabric. Buttonhole stitch over the loop of threads on the back of the work.

Sewing on a 4-hole button

This is stitched in the same way as for a two-hole button except that the threads make an X over the button on the front.

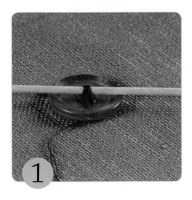

1 Position the button on the fabric. Place a cocktail stick on the button. Using double thread, stitch up and down through alternate sets of holes, over the cocktail stick. Make an X shape as you stitch.

2 Remove the cocktail stick. Wrap the thread around the thread loops under the button to make the shank.

3 On the reverse of the fabric, buttonhole stitch over the thread loops in an X shape.

Sewing on a shanked button

When sewing this type of button in place, use a cocktail stick under the button to enable you to make a thread shank on the underside of the fabric.

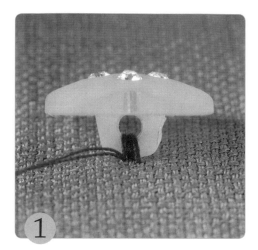

1. Position the button on the fabric. Hold a cocktail stick on the other side of the fabric, behind the button. Using double thread, stitch the button to the fabric, through the shank.

2. Be sure each stitch goes through the fabric and around the cocktail stick beneath.

3. Remove the cocktail stick. Work buttonhole stitching over the looped thread shank.

Sewing on a reinforced button

A large, heavy button often features a second button sewn to it on the wrong side and stitched on with the same threads that secure the larger button. The smaller button helps support the weight of the larger button.

1. Position the large button on the right side of the fabric. Hold a smaller button beneath the fabric, in line with the large button. Sew on the large button, stitching through to secure both buttons together.

2. When the stitching is complete, wrap the thread around the thread loops beneath the larger button. Secure with a double stitch.

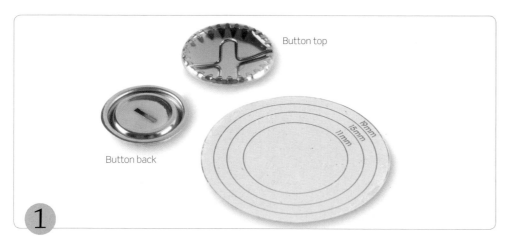

Button top

Button back

1

Covered buttons

Covered buttons are often found on expensive clothes and will add a professional finish to any jacket or other garment that you make. A purchased button-making gadget will enable you to create covered buttons very easily.

1 On the pattern, select the size of button you want to make.

2 Cut out the button pattern from interfaced fabric. Stitch a gather thread around the edge. Place the button top on the interfaced side of the fabric.

3 Pull up the gathers and secure with a double stitch around the shank of the button top.

4 Put the button in the correct hole in the button-maker. Push well in.

5 Place the button back on top of the button.

6 Take the other side of the button-maker and press down on the button back until it clicks into position.

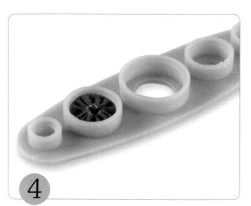

2

3

4

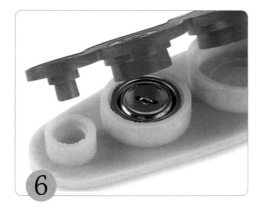

5

6

7 Remove the button from the button-maker and check to be sure the back is firmly in place.

8 The finished covered button.

7

8

Stages of a buttonhole

A sewing machine stitches a buttonhole in three stages. The stitch can be slightly varied in width and length to suit the fabric or item, but the stitches need to be tight and close together.

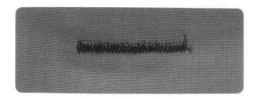

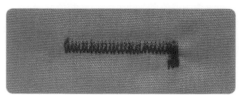

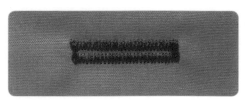

1 Machine the first side of the buttonhole.

2 Stitch a bar tack at one end.

3 Machine the second side and bar tack at the other end.

Positioning buttonholes

Whether the buttonholes are to be stitched by machine or another type of buttonhole is to be made, the size of the button will need to be established in order to work out the position of the button on the fabric.

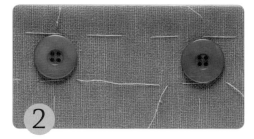

1 Place the button on a sewing gauge and use the slider to measure the button's diameter. On the right-hand side of the fabric, as the garment will be worn, work a row of tacking stitches along the centre front line.

2 Work a second row of tacks the diameter of the button away. Position the buttons between the tack lines. Stitch lines at right angles where the buttonholes are to be placed.

Vertical or horizontal?

As a general rule, buttonholes are only vertical on a garment when there is a placket or a strip into which the buttonhole fits. All other buttonholes should be horizontal. Any strain on the buttonhole will then pull to the end stop and prevent the button from coming undone.

Horizontal buttonholes

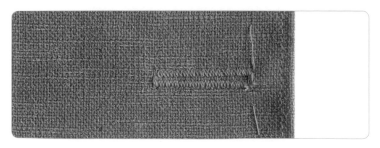

These are positioned with the end stop on the tacked centre line.

Vertical buttonholes

These are positioned with the buttonhole centred on the tacked centre line.

Machine-made buttonholes

Modern sewing machines can stitch various types of buttonholes, suitable for all kinds of garments. On many machines the button fits into a special foot, and a sensor on the machine determines the correct size of buttonhole. The width and length of the stitch can be altered to suit the fabric. Once the buttonhole has been stitched, always slash through with a buttonhole chisel, to ensure that the cut is clean.

Basic buttonhole

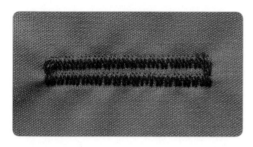

The most popular shape for a buttonhole is square on both ends.

Round-end buttonhole

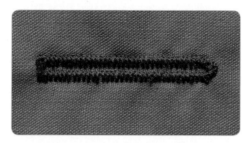

A buttonhole featuring one rounded end and one square end is used on lightweight jackets.

Keyhole buttonhole

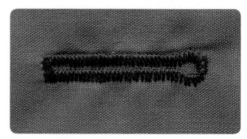

This is also called a tailor's buttonhole. It has a square end and a keyhole end, and is used on jackets and coats.

Corded loop

It is possible to make a very fine button loop that has a cord running through it. This type of loop is suitable for lightweight fabrics. Use a shanked button with a corded loop.

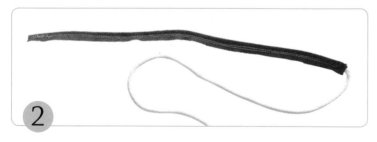

1 Cut a bias strip 4cm (1½in) wide. Cut a piece of cord twice the length of the strip. Wrap the cord in the bias strip, folded wrong side to wrong side. Pin. Make sure the bias strip is near to one end of the cord.

2 Stitch along the bias strip, next to but not too close to the cord. Machine another row 2mm (¹⁄₁₆in) away from the first stitching. Trim away the bias strip close to the stitching. Stitch through the cord and bias strip in the centre of the cord and near the end of the bias strip.

3 At the centre point, ease the fabric over the cord to turn it to the right side. Trim off the exposed ends of cord from the fabric loop.

Zips

Knowing how to add a zip is crucial if you want to progress to making projects such as purses (see pp.152–153), pencil cases, or cushion covers (see pp.154–155). But it isn't complicated.

Just ensure that if your fabric has a definite "top" and "bottom" that you are absolutely certain that you have it the right way up before you start to sew.

This is the right side of the fabric

Pin to the far edge of the zip

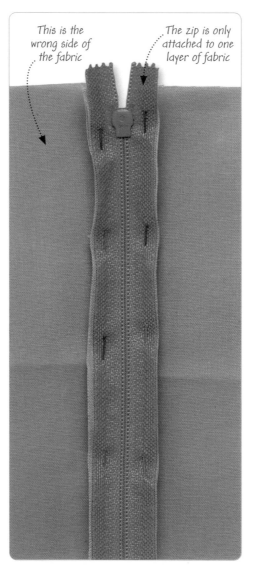

This is the wrong side of the fabric

The zip is only attached to one layer of fabric

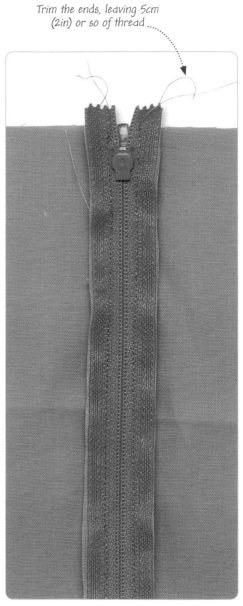

Trim the ends, leaving 5cm (2in) or so of thread

1 Place the right side of the fabric on top of the zip, aligning the edge of the fabric with the far edge of the zip. Pin the fabric in place. Position the pins close to the teeth of the zip. If you are making a purse or pencil case, bear in mind that the edge that you have pinned to the zip will sit at the top.

2 Move the pinned fabric to the right so that it is out of your way, then repeat the process to attach another piece of fabric to the other side of the zip. When you turn the zip and fabric over they will appear as shown above, with your pins visible through the fabric.

3 Move the fabric out of the way so you can position just one edge of the zip and its attached single thickness of fabric under the foot. Machine stitch from the top of the zip to the bottom, then repeat to sew down the other side of the zip. Trim the ends of the thread.

How to shorten a zip

Zips do not always come in the length that you need, but it is easy to shorten them. Skirt or trouser zips and concealed zips are all shortened by stitching across the teeth or coils, whereas an open-ended zip is shortened at the top and not at the bottom.

Shortening a skirt/ trouser or concealed zip

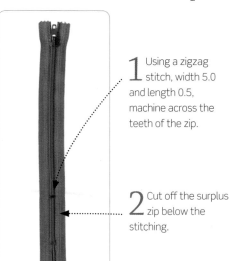

1 Using a zigzag stitch, width 5.0 and length 0.5, machine across the teeth of the zip.

2 Cut off the surplus zip below the stitching.

Shortening an open-ended zip

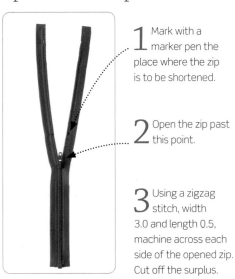

1 Mark with a marker pen the place where the zip is to be shortened.

2 Open the zip past this point.

3 Using a zigzag stitch, width 3.0 and length 0.5, machine across each side of the opened zip. Cut off the surplus.

Marking for zip placement

For a zip to sit accurately in the seam, the seam allowances where the zip will be inserted need to be marked. The upper seam allowance at the top of the zip also needs marking to ensure the zip pull sits just fractionally below the stitching line.

1 Stitch the seam, leaving a gap for the zip. Secure the end of the stitching.

2 Place a row of tacks along the stitching line through the opening. Place a row of tacks along the upper seam allowance.

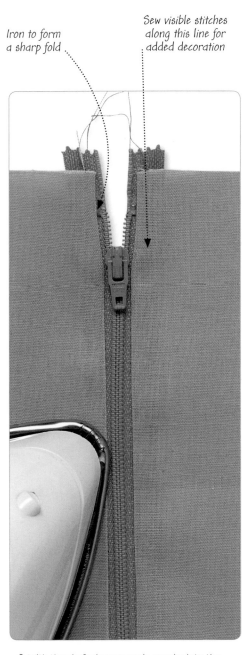

Iron to form a sharp fold

Sew visible stitches along this line for added decoration

4 With the zip facing upwards, manipulate the fabric with your fingers so that it sits flat, then iron to make a crisp fold either side of the zip. If you want, you can add a line of stitching on top of these folds – this will help to keep them in place and also makes a decorative feature.

Lapped zip

A skirt zip in a skirt or a dress is usually put in by means of a lapped technique or a centred zip technique (see page 95). For both of these techniques you will require the zip foot on the sewing machine. A lapped zip features one side of the seam – the left-hand side – covering the teeth of the zip to conceal them.

1 Stitch the seam, leaving enough of the seam open to accommodate the zip. Secure the end of the stitching.

2 Insert the right-hand side of the zip first. Fold back the right-hand seam allowance by 1.3cm (½in). This folded edge is not in line with the seam. Place the folded edge against the zip teeth. Tack.

3 Using the zip foot, stitch along the tack line to secure the zip tape to the fabric. Stitch from the bottom of the zip to the top.

4 Fold back the left-hand seam allowance by 1.5cm (⅝in). Place the folded edge over the machine line of the other side. Pin and then tack.

5 Starting at the bottom of the zip, stitch across from the centre seamline and then up the side of the zip. The finished zip should have the teeth covered by the fabric.

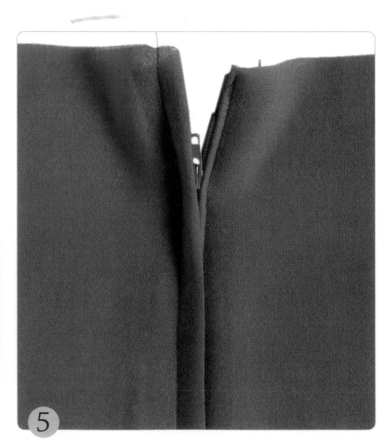

Centred zip

With a centred zip, the two folded edges of the seam allowances meet over the centre of the teeth, to conceal the zip completely.

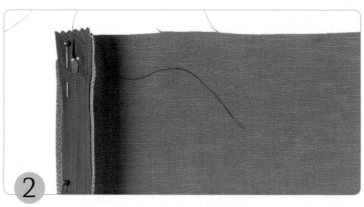

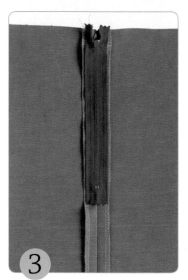

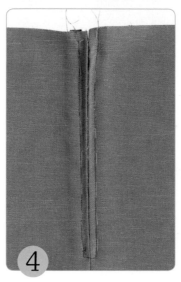

1 Stitch the seam, leaving a gap for the zip. Tack the rest of the seam allowance. Press the seam open lightly.

2 Centre the zip behind the tacked part of the seam. Pin and then tack in place along both sides.

3 On the wrong side, lift the seam allowance and the zip tape away from the main fabric. Pin. Machine the zip tape to the seam allowance. Make sure both sides of the zip tape are secured to the seam allowances. Stitch through to the end of the zip tape. Machine the zip tape to the seam allowance. Make sure both sides of the zip tape are secured to the seam allowances. Stitch through to the end of the zip tape.

4 Working from the right side of the work, stitch down one side, across the bottom, and up the other side of the zip. Remove the tacks.

5 The finished zip from the right side.

Concealed or invisible zip

This type of zip looks different from other zips because the teeth are on the reverse and nothing except the pull is seen on the front. The zip is inserted before the seam is stitched. A special concealed zip foot is required.

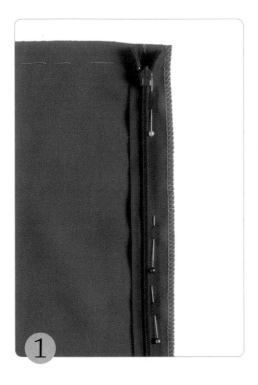

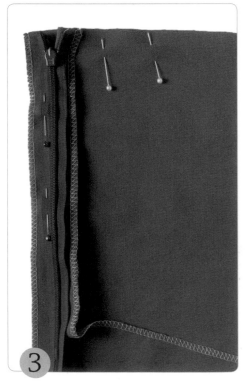

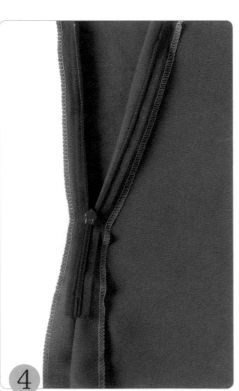

1 Mark the seam allowance with tacking stitches. Place the centre of the zip over the tack line, right side of zip to right side of fabric. Pin in place.

2 Undo the zip. Using the concealed zip foot, stitch from the top of the zip down as far as possible. Stitch under the teeth. The machine will stop when the foot hits the zip pull.

3 Do the zip up. Place the other piece of fabric to the zip. Match along the upper edge. Pin the other side of the zip tape in place.

4 Open the zip again. Using the concealed zip foot, stitch down the other side of the zip to attach to the second piece of fabric. Remove any tacking stitches.

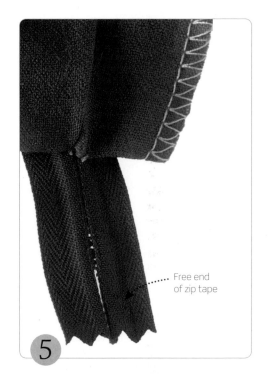

5 Close the zip. On the wrong side at the bottom of the zip, the two rows of stitching that hold in the zip should be finishing at the same place.

6 Stitch the seam below the zip. Use the normal machine foot for this. There will be a small gap of about 3mm (⅛in) between the stitching line for the zip and that for the seam.

7 Stitch the last 3cm (1¼in) of the zip tape to just the seam allowances. This will stop the zip pulling loose.

8 On the right side, the zip is completely concealed, with just the pull visible at the top. Apply waistband or facing.

Free end of zip tape

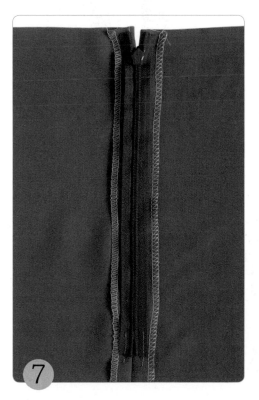

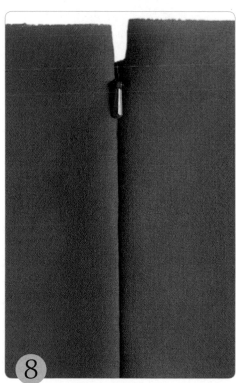

Fastenings
Tape fasteners

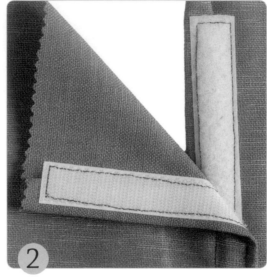

Velcro™

In addition to individual small fasteners, there are fastenings in the form of tapes that can be sewn on or stuck on. Velcro™, a hook and loop tape, is available in many colours and types. Sewn-on Velcro™ is ideal for both clothing and soft furnishings, while the stick-on variety can be used to fix curtain pelmets and blinds to battens on windows. Plain cotton tape with snap fasteners is used primarily in soft furnishings. Hook and eye tape is found in underwear or down the front of a shirt or jacket, where it can be very decorative.

1 Pin the Velcro™ in place. The loop side should be underneath and the hook side on top.

2 Stitch around all the edges.

Snaps

A snap is a ball and socket fastener that is used to hold two overlapping edges closed. The ball side goes on top and the socket side underneath. Snaps can be round or square and can be made from metal or plastic.

Metal snaps

1 Tack the ball and socket halves of the snap in place.

2 Secure permanently using a buttonhole stitch through each hole in the outer edge of the snap half.

3 Remove the tacks.

Plastic snaps

A plastic snap may be white or clear plastic and is usually square in shape. Stitch in place as for a metal snap (see above).

Hooks and eyes

There are a multitude of different types of hook and eye fasteners. Purchased hooks and eyes are made from metal and are normally silver or black in colour. Different shaped hooks and eyes are used on different garments – large, broad hooks and eyes can be decorative and stitched to show on the outside, while the tiny fasteners are meant to be discreet. A hook that goes into a hand-worked eye produces a neat, close fastening.

Attaching hooks and eyes

1 Secure the hook and eye in place with a tacking stitch. Make sure they are in line with each other.

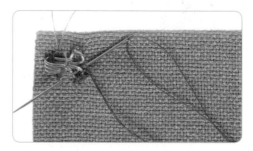

2 Stitch around each circular end with a buttonhole stitch.

3 Place a few over-stitches under the hook to stop it moving.

Hand-worked eye

1 Using a double thread, work several small loops into the edge of the fabric.

2 Buttonhole stitch over these loops.

3 The completed loop will have a neat row of tight buttonhole stitches.

Trouser hook and eye

1 The hook and eye fastener for trouser and skirt waistbands is large and flat. Tack the hook and eye in position. Do not tack through the holes that are used for securing.

2 Buttonhole stitch through each hole on the hook and eye.

Pockets

Pockets come in lots of shapes and formats. Some, such as patch pockets are external and can be decorative, while others, including front hip pockets, are more discreet and hidden from view. They can be made from the same fabric as the garment or from a contrasting fabric. Whether casual or tailored, all pockets are functional.

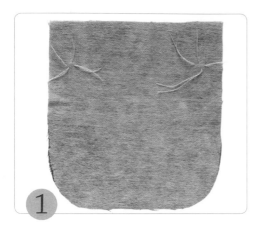

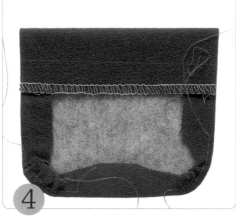

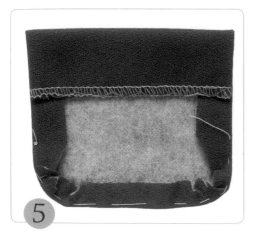

Unlined patch pocket

An unlined patch pocket is one of the most popular types of pocket. It can be found on garments of all kinds and be made from a wide variety of fabrics. On lightweight fabrics, such as used for a shirt pocket, interfacing is not required, but on medium and heavier fabrics it is advisable to apply a fusible interfacing.

1 If needed, apply an interfacing to the pocket fabric. Mark the fold lines with tailor's tacks.

2 Fold the top of the pocket down, folding where indicated by the tailor's tacks. Overlock or zigzag stitch the edge to neaten. Stitch down the sides of the turned-down top.

3 Stitch a long machine stitch through the corners. Trim away the fabric in the seam allowance in the curves. Remove the top corner.

4 Turn the top edge over to the wrong side. Pull up the stitching in the curves to tighten. Press. Turn under the curved edges.

5 Tack through the bottom edge and curves to secure. Using a herringbone stitch, hand stitch the top edge to the wrong side of the pocket.

6 Press. The pocket is now ready to attach.

Self-lined patch pocket

If a patch pocket is to be self-lined, it needs to be cut with the top edge of the pocket on a fold. Like an unlined pocket, if you are using a lightweight fabric an interfacing may not be required, whereas for medium-weight fabrics a fusible interfacing is advisable. A self-lined patch pocket is not suitable for heavy fabrics.

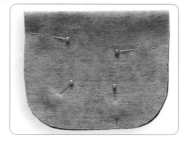

1 Cut the pocket fabric and apply a fusible interfacing, if needed. Fold the pocket in half, right side to right side. Pin to secure.

2 Machine around the three open sides of the pocket. Leave a gap of about 3cm (1¼in) for turning through. Remove bulk from the corners by trimming.

3 Trim one side of the seam allowance down to half its width. Use pinking shears to trim the corners.

4 Turn the pocket through the gap to the right side. Press. Hand stitch the gap in the seam using a flat fell or blind hem stitch. The pocket is now ready to be attached.

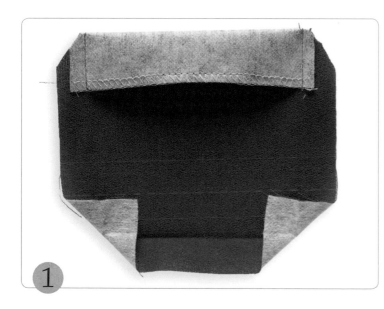

Square patch pocket

It is possible to have a patch pocket with square corners. This requires mitring the corners to reduce the bulk. Use a fusible interfacing on medium-weight fabrics.

1 Cut the pocket and apply interfacing, if needed. Neaten the upper edge of the pocket with overlock or zigzag stitching. Fold over the upper edge and stitch down the sides. Fold in the other three edges and press to crease. Remove the top corners. Fold in the bottom corners, then fold across these to give creases for the mitres.

2 Stitch the crease lines together in each bottom corner to mitre it. Cut off the surplus fabric, then press the corner seam open with the toe of the iron.

3 Turn the edges of the pocket to the wrong side.

4 The finished pocket is now ready to be attached.

Attaching a patch pocket

To attach a pocket successfully, accurate pattern marking is essential. It is best to do this by means of tailor's tacks or even trace tacking. If you are using a check or stripe fabric, the pocket fabric must align with the checks or stripes on the garment.

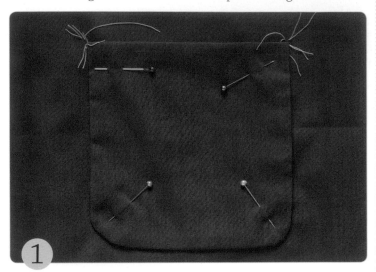

1 Mark the pocket placement lines on the garment with tailor's tacks. Take the completed pocket and place it to the fabric, matching the corners with the tailor's tacks. Pin in position.

2 To make sure the pocket remains in the correct position, tack around the edge along the sides and bottom. Keep the tacking stitches close to the finished edge of the pocket.

3 Machine stitch about 1mm (1/32in) from the edge of the pocket. Remove the tacking stitches. Press.

4 Alternatively, the pocket can be hand stitched in place, using a slip hem stitch into the underside of the pocket seam. Do not pull on the thread too tightly or the pocket will wrinkle.

How to make a kangaroo pocket

This type of pocket is a variation on a patch pocket, see page 101, and is made and attached in the same way. It is a large pocket that is often found on aprons, sports clothes, and children's dresses.

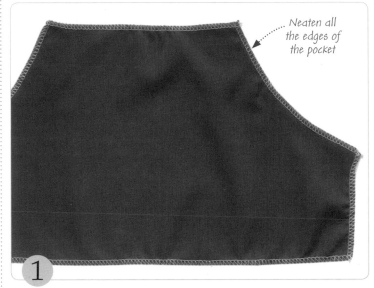

Neaten all the edges of the pocket

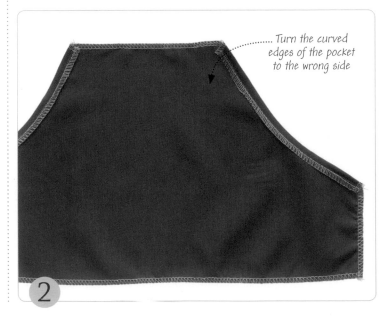

Turn the curved edges of the pocket to the wrong side

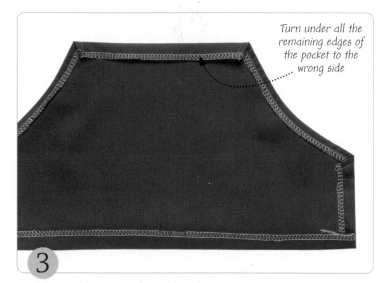

Turn under all the remaining edges of the pocket to the wrong side

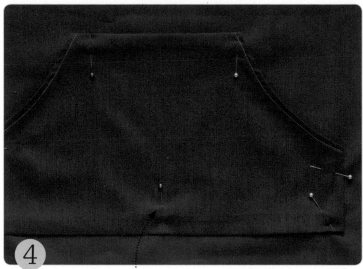

Pin the pocket securely in place

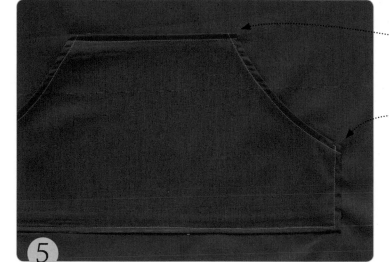

Stitch the pocket along the upper edge first

Then stitch the short straight sides and lower edge

Tip Sew very carefully around this irregular shape to ensure that your stitches don't run off the edge of the fabric.

1 Cut out your pocket to the correct size for your project, remembering that you will lose about 1cm (½in) from each edge when you turn them under. Neaten all the edges with a zigzag or overlock stitch (see p.55) to prevent them from fraying and creating a hole in the seam. Secure the ends of the thread carefully (see p.52).

2 The curved edges of the pocket will form the pocket opening after it is attached. Evenly turn these curved edges over to the wrong side – manipulate the fabric using your fingers if you need to – and iron the curve flat. Then, using a straight stitch with a matching thread colour, machine the turned, curved edges to secure.

3 Turn all the remaining edges of the pocket over by about 1cm (½in), so that they sit on the wrong side. If the fabric is bulky, trim the corners, then iron the edges in place.

4 Place the pocket on the garment, wrong side of the pocket to the right side of the garment. Make sure the pocket is flat, centred, and straight. Pin the pocket in place.

5 Machine sew the upper edge of the pocket, then down one short straight side, pivot at the corner (see p.57), stitch along the bottom, pivot again, then stitch up the other side.

6 Reinforce the corners with some diagonal stitches. If required, stitch one or two vertical lines down the centre of the pocket, to divide into two pockets. Iron again.

A diagonal stitch will strengthen the corners

Waistbands

Elasticated waistbands feature on many items of clothing, from skirts and trousers, to casual jackets and dresses. Knowing how to add an elastic waistband to garments is therefore a very useful skill and one you will use time and time again. The technique below shows you how to make a deep waistband to thread your elastic through.

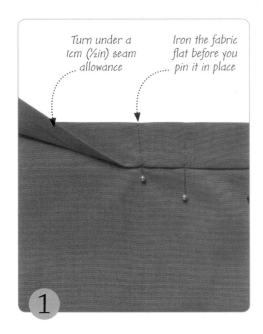

Turn under a 1cm (½in) seam allowance

Iron the fabric flat before you pin it in place

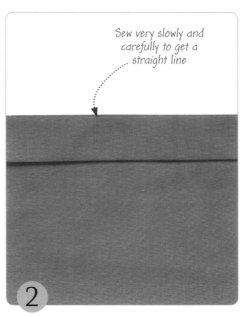

Sew very slowly and carefully to get a straight line

1 Turn over 1cm (½in) and iron it flat. Measure your elastic to work out how deep you need to make your waistband and add 1cm (½in). Turn this over, iron, and then pin in place.

2 Machine stitch a straight line along the top, 2mm (¹⁄₁₆in) from the edge of the fold. This is the top edge of the channel that will enclose the elastic.

3 Machine stitch the lower edge of the fold 2mm (¹⁄₁₆in) from the edge to create the bottom of the channel. Leave a gap of about 7cm (3in) so that you can insert the elastic.

4 Cut a piece of elastic long enough to fit round the waist comfortably. Pin one end of the elastic to the fabric. Pin a safety pin to the other end and feed it through the channel.

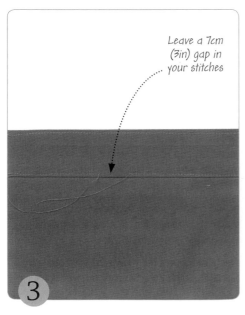

Leave a 7cm (3in) gap in your stitches

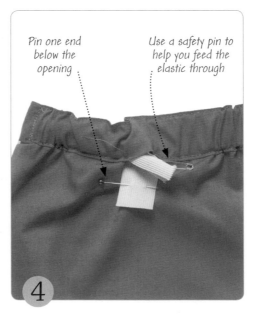

Pin one end below the opening

Use a safety pin to help you feed the elastic through

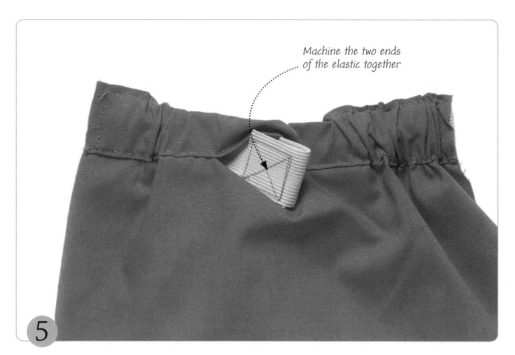

Machine the two ends
of the elastic together

5 When you have fed the elastic right the way through the channel, pull the two ends of the elastic together. Pin them securely to each other so that they can't come apart as you sew. Machine stitch a square shape with an "X" across it to join the two ends. This will strengthen the join so it doesn't come apart with everyday wear.

6 Push the elastic back into the channel and work it round with your fingers to make sure that the waistband is evenly gathered. Pin the gap closed then stitch it up to enclose the elastic inside the channel. Sew neatly in a matching thread colour so that the stitches will be hard to spot once you are wearing the skirt.

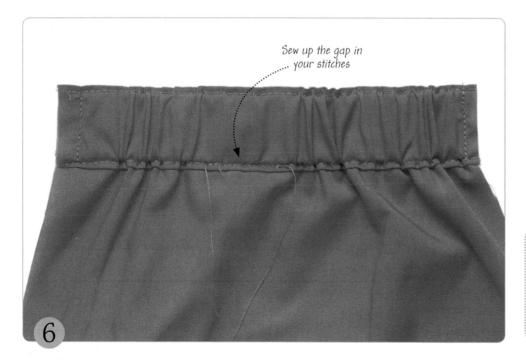

Sew up the gap in
your stitches

Tip Elastic stretches as you sew and can be fiddly to work with. As long as you are happy that your stitches are secure it won't matter if they are untidy.

A waist with a facing

Many waistlines on skirts and trousers are finished with a facing, which will follow the contours of the waist but will have had the dart shaping removed to make it smooth. A faced waistline always sits comfortably to the body. The facing is attached after all the main sections of the skirt or trousers have been constructed.

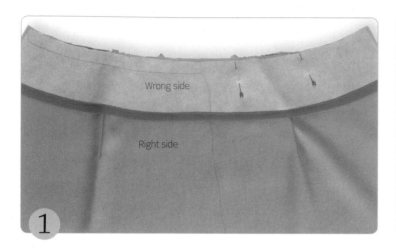

Wrong side

Right side

1

2

3

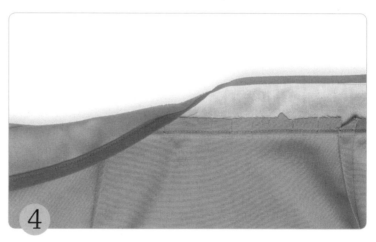

4

1 Apply a fusible interfacing to the facing. Neaten the lower edge of the facing with bias binding. Pin the interfaced facing to the waist edge, matching notches. Stitch the facing in place using a 1.5cm (⅝in) seam allowance.

2 Layer the seam allowance on the facing side of the seam to reduce it by half. Clip the seam allowance by using straight cuts at 90 degrees to the stitching line.

3 Press the waist seam up into the facing. Stitch the seam allowance down on to the facing at a distance of about 3mm (⅛in) from the original stitching (this is called understitching).

4 Turn the facing to the inside of the garment and press. Reduce the bulk from the top of the dart.

5 The right side of the waistline.

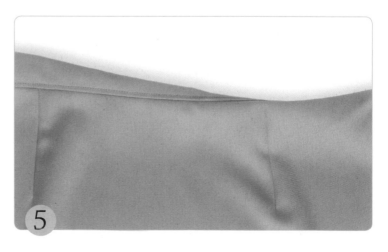

5

Petersham-faced waist

Petersham is an alternative finish to a facing if you do not have enough fabric to cut a facing. Available in black and white, it is a stiff, ridged tape that is 2.5cm (1in) wide and curved – the tighter curve is the top edge. Like a facing, petersham is attached to the waist after the skirt or trousers have been constructed.

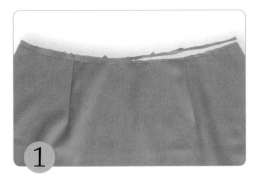

Right side

Wrong side

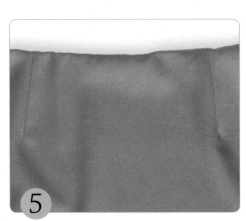

1 Stay stitch around the waist 1.2cm (½in) from the raw edge. Trim back raw edge to 6mm (¼in).

2 Pin the top edge of the petersham (the tighter curve) to the waist so that it overlaps the stay stitching by 2mm (¹⁄₁₆in). Tack in place.

3 Machine the petersham in place, stitching about 2mm (¹⁄₁₆in) from the edge of the petersham. Do not worry if the other edge looks wavy.

4 Turn over and roll the petersham to the inside of the waist.

5 Press the petersham flat to the fabric, making a neat pressed edge along the top of the seam.

Finishing the edge of a waistband

One long edge of the waistband will be stitched to the garment waist. The other edge will need to be finished, to prevent fraying and reduce bulk inside.

Turning under

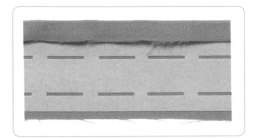

This method is suitable for fine fabrics only. Turn under 1.5cm (⅝in) along the edge of the waistband and press in place. After the waistband has been attached to the garment, hand stitch the pressed-under edge in place.

Overlock stitching

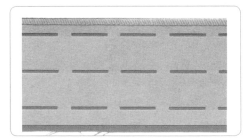

This method is suitable for heavier fabrics as it is left flat inside the garment after construction. Neaten one long edge of the waistband with a 3-thread overlock stitch.

Bias binding

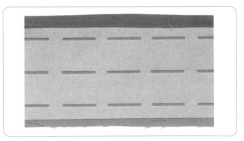

This method is ideal for fabrics that fray badly and can add a feature inside the garment. It is left flat inside the garment after construction. Apply a 2cm (¾in) bias binding to one long edge of the waistband.

Upcycle clothing

Many people nowadays have taken upcycling, or re-purposing, clothing and other fabric to their hearts. Quite simply, instead of chucking old items out, you find a new use for them. You could transform an old jumper into a cushion cover, use a teeshirt to make a bag (see opposite, below), or even turn an old pillowcase into a child's dress (see pp.179–181).

Wanting to save the planet is one reason why you might do some upcycling. Other reasons are that you can't bear to throw away the much-loved dress that you no longer fit into, that worn-out-in-places jacket that holds happy memories, or the pillowcase whose matching duvet cover has long since vanished. And if those reasons aren't enough, being thrifty is another.

WHAT WORKS

So what sort of item lends itself to upcycling? The answer is, almost anything – from coats, dresses, and skirts, through trousers, jumpers, ties, and jackets to teatowels, tablecloths, curtains, sheets, and pillowcases. The only limits are your creative and technical skills. For your first upcycling projects, it's best to choose fabrics that are easy to work with, such as cotton, linen, wool, and mixes made from these. As with any other sewing project, avoid very fine, very thick, very stretchy, and very slippery fabrics, especially if you are a beginner sewer. Experiment with charity shop buys before you sew any treasured fabrics.

MAKING USE OF WHAT'S ALREADY THERE

As you get into upcycling, you'll see how easy it can be to incorporate the elements of an old item – such as pockets, an elasticated waistband, a seam, a neckline, or some buttons – into your upcycled project. Jeans pockets could become apron pockets, an elasticated waistband could be stitched together to make a neck opening for a tunic top, a seam could become the bottom of a bag, while a neckline becomes its opening.

Sources of upcycling material

Once you've been hit by the upcycling bug, you'll find yourself looking at the clothes in your wardrobe, at your household linens, and at the clothes in charity shops and car boot sales in a new light. Everything and anything that's pre-loved can enjoy a second use – right down to its buttons. If you can't incorporate the buttons from a garment in your new project, don't throw them away. It probably won't be long before you can use them to decorate an upcycled bag or hat. And if your own wardrobe and the charity shops weren't enough, the oddments bin in your local fabric shop will start to exert a strange fascination. If the oddments are too small to make a garment, they'll surely be big enough to make an appliqué motif, a pair of apron ties, some dainty drawstring bags, a length of bias tape to trim the armholes and hem of a blouse, or a bunch of fabric puffs you can join together to make a throw.

Upcycling ideas

Part of the fun of upcycling is seeing the possibilities in items that you normally wouldn't think twice about giving to the charity shop or leaving on the sale rail. Here are a few ideas to get your creative juices flowing.

If your child has grown out of an old, much-loved dress, sew up the bottom and transform it into a peg bag that you can hang on the washing line (see right, above).

Instead of shortening an old skirt to a more fashionable length, why not turn it into an apron or a child's skirt?

When your boyfriend cardigan has finally seen better days, transform it into a cosy pillow or a decorative ruffled bib for a tank top.

If your wardobe is full to bursting with colourful printed teeshirts and you finally realise there just aren't enough days in the year to wear them all, cut them up, stitch them together again and you'll have a unique jersey shift dress. Alternatively, sew up the bottom of one, snip off the sleeves, and transform it into a useful bag (see right, below). Personalize with handmade flowers (see pp.139–141).

When your local upholstery shop is throwing out its old swatch books, gather them up, stitch fabric swatches of the same weight together and make yourself a patchwork dress or jacket.

If you see a bargain dress in the sales in a fabric you adore but that's two sizes too big and a weird shape to boot, use one of your own dresses as a template to cut the dress down to size, remove any sleeves, and use the excess fabric to make a glamorous ruffle at the shoulder.

Has an old shirt finally lost its appeal? Are the collar and cuffs too worn to be respectable? Cut up the back and fronts and use the fabric to line a tote bag or a makeup purse.

Rather than rejecting a charity-shop dress because although you love the fabric, you'd never wear that style, cut it into strips and turn them into a bow-tie turban and matching belt or clutch bag.

Peg dress bag

Teeshirt bag

How to make patchwork squares

This simple technique will open up a world of beautiful projects to you, from quilts and bags to cushion covers and clothing. The key thing to remember with patchwork is to iron, iron, iron! It's crucial to keep the seams flat so that the patchwork is smooth. Mix and match patterns, colours, and even textures to create your own unique patchwork.

Position the needles so they are perpendicular to the join

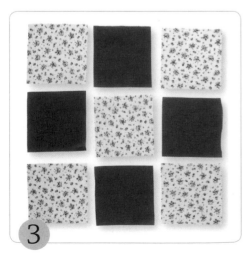

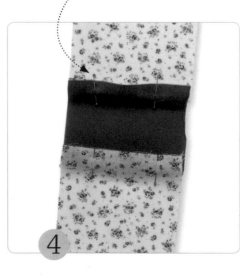

1 Decide how large you want your squares to be, allowing 2cm (³⁄₄in) extra for the seams between the patches. Draw the shape on stiff card and cut it out. Lay it on your fabric and draw round it.

2 Cut your squares out using fabric scissors. The number you need will depend on the size and pattern of your patchwork. Cut out some to start and then cut more as you need them.

3 Lay out your fabric squares and work out how you want to arrange them. Mix up the patterns and colours for a mismatched look, or alternate the colours and patterns, as shown.

4 Pin the patches together in strips of three. Position your pins so that the sewing machine can sew over them easily and you won't have to remove them as you go.

5 Sew along the two seams, 1cm (¹⁄₂in) from the edge. Press the patches with an iron - position the seams so that wherever possible you are ironing the lighter fabric behind the darker fabric.

6 Repeat Steps 4 and 5 twice more so you have three strips of three patchwork pieces. Pin these together to create a three by three square and then machine the seams.

7 Tie off any loose ends, remove all the pins and trim any loose threads or scruffy edges. Iron he patchwork face down to get the seams as flat as possible.

8 Flip the patchwork over and iron it again. You can use this technique to create a patchwork of any size. It is ideal for making cushion covers and quilts (see pp.112-113).

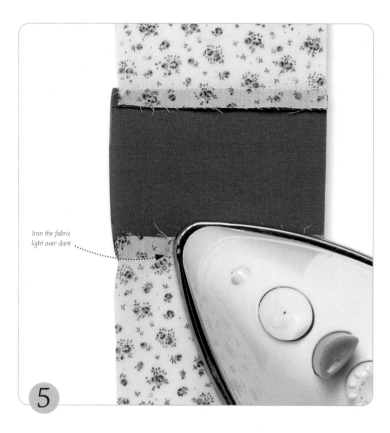

Iron the fabric light over dark

5

6

7

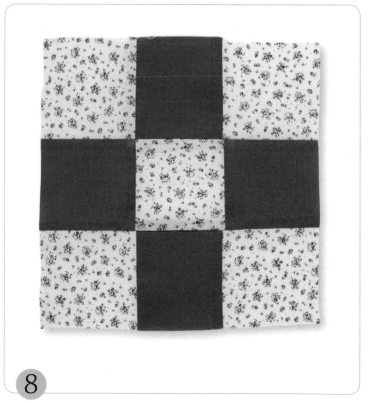

8

Patchwork cushion and quilt

If you mastered how to make patchwork and are looking for some exciting projects so that you can put your new skills into action, why not make a patchwork cushion or blanket? These gorgeous items are easy to make and will add a warm touch to your lounge or bedroom. Use vintage flower prints in soft pastel shades for a designer look.

Creating your cushion

This cushion is incredibly easy to make – all you need to do is sew nine patchwork squares together for each side of the cushion; the patchwork squares used for the example shown are 13 x 13cm (5 x 5in). Lay the sewn-up pieces on top of each other, right sides together, and then sew around three of the edges leaving a 10-cm (4-in) gap in the fourth. Gently turn the cushion inside out through this gap, making sure that you poke out all the corners neatly. Stuff the cusion with wadding until you are happy that it is plump enough, and then sew up the gap using slip stitch (see p.50). If you want to create a patchwork cushion with a zip, see pp.154–155 to learn how.

Creating your quilt

Decide how large you want your quilt to be, and how large your patchwork squares should be for your design. There are no hard and fast rules here – just have a play around with different sizes and colours until you work out a design you like. Here,

sixteen large 30-cm (12-in) squares were used to form four rows of four. To add a bit of extra interest and to make the quilt look more professional, narrow strips were added between each row and around the edges. The width of this strip can be as wide or narrow as you like – the strips in the example opposite are 5cm (2in) wide.

Sew four patchwork squares together, as in Steps 1–4 on p.110, and then repeat this three times to create four strips of four. Iron them flat. Attach a 5-cm (2-in) wide band of fabric along one long edge of three of the four patchwork strips, then sew all the strips together so that the three bands of fabric alternate with the four patchwork strips. To add the border, cut another four lengths of fabric and sew them around the four sides of the quilt.

To give the quilt some weight, pad it with sheet wadding of your chosen thickness. Measure the length and width of the patchwork and cut a piece of backing fabric and a layer of wadding to this size. Place the three layers together so the patchwork and backing fabric are next to each other, right side to right side, and the wadding is on top. Pin around one short side and the two long sides, and pin around the other short side, leaving a gap of 30cm (12in) that you will use to turn the quilt to the right side. Machine sew all the sides 1cm (½in) from the edge. Trim away excess wadding and fabric from the corners, then turn the quilt to the right side through the gap. Push the corners out, press well and use slip stitch to close the gap.

If you want a quilted effect, stitch through all the layers along the patchwork seams.

Mending
How to unpick a stitch

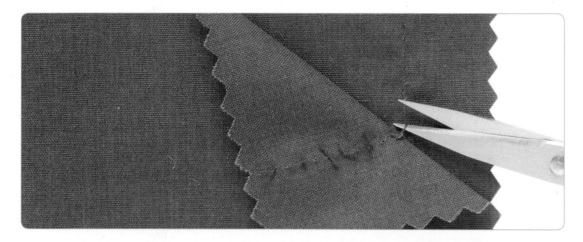

Small scissors

This is a simple method for unpicking stitches. Gently pull the two pieces of fabric apart and, using small, sharply pointed scissors, snip through the stitches. Remove all the tiny pieces of cotton before restitching the seam.

Seam ripper

A seam ripper is a useful tool for removing stitches from seams in light to heavyweight fabrics. Carefully slide its thin, sharp blade under a stitch to cut it through. If you cut through every fourth or fifth stitch, it will encourage the whole seam to unravel.

Pin and scissors

If your stitches are too small for a seam ripper or scissors, use this technique instead. Slide a pin into the stitch and wiggle it around to loosen it. Once it is loose, insert a pair of small, sharp scissors and snip through the thread. Repeat every few stitches.

How to darn a hole

It is important to know how to darn holes in knitted garments such as socks or jumpers, because a stitch in time could indeed prevent nine.

If you find a hole in a jumper or pair of socks, it is always worth darning it while it is still small so that you can stop it from unravelling even further. Simply stitch vertical stitches to strengthen the fabric, then close the hole by stitching horizontally.

1 A small hole could get bigger

2 Stitch several rows of running stitches vertically around the hole

3 Stitch horizontal rows of running stitches through the vertical stitches

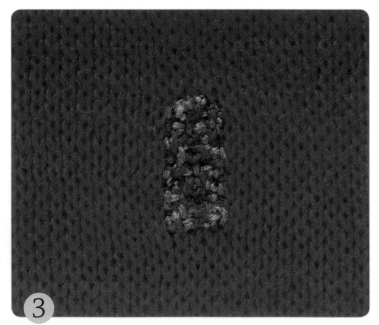

How to mend a tear

When a garment gets a tear in it, it might seem as though it is ruined. However, a tear can be very quickly remedied with the help of some fusible mending tape and some new stitching. By applying the fusible mending tape to the wrong side of the fabric, it will be hardly noticeable once you've finished.

Measure the length of the tear

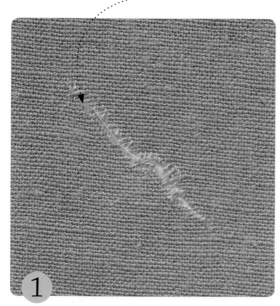

Ensure that the mending tape completely covers the tear before you iron

1 Measure the length of the tear in your garment, being careful not to rip it further as you handle it. Cut a piece of fusible mending tape that will fit over the tear, leaving about 1cm (½in) extra on either end.

2 On the wrong side of the fabric, carefully place the fusible mending tape over the tear, ensuring that the tear is "closed" and not gaping open under the tape. Use an iron to fuse the tape in place (see p.82). Make sure it is securely attached.

3 Turn the fabric over so that the tear is face up. Using a zigzag machine stitch, carefully sew along the tear line – this will bind the fabric to the mending tape so that the hole cannot reopen. Use a matching thread colour so that the join is as invisible as possible.

4 Turn your fabric over and carefully trim away any excess mending tape from around the line of stitches. Take care not to snip too close to the stitches or through the fabric. Your tear is now mended.

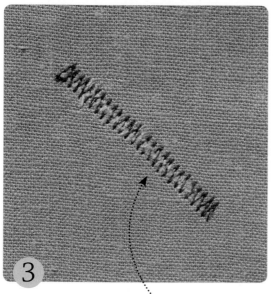

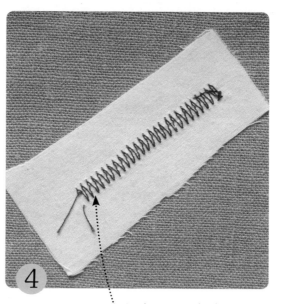

Use a closely worked, narrow zigzag stitch

On the wrong side, the zigzag stitching will be visible on top of the fusible tape

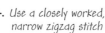

Finishing touches

Simple finishing touches can be used to good effect on many items. The term appliqué applies to one fabric being stitched to another in a decorative manner. The fabric to be appliquéd must be interfaced to support the fabric that is to be attached. Appliqué can be drawn by hand, then cut and stitched down, or it can be created by a computer pattern on the embroidery machine. The embroidery machine can also be used to create quilting, or this can be done by hand or with a sewing machine.

Hand-drawn appliqué

This technique involves drawing the chosen design on to a piece of double-sided fusible web, after which the design is fused in place on fabric prior to being stitched.

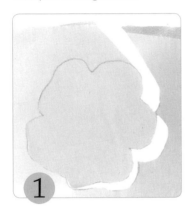

1 Draw a decorative shape, such as a flower, on to a piece of double-sided fusible web. Using the iron, fuse the web on to your chosen fabric. Cut out the shape from the fabric.

2 Place the shape, fusible web side down, where it is to be positioned on fabric and fuse in place. Using a wide, close zigzag stitch, stitch around the shape.

3 For a flower, stitch on top of the fabric appliqué to make petal shapes.

Machine appliqué

There are designs available for appliqué if you have an embroidery machine. You will need to use a special fusible embroidery backer on both the fabric for the appliqué and the base fabric.

1 Place the base fabric and appliqué fabric in the embroidery hoop and stitch out the first part of the design.

2 Trim the appliqué fabric back to the stitching lines.

3 Complete the computerized embroidery.

Quilting

This is a technique that involves stitching through two layers of fabric, one of which is a wadding. The stitching sinks into the wadding, creating a padded effect. Quilting can be done by hand, with a sewing machine, or using computerized embroidery.

Components of quilting

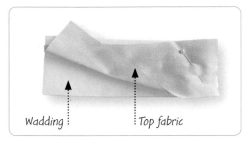

Wadding   Top fabric

Horizontal quilting

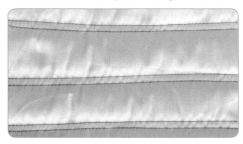

Tack the wadding and top fabric together. Stitch double lines with spaces between. Use a stitch length of 4.0 on your machine.

Diamond quilting

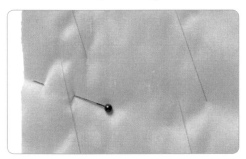

1 Diagonally tack the wadding and top fabric together.

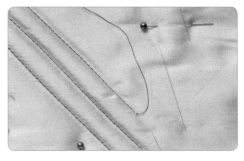

2 Set the machine to a stitch length of 4.0, with the needle on the one side of the foot. Stitch rows of machining diagonally across. Use the width of the machine foot as a guide to keep the rows parallel.

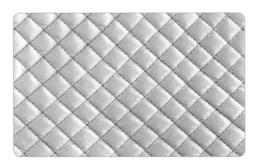

3 Stitch parallel rows in the opposite diagonal directions, to create diamond shapes.

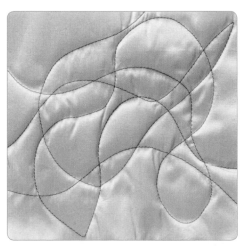

Computerized quilting

Tack the wadding and top fabric together, then stitch on a quilted pattern with the embroidery machine.

Freeform quilting

Tack the wadding and top fabric together. Stitch at random.

Projects

- Three templates from p.203, Lavender Hearts A, B, and C
- Pencil
- Three fabrics: two cotton, one felt
- Fabric scissors
- Pins
- Pinking shears
- Embroidery silk
- Needle
- Circle of muslin 10cm (4in) in diameter
- Dried lavender
- Wadding
- Rustic twine or ribbon

Lavender heart

Lavender has been used for centuries to perfume clothing and ward off moths. This simple hand-sewn project brings the old-fashioned lavender bag bang up to date. Once you've made it, you won't want to hide it away in a drawer or cupboard.

❧ how to make

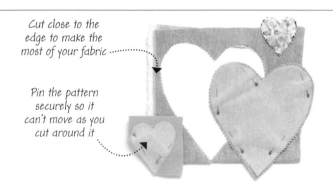

Cut close to the edge to make the most of your fabric

Pin the pattern securely so it can't move as you cut around it

1 Trace the templates onto a piece of paper using a pencil and cut out the heart pattern pieces. Fold the main fabric in half, wrong sides together, and pin template A to it. Cut around the template with pinking shears – by cutting the front and back out together you ensure that they are exactly the same size and shape. Use templates B and C to cut out two small heart appliqués – one from felt, one from cotton.

Use a bright thread colour to make a feature of your stitches

2 Using three strands of embroidery silk, stitch the appliqué shapes onto the piece that will form the front of your heart, placing as shown. Use a simple running stitch. Don't feel limited to using running stitch – why not try out some of the other embroidery stitches given on pp.62–65.

3 Pin the front and back pieces together securely and using three strands of embroidery silk, stitch around the outside edge using a small running stitch. Start and end on a straight edge. Leave a 6-cm (2½-in) gap and enough thread to finish the seam later on. Secure your thread at the start of your line of stitches, otherwise the front and back pieces will start to come apart.

Keep the stitches an equal distance from the edge of the fabric

4 Sew around the outer edge of the circle of muslin using a running stitch. Leave the needle attached. Place a pinch of lavender in the centre of the muslin and then pull the thread to gather the edges inwards, enclosing the lavender. Sew the pouch closed. Securing the lavender in this way keeps it in place and prevents it showing through the outer fabric.

Add the lavender once you are ready to tighten the thread

Allow the fabric to concertina slightly as you sew

5 Using wadding, begin to stuff the heart through the gap you left in the stitching. Once the heart is about half full, insert the lavender muslin ball. Continue to fill, pushing wadding around the ball so that it is firmly held in the centre of the heart. Make sure the heart is plump and evenly stuffed.

The lavender ball needs to sit in the centre of the heart

Push wadding right into the point of the heart

6 Once you are happy that you have inserted enough wadding, pin up the gap and stitch it closed, continuing the line of running stitch. Secure the thread firmly at the end of your stitches so that the front and back of the heart cannot come apart. If the heart feels lumpy, manipulate it with your fingers to get an even shape.

Pin the gap closed so that the edges stay aligned as you sew

Try to keep the loops of the bow the same size

This piece of twine will form the hanging loop

Twist the twine to make a loose bow

Insert the loop into the bow and stitch the two pieces of twine together

Trim off the excess twine once the hanging loop is secure

7 There are many materials you could use to hang your hearts, such as rustic-looking twine, ribbon, or embroidery silk. To create a hanging loop from rustic twine, twist a length into a loose bow. Work out how long you want your hanging loop to be, cut another piece of twine to this length, and feed both ends through the centre of the bow. Stitch through the centre of the bow to secure the loop in place and then trim off the ends of the loop. Sew the bow onto the top corner of your heart – stitch it so that it sits on top of the line of stitches around the edge.

Make alternative shapes

Once you have mastered the technique for making lavender hearts, why not adapt the heart shape and embellish it in different ways, or make other decorative shapes? You could make a smaller heart, using template B (see p.203), or you could lengthen the point of the heart and add a little curve to it (below right). Alternatively, you could make a completely different shape, such as the bird (right), which uses the templates on pp.202 and 205. Its contrasting felt wing and ribbon legs make an attractive decoration to hang around the house.

CUTTING YOUR PATTERN

You can use almost any simple outline you like as long as you make sure that the front and back pieces are exactly the same shape and size. The best way to do this is to cut one paper pattern and pin it to your fabric, which should be folded in half, right sides inwards. Use pinking shears to give a zigzag edge, or use fabric scissors for a straight edge.

CREATING YOUR SHAPE

Before sewing the front and back together, add any decoration you want, such as the bird's wing and eye, or any other embellishments. Secure these neatly using embroidery thread. Using the same techniques as for the lavender heart, stitch your front and back pieces together leaving a 6-cm (2^1/$_2$-in) gap along one edge. If you are making a bird and wish to attach ribbon legs, pin these into position before you sew – place them so that 1cm (^{1}/$_2$in) of the ribbon sits inside the bird – this will secure them. Stuff the shape with wadding and then neatly sew up the hole.

TIP

A hanging loop of ribbon secured with a button in a contrasting colour can look very attractive. Choose a contrasting ribbon, make it into a hanging loop, cross the ends over, and pin them in position at the top of the heart. Make sure that when the button is on top, the ends of the ribbon poke out a little way beyond the edge of the button. Stitch the button in place where the ends of the ribbon cross and through the stitching round the edge of the heart. Trim the ends of the ribbon so they are of equal length.

Lavender bird

Lavender hearts

Drawstring bag

Fed up with characterless plastic storage boxes? Make this simple drawstring bag in a printed cotton of your choice for a more personalized way to store small toiletry items or a collection of hair accessories.

❦ how to make

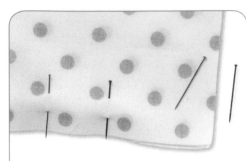

... Make sure the line of stitches is parallel to the edge

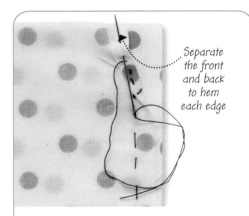

Separate the front and back to hem each edge

1 Fold your oblong of fabric in half along the long edge, right side to right side. With the fold to your left, pin the doubled fabric together along the bottom edge and up the right-hand edge, stopping 2.5cm (1in) from the top – this will allow you to create the channel for the drawstring in Step 4. Place the pins facing outwards – this will make them easy to remove as you sew – and space them 2.5cm (1in) apart. Make sure all the edges are neatly aligned.

2 Starting in the bottom left-hand corner, secure the thread and sew along the bottom edge and up the right-hand side, stopping at the pins. Use a short, even hand running stitch about 1cm (½in) from the edge. Remove each pin as you reach it. Your bag now has a front and a back.

3 At the top of the seam, in the unstitched area, fold the edge of the fabric over to make a narrow hem and sew in place. Repeat for both the front and the back. Keep your stitches as neat and even as possible, as these narrow hems will form the opening of the drawstring channel.

4 Fold the top 2cm (¾in) of the fabric over to make a hem, and pin securely into place. You will thread your ribbon through this channel, so ensure that the ribbon is narrow enough to fit. Once you have pinned the fabric in place, doublecheck that the turnover is an even depth all the way round.

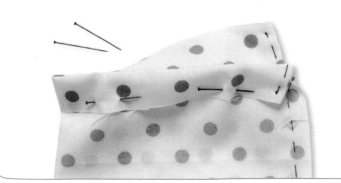

5 Beginning on the front right hand side, use short, even hand running stitches to secure the folded fabric in place. Remove the pins as you go. Secure the end of the thread once you reach the end of the turnover.

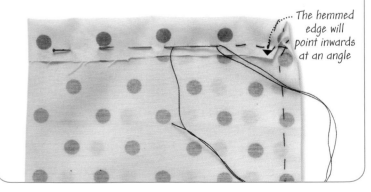

... The hemmed edge will point inwards at an angle

6 Attach a safety pin to one end of your piece of ribbon and slide it into the channel. Work the safety pin along with your fingers until it comes out at the other end.

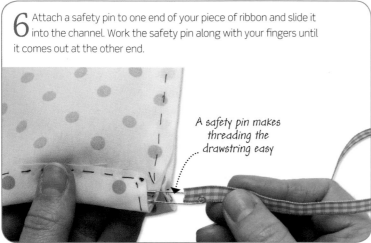

A safety pin makes threading the drawstring easy

7 Knot the ribbon at the length you want and then turn the bag inside out so that it is ready to use. To work out how long you want your drawstring to be, pull the bag closed before you knot the end – you will see how much excess ribbon you are left with.

Beaded silk bag

This pretty silk bag is suitable for evening wear and special occasions, especially for a bride or flower girl. Try using silk or satin for this – using two slightly different colours as the fabrics will provide lots of contrasting shadows. However, it would look very different if made in a floral cotton. The size of the bag can easily be adjusted by cutting the initial pattern larger or smaller.

🌱 you will need

- 1.5m × 60cm (60 × 24in) non-woven fusible interfacing
- 75 × 115cm (30 × 46in) silk dupion
- 75 × 115cm (30 × 46in) contrast silk dupion
- 1 reel thread
- Beads, to decorate
- 2m (80in) organza or satin ribbon, 12–15mm (½–⅝in) wide

❧ how to make

1 Draw around a large plate on a 75cm (30in) square of pattern paper. Mark bold lines that can be traced.

2 Draw two more circles around this circle, the first one 2.5cm (1in) larger and the second one 5cm (2in) larger.

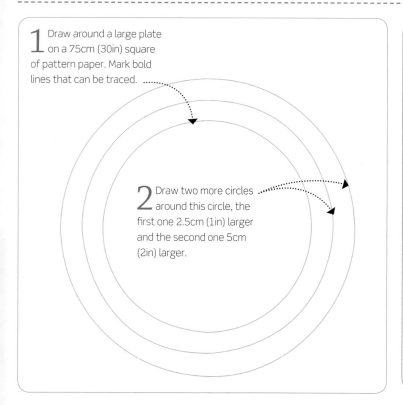

3 Find the centre of the circle by folding the paper, and then divide the circle into 16 segments.

4 Extend these lines 10cm (4in) beyond the pattern.

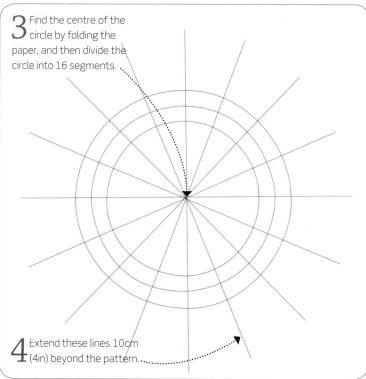

5 Join the ends of alternate lines to the circle to make points.

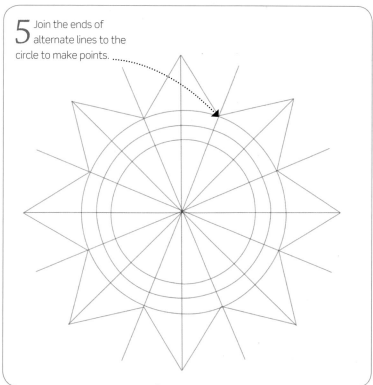

6 This is your pattern. Cut out carefully.

7 Cut the interfacing (see p.46) in half. Take one piece of interfacing and place it over the paper pattern. Using a soft pencil or water-soluble marker pen, trace the pattern on to the interfacing.

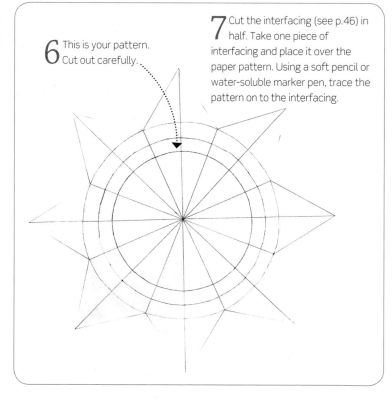

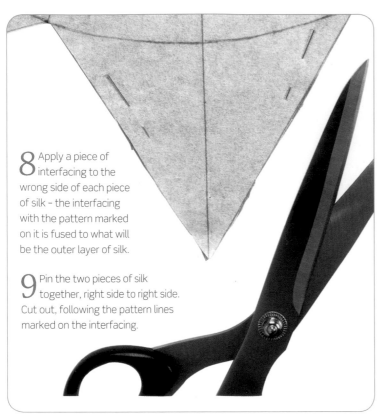

8 Apply a piece of interfacing to the wrong side of each piece of silk – the interfacing with the pattern marked on it is fused to what will be the outer layer of silk.

9 Pin the two pieces of silk together, right side to right side. Cut out, following the pattern lines marked on the interfacing.

10 Trace tack the two inner circles on the pattern. Cut through the thread loops.

11 Carefully separate the two pieces of silk, snipping through the trace tackings.

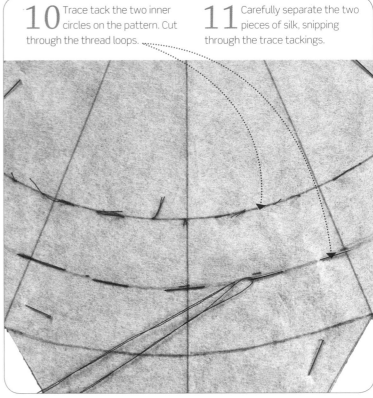

12 On the interfaced side of the outer layer of silk, mark the position of the two buttonholes. They should be on opposite sides of the bag, between the two trace-tacked lines.

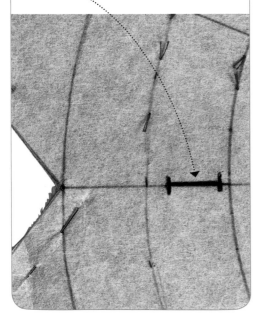
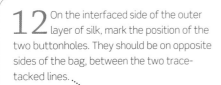

13 Tailor tack the position of the button holes.

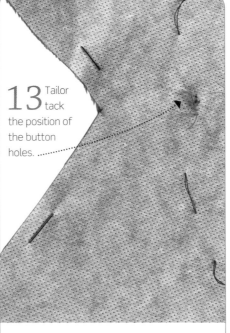

14 Make the buttonholes on the sewing machine in just the top layer of fabric (see pp.90–91).

15 Place the two pieces of silk together again, right side to right side.

16 Stitch around the outer edge, leaving a gap the width of one point on one of the sides, for turning through. Reinforce the sides of the gap with a slip hem stitch.

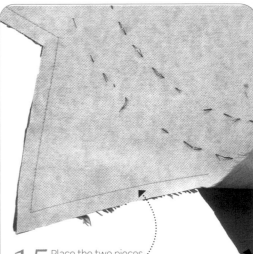

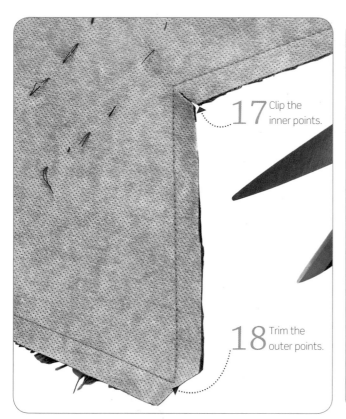

17 Clip the inner points.

18 Trim the outer points.

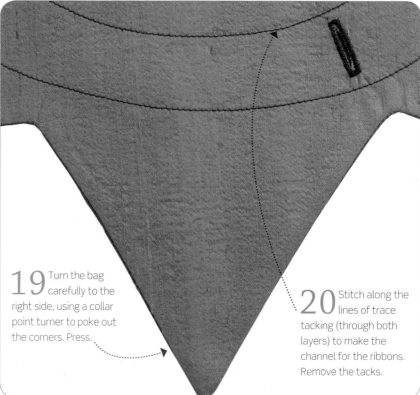

19 Turn the bag carefully to the right side, using a collar point turner to poke out the corners. Press.

20 Stitch along the lines of trace tacking (through both layers) to make the channel for the ribbons. Remove the tacks.

21 Embellish each point by sewing on a few beads.

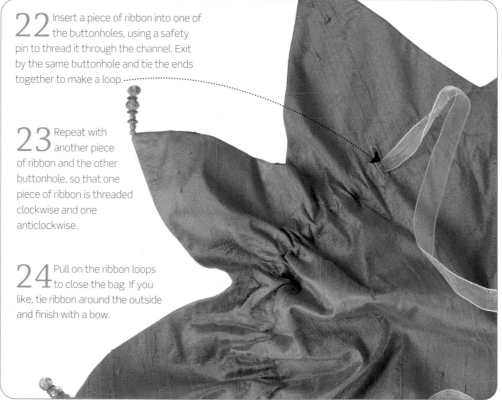

22 Insert a piece of ribbon into one of the buttonholes, using a safety pin to thread it through the channel. Exit by the same buttonhole and tie the ends together to make a loop.

23 Repeat with another piece of ribbon and the other buttonhole, so that one piece of ribbon is threaded clockwise and one anticlockwise.

24 Pull on the ribbon loops to close the bag. If you like, tie ribbon around the outside and finish with a bow.

♥ you will need

- Template page 208
- 30 × 115cm (12 × 46in) cotton fabric
- 30 × 115cm (12 × 46in) heavy fusible interfacing
- 1 reel machine embroidery thread
- 30 × 90cm (12 × 36in) polyester wadding
- 2m (80in) ribbon, about 5mm (³⁄₁₆in wide)
- 2 squares felt, about 15 × 12cm (6 × 5in)
- Small amount polyester stuffing, about 85g (3oz)

Sewing aids

Here's a perfect starting point if you are new to sewing – make yourself some matching sewing aids: a scissor cover, needle case, and pin cushion. This project allows you to practise your machine stitching and experiment with a range of decorative stitches. Cotton fabric and machine embroidery thread will work well, but you could always try silk fabric or variegated embroidery thread.

🍃 how to make

1 Cut the piece of fabric in half through the fold. The top layer is to be embroidered and the under layer is the lining. Before cutting out the individual pieces, apply a heavyweight fusible interfacing to the top fabric layer. ....

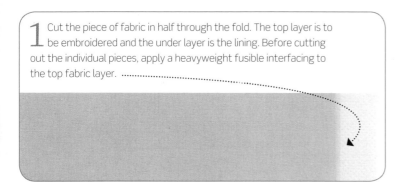

2 Choose four or five decorative stitches (see p.53) and stitch vertical rows on the top layer. Use the width of the machine foot as a guide.

3 Now cut out the pieces from the embroidered fabric and the lining according to the template on p.208.

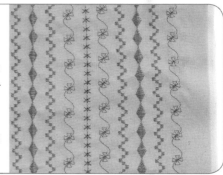

Pin cushion

1 Place lining piece 2 to the embroidered piece 2, right side to right side.

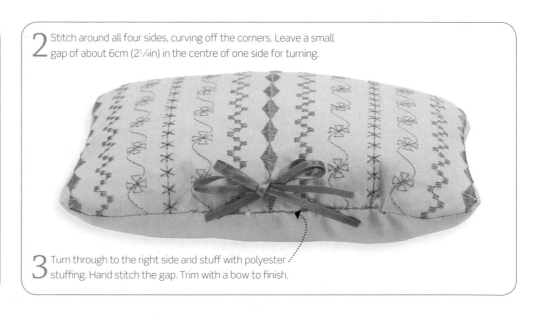

2 Stitch around all four sides, curving off the corners. Leave a small gap of about 6cm (2¼in) in the centre of one side for turning.

3 Turn through to the right side and stuff with polyester stuffing. Hand stitch the gap. Trim with a bow to finish.

Scissor holder

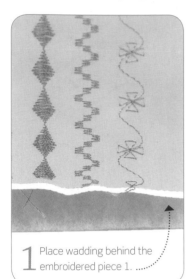

1 Place wadding behind the embroidered piece 1.

2 Place lining piece 1 over the embroidered fabric, right side to right side.

3 Stitch all around the edge, leaving a gap of about 10cm (4in) on one side for turning.

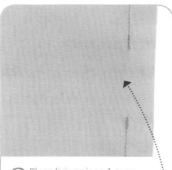

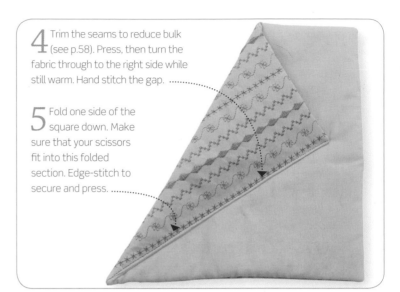

4 Trim the seams to reduce bulk (see p.58). Press, then turn the fabric through to the right side while still warm. Hand stitch the gap.

5 Fold one side of the square down. Make sure that your scissors fit into this folded section. Edge-stitch to secure and press.

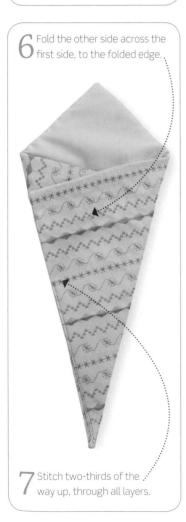

6 Fold the other side across the first side, to the folded edge.

7 Stitch two-thirds of the way up, through all layers.

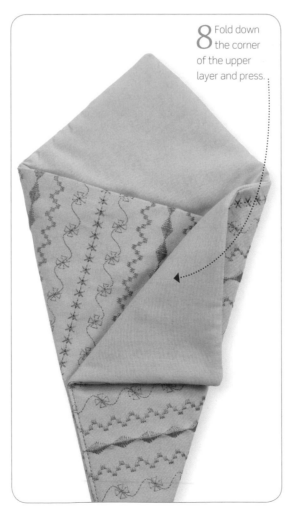

8 Fold down the corner of the upper layer and press.

9 Sew on a ribbon bow to trim the edge.

Needle case

1 Trim 2cm (¾in) off one short side of lining piece 3.

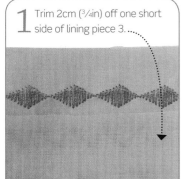

2 Stitch the short edges of the lining and embroidered piece 3 together, right side to right side. (The embroidered fabric will appear too big – just let it bulge out.) Stitch ribbon ties in to the middle of each side as you sew.

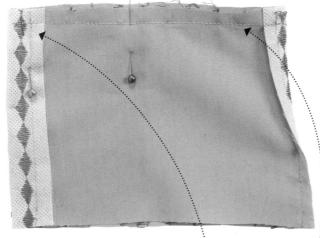

3 Fold the short ends of the embroidered fabric towards the lining so that the fabric lies flat.

4 Stitch along the long edge.

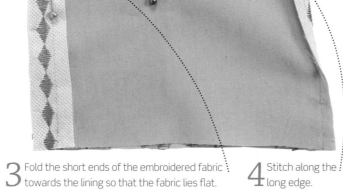

5 Turn through the other long edge. Hand stitch the lower edge with a blind hem or flat fell stitch (see pp.50–51).

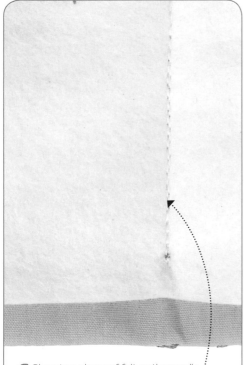

6 Place two pieces of felt on the needle case and attach by stitching down the centre with the sewing machine.

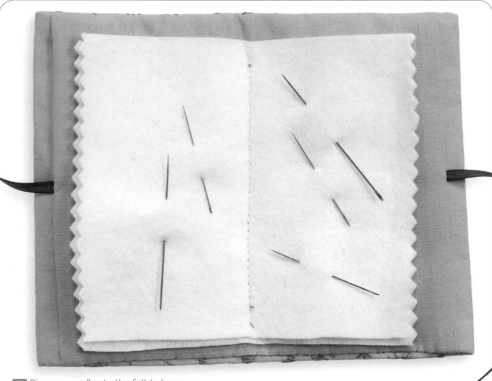

7 Pin your needles to the felt to keep them safe and tidy.

you will need

- Templates from p.204
- Fabric: black felt and polka dot cotton
- Fabric scissors
- Needle
- Pins
- White pearl-headed pins
- Wadding

Ladybird pin cushion

No insects were harmed during the making of this cute ladybird pin cushion! Whether you're a beginner sewer or a pro, a pin cushion helps you keep your pins to hand. Our ladybird version will bring a smile to your face every time you reach for a pin.

how to make

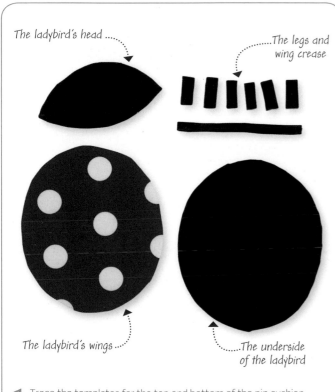

The ladybird's head .....

.....The legs and wing crease

The ladybird's wings .....

.....The underside of the ladybird

1 Trace the templates for the top and bottom of the pin cushion, the ladybird's head, the six legs, and the wing crease. Cut out your fabric pieces: use black felt for the body, head, six legs, and the wing crease. Use polka dot fabric to form the wings. When using the polka dot fabric for the ladybird's wings, position your template carefully before you pin it to get an equal number of spots on each wing.

2 Position the ladybird's head and the wing crease on top of the polka dot body and pin them in place. Hand sew around the lower edge of the head and down the central wing crease to attach them to the polka dot body. Use a running stitch and a black thread, so that your stitches are camouflaged. You don't need to sew around the top edge of the head as this will be sewn in place when you join the top and bottom layers.

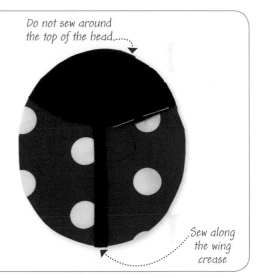

Do not sew around the top of the head......

Sew along the wing crease

3 Arrange the six ladybird legs on either side of the polka dot body, facing inwards, towards the centre of the ladybird's back. When you turn the pin cushion inside out in Step 5, they will face outwards. Space them evenly. Position the legs closer to the ladybird's head than to its bottom. You will square it all up in Step 6 when you finish sewing the ladybird up.

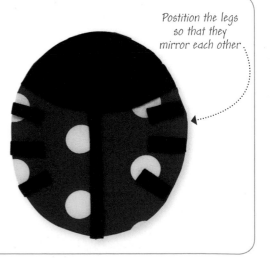

Postition the legs so that they mirror each other.

4 Very carefully, place the underside of the ladybird on top, sandwiching the legs between the top and bottom. Take care not to move the legs as you pin through all the layers. Carefully turn the whole thing over and use a running stitch to hand sew round the entire ladybird, 1cm (½in) from the edge. Leave an 8-cm (3-in) gap in your stitching at the bottom of the body.

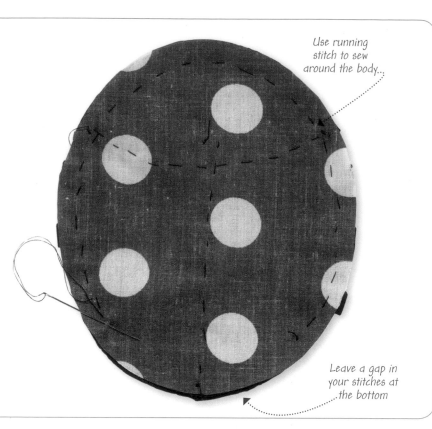

Use running stitch to sew around the body...

Leave a gap in your stitches at the bottom

Lay the felt gently so that the legs do not move out of position....

....Pin through all the layers

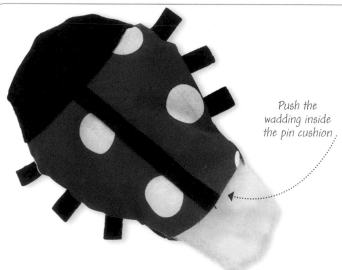

Push the wadding inside the pin cushion

5 Remove all the pins and carefully turn the ladybird inside out through the gap that you left in your stitches. Push your fingers right inside the body and along the seam, to make sure the fabric is stretched right out and that the shape is as round as possible. Stuff the ladybird with wadding through the gap in the bottom of the body. Fill your pin cushion with stuffing until it is plump and rounded. Manipulate the stuffing from the outside if you need to, to make sure that the shape is even.

Red thread will be hardest to spot against the polka dot fabric

.Hide all the untidy or raw edges by tucking them inside the pin cushion

6 When the pin cushion is full of stuffing and the fabric is taut, turn in the raw edges at the bottom of the body and pin them together. Use red thread and slip stitch to sew up the gap (see p.51). Use two white pearl-headed pins to make the eyes for your ladybird. Alternatively, use white embroidery silk and work two French knot stitches (see p.65).

Alternative shapes

This cheerful sunflower pin cushion will brighten up any desk or workspace and is very simple to make. You can stand it upright in a terracotta pot, or use it without its stalk and keep it in your sewing box.

PREPARING

Begin by cutting out your template pieces (see pp.204–205). Use pinking shears to cut out one inner circle of fabric and straight-bladed scissors for the two outer circles and the petals. Try to keep your petals as similar in size and shape as possible, but don't worry if they are slightly irregular – this will add to the charm!

SEWING

Using hand running stitch, sew the inner circle to the front of one of the outer circles to form the centre of the sunflower.

Arrange all the petals except two adjacent ones evenly around the edge of the second outer circle (this is the back of the sunflower), on the wrong side of the fabric. Ensure that each petal overlaps the edge by about 2cm (3/4in) so that they are firmly anchored in place when you sew the front of the sunflower to the back. Carefully lay the front of the sunflower with its contrasting centre right side up on top of the wrong side of the back. Pin the front to the back all the way round, except in the area of the missing petals. You should have a gap of about 8cm (3in). This is where you will insert the wadding. If any petals feel loose, unpin them, slide them a little further in, and pin again.

Using hand running stitch, sew around the edge of the sunflower through all the layers, 1cm (1/2in) from the edge. Remove the pins as you go. When you reach the last pin, secure the thread. Fill the sunflower head through the gap with wadding until the fabric is taut. Pin your last two petals in place in the gap, ensuring that all the wadding is trapped inside the flower.

Sew up the gap using running stitch. If you want to add a stalk (see above, right) leave a gap of 1cm (1/2in) in your stitches.

Leave these two petals until last

CREATING A STALK

Cut a piece of bamboo cane about 20cm (8in) long. Cut a piece of green felt to the same length and about 4–5cm (11/2–2in) wide. Lay the cane on top of the felt and fold in half lengthways so that the cane is completely enclosed. Sew the edges of the felt together around the cane using running stitch. The felt tube should be a snug fit. Insert the "stalk" through the gap in the edge of the flower. Add a few more stitches to hold the stalk securely. Fill your pot with a block of floristry foam and insert the sunflower in it. Alternatively, providing your pot doesn't have any holes, fill it with plaster of Paris, insert the sunflower, and leave to set.

Bug bags and simple cushions

Using exactly the same techniques as you used for your ladybird pin cushion, you can now progress to making some jolly bug bean bags, colourful ladybird seat cushions, or any other simple cushion shapes.

CREATING A BEAN BUG
You can use polka dot fabric for the top of your bug bean bag if you like, but why not use a cheery gingham fabric instead? With a head, underside, and wing crease made from black felt, your bug bean bag will still give the impression it's a ladybird, but you'll be able to indulge your creativity.

Make the bug bean bag in exactly the same way as you made the ladybird pin cushion (see pp.134–136), but when it comes to adding the stuffing, use bean-bag filling instead of wadding. You can buy these small polystyrene balls online, from specialist craft and haberdashery suppliers, or from department stores.

TIP
Be careful not to over-fill your bug bean bags or there is a risk that when you throw them around, they will burst on impact and scatter their contents everywhere.

LADYBIRD CUSHIONS
You can make a ladybird cushion any size you like simply by scaling up the templates for the ladybird pin cushion (see p.204). Follow the instructions as for the pin cushion (see pp.134–136). The cushions are sure to get grubby over time, so choose durable fabrics that you can spot-clean. You don't want to be opening the cushions up every few months to remove the stuffing and wash the covers.

ALTERNATIVE CUSHIONS
You don't have to stick to ladybird cushions. Almost any simple shape will work well, from circles to squares to rectangles. Just decide on the shape and size you want, make a template, cut your fabric (making sure of course that your front and back pieces are both exactly the same size and shape), and off you go!If you are feeling adventurous, you can decorate the front of

your cushion with ribbon, upholstery or lace trim, buttons of various shapes, sizes, and colours, fabric puffs, embroidery (see pp.62–63), or felt flowers (see pp.139–141). Just make sure that you always add your decoration to the front of the cushion before you sew the front and back together, and attach it very securely. Once the two are joined, it will be much more tricky to add your decoration.

If you don't yet feel quite ready to add this sort of decoration, why not simply make the front and back of your cushion from contrasting fabric for a reversible cushion? For instance, you could use a plain cotton fabric on one side and a small floral print or gingham on the other.

Felt flower brooches

If you buy these in the shops you can spend a small fortune, but felt flower brooches are deceptively easy to make. Use individually or in a group to add some pizazz to clothes or anything you care to pin them to.

how to make

Daisies

1 Cut an oblong of felt 13cm (5in) long and 5cm (2in) wide. Fold the felt in half lengthways and crease it using your fingers. Secure the top edge with a few stitches and leave the needle in place. Hold the fabric with the crease towards you, and snip upwards along the entire length. Do not snip right through.

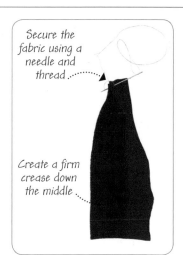

Secure the fabric using a needle and thread

Create a firm crease down the middle

Snip 2cm (¾in) cuts to form the petals

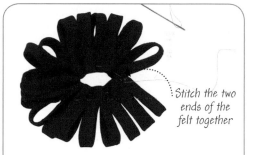

Stitch the two ends of the felt together

2 Using the needle and thread, sew along the long uncut edge of the felt with a running stitch. Once you reach the other end, pull the thread tight so that the felt gathers up into a tight circle. Sew the two ends together to form your ring of petals.

3 Cut a circle of fabric about twice the diameter of your button. Sew up the circle into a puff. Using a thread that will camouflage well with your fabric, sew the button to the backing fabric and secure it well. Felt can be quite a stiff fabric, so take care not to prick your fingers when passing your needle through it.

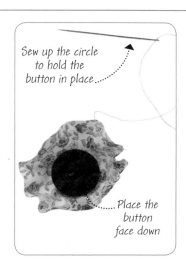

Sew up the circle to hold the button in place

Place the button face down

Sew through the button's holes to hold it in place

Attach the felt square using PVA or strong fabric glue

4 If you want to add leaves to your flower, use pinking shears to cut out two teardrop shapes using the Leaf A and B templates on p.202. Using a matching thread colour, sew your brooch fastening to a square of felt, attaching it at both ends and in the middle, to make sure it is firmly held in place. Glue or sew the square of felt to the back of your flower to finish.

you will need

- Templates from pp.200–203
- Fabric: felt in assorted colours; contrasting fabric to cover buttons and make leaves
- Fabric scissors
- Embroidery thread
- Needle
- Pins
- Buttons
- Pinking shears
- Brooch fastenings
- Fabric or PVA glue

Layered petals

1 To create a layered flower, choose a a button for the centre and a selection of fabrics, including two colours of felt. Trace the patterns from p.200 and p.201 and cut out your flower shapes. Use pinking shears to cut out two circles for the flower centre. Felt is ideal for the petals as it won't bend or sag once in place.

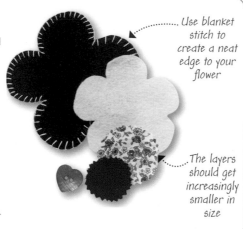

Use blanket stitch to create a neat edge to your flower

The layers should get increasingly smaller in size

2 Lay out the shapes on top of each other, in decreasing size order. End with the button in the centre. Hold the layers in place as you sew through the holes in the button to secure them. Finish the flower off with a brooch fastening or attach it to a bag or hairband as decoration.

Sew the button in place, pushing the needle through all the layers

Roses

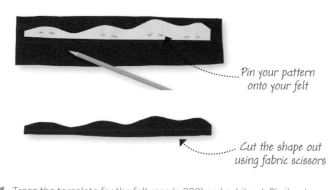

Pin your pattern onto your felt

Cut the shape out using fabric scissors

1 Trace the template for the felt rose (p.202) and cut it out. Pin it onto your felt and cut around it. Don't feel you have to play safe with rose-red felt. Why not experiment with any other coloured scraps of felt you have in your sewing basket?

2 Beginning at the narrower end, start to roll up the felt. Secure the initial twist at the bottom with a couple of stitches. Continue to roll, twisting the felt to form the rose shape, and securing at the bottom of the rose regularly with little stitches.

Stitch the rose in place as it grows

Stitch through the initial twist

3 Using the templates on p.202, cut out some felt leaves using pinking shears. Embroider leaf markings using a running stitch (see p.50). Stitch the leaves onto the back of your roses and attach a brooch fastening onto the back. For a multi-coloured rose, snip the template in half and cut each half from a different colour felt. Stitch the pieces together to form one strip then roll up as in Step 2.

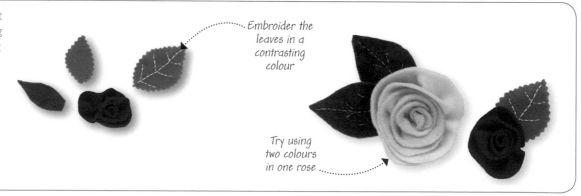

Embroider the leaves in a contrasting colour

Try using two colours in one rose

Bolster pillow

This is such an easy project to make, even though it looks quite complicated. They look great on a bed or nestling along the sides of a sofa. Experiment with contrast piping and look in the shops for decorative tassels that can be sewn on to the ends.

❧ how to make

1 Using the template on p.210, make two bias strips (see pp.80-81), 4cm (1½in) wide and 60cm (24in) long, from piece 4.

2 Wrap each bias strip around a length of piping cord and pin in place.

3 Machine stitch using the zip foot.

4 Stitch the piping to the two long sides of piece 1 (see p.86). Align all the raw edges, then pin. Machine in place.

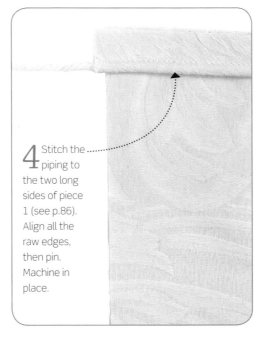

5 Place pieces 2 and 3 over the piping cord, one at either end, right side to right side. Pin in place.

6 Machine close to the piping using the zip foot.

7 Turn under the unattached edges of pieces 2 and 3 to the wrong side by 1.5cm (⅝in) and press. Using a long stitch on your sewing machine, insert two rows of gather stitches.

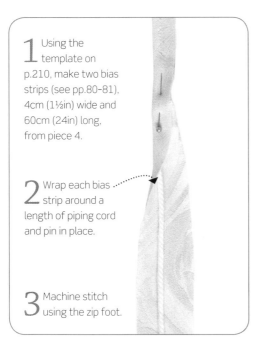

8 Fold the cushion fabric in half lengthways, right side to right side, matching the piping with the ends.

9 Machine a 1.5cm (⅝in) seam. Press the seam open.

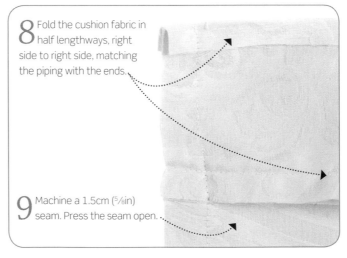

10 Turn to the right side.

🌿 you will need

- Template (see page 210)
- 50 × 115cm (20 × 46in) fabric
- 1.5m (60in) piping cord
- 1 reel matching thread
- 1 bolster pad, 42 × 17cm (17 × 7in)
- 2 tassels

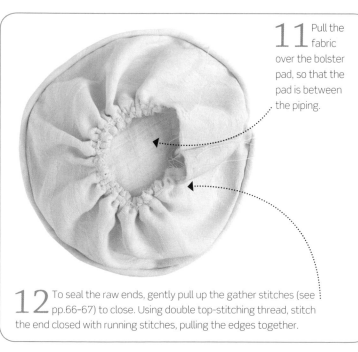

11 Pull the fabric over the bolster pad, so that the pad is between the piping.

12 To seal the raw ends, gently pull up the gather stitches (see pp.66–67) to close. Using double top-stitching thread, stitch the end closed with running stitches, pulling the edges together.

13 To finish, sew a tassel on to each end.

Bunting

A line of bunting flapping gently in the breeze conjures up sun-filled images of summer parties. Make our simple bunting in fabrics of your choice to personalize your party and make it an event your guests will remember long after it's over.

❧ how to make

Cut two triangles out at the same time

1 Fold the fabric in half, making sure that you fold one selvedge up to meet the other so that the pattern – if your fabric has one – aligns perfectly. Trace the template, cut it out, and pin it onto the fabric through both layers. Cut the triangles out using fabric scissors. Repeat until you have enough triangles.

2 Pin two triangles together, right sides facing, along the two diagonal sides. Beginning at the top of the triangles, machine stitch down towards the point about 1cm (½in) from the edge of the fabric. When you reach the point, lower the needle into the fabric, raise the presser foot, and turn the fabric so the foot is facing along the adjacent side. Lower the foot and continue stitching along the second side.

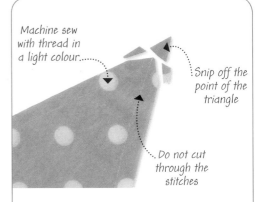

Machine sew with thread in a light colour

Snip off the point of the triangle

Do not cut through the stitches

3 Once you have secured your thread, trim away any excess fabric at the point of the triangle using fabric scissors. Repeat for all of your pairs of triangles. Trimming away the excess fabric means that when you turn the triangle inside out, it will form a neat point.

4 Turn the triangles the right way out and use a knitting needle or similar pointed item to gently push out the points. Push gently, as you don't want to burst through the stitches.

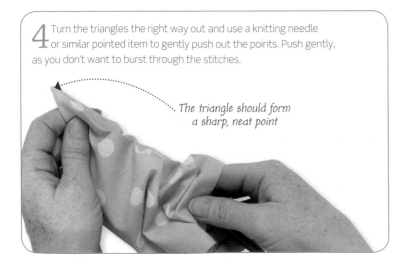

The triangle should form a sharp, neat point

5 Iron all the triangles flat. Ensure that when you iron them you don't allow the fabric to twist from the point – the seams should run very precisely down the sides of the triangle.

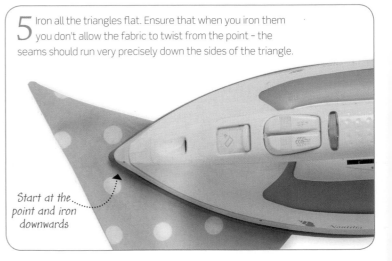

Start at the point and iron downwards

🍃 **you will need**

- Template from p.201
- Fabric: floral or polka dot cotton
- Fabric scissors
- Pins
- Sewing machine
- Thread
- Knitting needle
- Iron and ironing board
- Bias binding
- Buttons

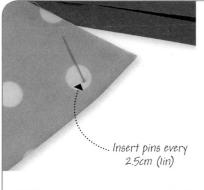

Insert pins every 2.5cm (1in)

6 If you need to, trim along the top of the triangle to make it level, ready for attaching the bias binding or ribbon. Fold bias binding or ribbon over the top edge of the triangle. Ensure that the triangle is pushed right into the fold, then pin in place. Space the triangles evenly along the bias binding. In this project the triangles were spaced 1cm (½in) apart.

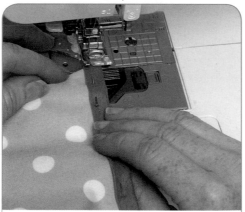

7 Machine stitch along the edge of the bias binding. Use a straight stitch and choose a thread in a matching colour. If you position the pins so that they point towards the sewing machine, you will easily be able to pull them out as you go.

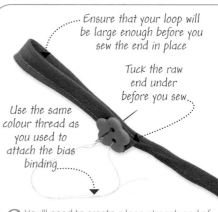

Ensure that your loop will be large enough before you sew the end in place

Tuck the raw end under before you sew.

Use the same colour thread as you used to attach the bias binding.

8 You'll need to create a loop at each end of the bias binding so that you can hang it up. Fold over the end of the bias binding to create a loop of about 2.5cm (1in). Tuck the raw end under and stitch it in place. For a decorative touch, stitch a pretty button over the folded end of the bias binding.

Tea towel

This apple print tea towel will brighten up any kitchen. It's one of the simplest machine-sewn projects you could possibly tackle, so why stop at making only one? A homemade tea towel also makes a great present for a friend.

🍃 how to make

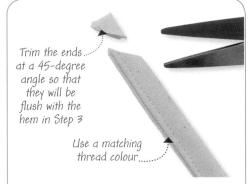

Trim the ends at a 45-degree angle so that they will be flush with the hem in Step 3

Use a matching thread colour

1 First, make your fabric loop. Fold the fabric rectangle lengthways in half and crease a line down the centre. Fold the edges inwards to meet this line and iron it into place. Then press these folded edges inwards to create one four-ply strip of fabric. Pin the fabric to prevent it moving, and machine stitch along the open edge using a straight stitch.

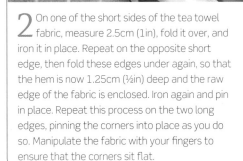

Fold over the two short edges first, then repeat on the two long sides

2 On one of the short sides of the tea towel fabric, measure 2.5cm (1in), fold it over, and iron it in place. Repeat on the opposite short edge, then fold these edges under again, so that the hem is now 1.25cm (½in) deep and the raw edge of the fabric is enclosed. Iron again and pin in place. Repeat this process on the two long edges, pinning the corners into place as you do so. Manipulate the fabric with your fingers to ensure that the corners sit flat.

Push the hanging loop right under the hem

The corners should be neatly flattened before sewing

3 Decide which corner you want your hanging loop in. Pin it securely across the corner, tucking it right into the hem. You may have to unpin a bit of each hem to make space for the ends of the loop. Pin again when the loop is in position. If your fabric has a pattern on it with an obvious "right way up", make sure you attach your loop to one of the top corners.

4 Rather than sewing around the edge of the tea towel in one go, you need to sew the two short edges first and then sew the two longer sides – that way the fabric is less likely to twist as you sew. Use a straight stitch and a matching thread colour. Try to get your line of machine stitching to run straight down the middle of the hem. Use the guides on the needle plate to help you.

5 When you come to the corner with the hanging loop, sew as slowly as you can, to ensure that you have stitched through both the hem and the ends of the loop. You don't want your hanging loop to give way when you use it. For added strength, you can machine a second time over the the hanging loop at the points where it slips under the hem.

The hanging loop must be pinned into position so that it cannot move as you sew over it

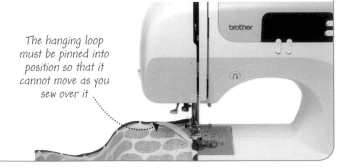

you will need

- Fabric: printed cotton, 50 × 75cm (20 × 30in)
- hanging loop fabric, 13 × 4.5cm (5in × 1¾in)
- Fabric scissors
- Iron and ironing board
- Pins
- Sewing machine
- Thread

Creating napkins

Napkins are really simple to make. You make them in the same way as tea towels but without the hanging loop. Choose cotton fabric that is relatively thick but also soft to the touch. You could make your napkins to any size you want, but the ones shown here measure 50 x 50cm (20 x 20in). Cut your squares of fabric, ensuring that the edges are parallel to or at right angles to the selvedges. Turn two opposite edges over by 2cm (¾in) and iron them flat. Tuck the raw edges under and into the fold and then iron flat again so that the hems now measure about 1cm (½in). Pin the hems into place, spacing the pins every 5cm (2in), positioning them perpendicular to the fabric. Repeat this on the other two edges, folding the fabric neatly in place at the corners. Machine sew two opposite edges first, secure the thread and then sew the other two opposite edges. Use a straight machine stitch, and sew as close to the edge of the hem as you can. Why not personalize your napkins with some appliqué shapes (see p.116) or embroidery stitches?

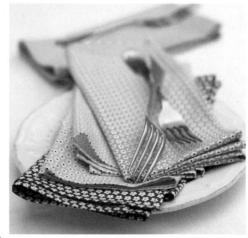

Table runner and tablecloth

Once you've mastered making tea towels and napkins, complete the set with a tablecloth and table runner. Choose hardwearing cotton, as they will need to withstand a lot of wear and tear.

Creating a table runner

This project uses the same simple techniques as the tea towel but features panels of contrasting material and decorative trimming along the ends. For this project you will need a length of patterned fabric for the main part of the runner, 110 x 35cm ($3^{1}/_{2}$ft x 14in), two plain panels, 6 x 35 cm ($2^{1}/_{2}$ x 14in), and two pieces of trimming, 35cm (14in) long.

To insert the plain panels, cut off 8cm (3in) from each end of the patterned fabric and put these pieces to one side. Lay the remaining patterned fabric wrong side down and place a band of plain fabric wrong side up on top of it so the long edge of the plain band aligns with the cut edge of the patterned fabric. Pin in place and, using a straight stitch, sew the two together 1cm ($^{1}/_{2}$in) from the edges. Open up the joined pieces of fabric and lay them right side down, then place one of the spare pieces of patterned fabric to the free edge of the plain band, wrong side to wrong side. Pin in place and stitch as you did on the other edge of the band.

Repeat at the other end of the patterned fabric to insert the second plain panel. Iron all the seams flat. If one fabric is lighter than the other, make sure that the lighter fabric overlaps the darker one. Create a double hem along the two short sides (see p.74), then repeat along the two long sides. To finish, pin your trimming to the underside of the two short ends, and sew it carefully into place.

Creating a tablecloth

Make your tablecloth to fit your table – simply measure the table and add about 30cm (12in) to the length and width so that the fabric can overhang on all sides. Decide how long or short you want your panels of patterned fabric on each end to be and then work out how much plain fabric you will need to go between them, allowing about 6cm (2¹/₂in) for making the seams. Cut your fabric to size, ensuring that the widths of both the patterned and plain fabrics are the same. Sew the pieces of fabric together using the method described opposite for making the table runner, then iron all the seams flat. Make a double hem along the two short sides (see p.74), then repeat on the other two, so that all four sides are neatly hemmed. To decorate, sew a length of ribbon over the join between the fabrics – this will give a really neat finish. Turn the ends of the ribbon under at either end so that there are no raw edges on show. To ensure that the ribbon lies flat, sew along the top edge first and once you reach the end, sew back along the bottom edge. Finish by machining the turned-under ends.

Apron

This apron is as stylish as it is practical. Make it in a print or striped fabric that co-ordinates with your kitchen or choose a heavy-duty cotton to make an apron for working in the garden. Just follow these nine simple steps.

❧ how to make

1 Cut out your fabric pieces using the templates given on p.206. If you choose to make your own bias binding (see p.80), make it from the same fabric as your kangaroo pocket. Neaten the two straight sides and the bottom of Apron Piece 1, using a zigzag, overedge, or overlock stitch.

.... *Neaten the three sides that won't be edged with bias binding*

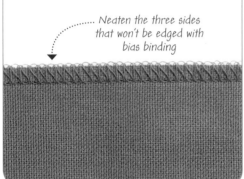

2 Turn over the three straight edges that you have just neatened by about 2cm (³⁄₄in), folding them to form a hem on the back of the fabric. Iron this hem flat and then pin it in place. Using a straight stitch, machine sew in place. Sew alongside the overlock or overedge stitching. Place the pins perpendicular to the edge of the fabric so that you can machine sew over them.

Insert pins every 10cm (4in) to hold the hem securely

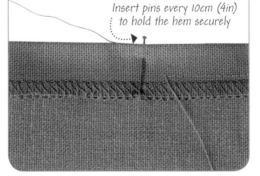

3 Pin homemade bias binding at the top edge of Piece 1, right side to right side, aligning the edge with the edge of the apron. If using bought bias binding, open one of the creases and pin the unfolded binding to the edges. You will sew along this open crease. Position the pins closely so that the bias strip cannot move.

Make sure the ...two top edges align

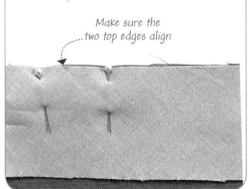

4 Machine sew the bias binding in place. For homemade binding, sew about 1cm (½in) from the edge; for bought binding, sew along the crease. Fold the binding over the stitching and under the fabric to the wrong side. Pull it tight and pin it in place. Tack, then remove the pins. On the right side, machine along the groove to secure. Repeat Steps 3 and 4 above to apply binding to the two arm holes.

This is the outside of your fabrice ...

...*Your stitches will create a neat edging*

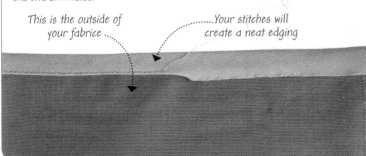

5 In order to create the two compartments of your pocket, you will need to mark a line that runs down the centre. Use a tape measure to ensure that your line is straight and centred, then mark it using a line of long tacking stitches (see p.49).Use a brightly coloured thread so that your tacking stitches stand out.

The curved edges will be the openings of the pocket......

Mark the centre of the pocket

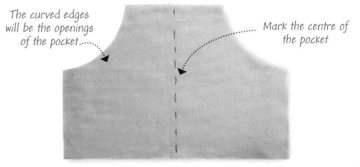

6 Prepare the pocket by machining a zigzag or overlock stitch around the entire edge. Fold the curved edges under by 5mm (¼in) and the top, bottom, and two straight edges by about 2cm (¾in). Pin all the folded edges in place, then press. Sew the curved edges in place.

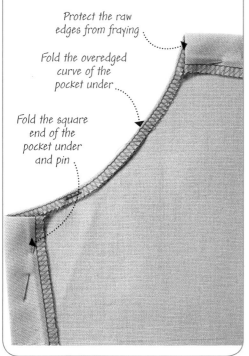

Protect the raw edges from fraying

Fold the overedged curve of the pocket under

Fold the square end of the pocket under and pin

7 Position the pocket 32cm (13in) from the top edge and centre it horizontally. Pin it in place and sew along the straight edges with a matching thread. Add diagonal stitches to reinforce the corners and sew two rows of stitches down the centre of the pocket. Remove the tacking stitches.

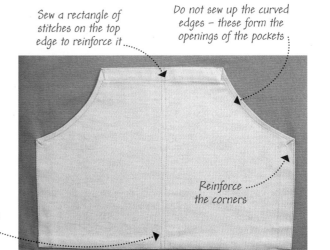

Sew a rectangle of stitches on the top edge to reinforce it

Do not sew up the curved edges – these form the openings of the pockets

Reinforce the corners

Follow your tacking stitches to create the two halves of your pocket

8 Create the apron strings and the neck tie: fold the fabric strips down the centre, lengthways. Fold the edges in to the centre, then fold each strip in half again so that it is four layers thick. Pin, then machine sew along the open edges.

Fold the raw edges inwards

Pin the end under before attaching

9 Attach the two apron strings first by pinning them in place to the back of the apron. Machine sew, creating a rectangle of stitches, then join the four corners with an "X". Attach the neck tie to the corners at the top of the apron using the same technique. Ensure that the neck tie isn't twisted before you sew.

Overlap at least 2.5cm (1in) so that the straps are secure

🌿 you will need

- Templates from p.206
- Fabric: heavy duty cotton or linen in two contrasting colours – for dimensions see p.206; apron strings fabric, two strips of 90 × 8cm (36 × 3in); neck tie fabric, 60 × 8cm (24 × 3in)
- Bias binding, three pieces 50cm (20in) long – buy ready-made or make it yourself
- Fabric scissors
- Sewing machine
- Overedge foot
- Thread
- Pins

Purse with a zip

Make this cute little purse from remnants of your favourite fabric to keep your loose change safe in your bag. Or, if you prefer, use the purse to store spare buttons, beads, or safety pins for your sewing projects.

❧ how to make

1 Trace the leaf templates given on p.202. Pin them to your felt, and then use pinking shears to cut out the shapes. Don't feel limited to using leaves as a decoration – you could cut out hearts or stars, or customize the purse with the first letter of your name.

Check that the pattern on the fabric is square with the selvedges

Cut your decorative shapes from felt

2 Iron a piece of fusible interfacing to the wrong side of each piece of lining. Don't move the iron but press firmly in one place. Make sure the interfacing doesn't overhang the lining before you apply your iron.

Press the iron firmly to bind the interfacing to the lining

3 Add your decoration to the piece of fabric that will become the front of the purse. If the pieces are too small to pin, hold them firmly in place as you sew. Use three strands of embroidery silk in a contrasting colour to make your stitches stand out against the felt.

Use a lighter thread to contrast

4 Lay one piece of lining onto the table with the interfaced side facing down. Position the zip on top of this so that their edges align, then lay a piece of the outer fabric face down on top. The lining and fabric will be right side to right side with the zip face up between. Pin the three layers together, inserting the pins close to the zip. Repeat to pin the second pieces of lining and fabric to the other side of the zip. The edge of the fabric that gets pinned to the zip will be the top of your design.

This will be the top of your purse

Pin close to the teeth of the zip

The outer side of the fabric must be facing down

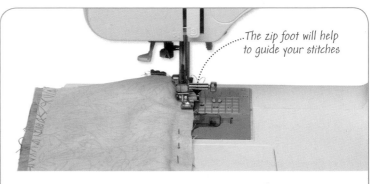

The zip foot will help to guide your stitches

5 Ensure that you have attached a zip foot to your sewing machine. Move the fabric clear so you can position one edge of the zip, one layer of outer fabric, and one piece of interfaced lining under the foot. Carefully sew along one side of the zip, following the line of pins. Use a straight stitch and try to keep the lines as straight as possible. Tie the threads off then turn the purse round and sew along the line of pins on the other side of the zip.

6 Open the purse out and place it on the table with the front and back pieces and the zip facing upwards. Iron the fabric firmly so that it sits neatly next to the zip and forms a crisp fold. If you want, machine sew a line of stitches down the sides of the zip to hold the folds in place. Before you move on to Step 7, you must open the zip about three-quarters of the way. This is really important – if you leave it closed you won't be able to turn your purse the right way out in Step 9.

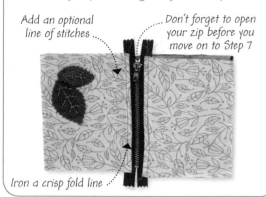

Add an optional line of stitches

Don't forget to open your zip before you move on to Step 7

Iron a crisp fold line

7 Flip the front and back pieces so that their right sides meet and do the same to the lining pieces. Pin the front to the back round the top and two sides but leave a 7-cm (3-in) gap in the lining. You will use this gap to pull the purse through in Step 9 Space your pins closely to ensure that the layers of fabric stay perfectly aligned as you sew.

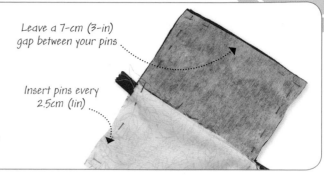

Leave a 7-cm (3-in) gap between your pins

Insert pins every 2.5cm (1in)

8 Sew around the edge of the purse leaving the 7-cm (3-in) gap unsewn; stitch about 1cm (½in) from the edge. Cut off any excess fabric at the corners so that they will turn inside out neatly without being bulky, being careful not to cut into your stitches. Trim away any excess zip fabric at either end. If you have used a metal zip, be really careful not to sew over it too fast or you could break your needle – go slowly to be on the safe side.

Cut off the excess zip fabric

Trim away the corners

9 Reach through the gap you left in the lining and through the open zip, and gently pull the purse the right way out. Carefully push the corners out so that they are square. Use a slip stitch (see p.51) to close up the gap in the lining, with thread in a matching colour. Push the lining into place inside the purse and it is ready to use. You could use a knitting needle to push the corners out, as long as you are gentle.

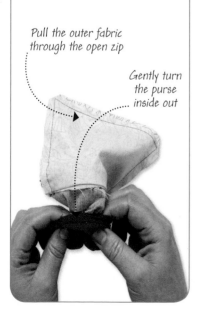

Pull the outer fabric through the open zip

Gently turn the purse inside out

you will need

- Templates from p.202, Leaf A and Leaf B
- Fabric: two pieces of patterned outer, two pieces of plain lining, two pieces of fusible interfacing, all 10 ×12.5cm (4 × 5in); felt to decorate
- Fabric scissors
- Pinking shears
- Iron and ironing board
- Needle
- Embroidery silk
- Pins
- Zip: 15cm (6in)
- Sewing machine
- Zip foot
- Thread
- Elastic and beads

Pencil case and cushion cover

Once you've mastered the technique of inserting a zip, there are any number of different items you can make that use exactly the same method. This lovely pencil case is made from black and white fabric that can be coloured in with fabric pens. Or why not choose a graphic printed fabric for a cushion cover and appliqué some birds and leaves on top?

Creating a pencil case

Choose fabrics that are hardwearing, such as thick cotton or canvas, and use a brightly coloured lining. Make the case using the method given on pp.152–153 – the only difference is the dimensions. This case uses fabric that is 24 x 16cm (10 x 6in). For a colour-in case, choose a monochrome, line-drawn print and invest in some fabric pens. Make sure that the case is long enough to hold your pens or pencils – the average pencil is about 20cm (8in) long.

Creating a cushion case

The advantage of creating a cover with a zip is that it can be removed and washed – so don't stuff the cushion with wadding, use a cushion pad instead. Choose a hardwearing fabric with a graphic monochrome print and cut it 2.5cm (1in) larger than the length and width of your pad. Trace the shapes from the monochrome fabric then cut them out of floral fabric. Pin them in place on the cushion front then machine sew around the edges with zigzag stitch. Make the cushion using the method on pp.152–153, but without the lining.

🌿 you will need

- Fabric: two pieces of floral fabric,
  33 × 28cm (13 × 11in); two pieces of plain
  fabric, 33 × 11.5cm (13 × 4½in) lining
  fabric, 70 × 33cm (27½ × 13in); two
  pieces of interfacing, 70 × 33cm
  (27½ × 13in) two pieces of strap fabric,
  56 × 6.5cm (22 × 2½in); two lengths of
  webbing, 56 × 4cm (22 × 1½in)

- Ribbon: 33cm (13in)
- Fabric scissors
- Pins
- Sewing machine
- Thread
- Iron and ironing board
- Needle

Tote bag

Want to stand out in the crowd as you do your weekly shop – and boost your environmentalist street-cred at the same time? Then make this irresistible, easy-to-sew tote bag. You could push the boat out and decorate your finished bag with a homemade felt flower.

how to make

1 Cut out your fabric and lay the pieces out to make sure that the lengths of floral fabric, the plain fabric, the lining fabric, and the panels of interfacing are all exactly the same width. Webbing is a strong tape-like fabric that is used for strengthening items like straps or handles. If you are unable to find any, you can substitute it with stiff interfacing.

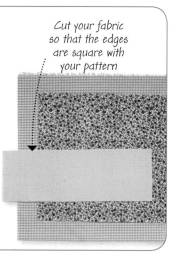

Cut your fabric so that the edges are square with your pattern

2 To create the tote straps, fold each long side of both pieces of strap fabric in by 1cm (½in) and iron in place. Lay the webbing or interfacing along the centre of the straps, tucked under the folded edges. Fold each strap in half lengthways and pin. Turn up 5mm (¼in) at the ends of each strap, to finish them neatly. Machine stitch along the straps, close to the open edge, using a straight stitch.

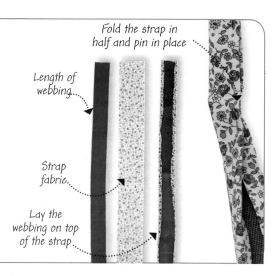

Fold the strap in half and pin in place

Length of webbing

Strap fabric

Lay the webbing on top of the strap

3 Next, join the floral and plain fabrics to make the front and back of the tote. With the right sides together, pin one short edge of each floral length to the long edge of each plain piece. Using a straight stitch, machine sew the floral fabric to the plain fabric, 1cm (½in) from the raw edges. Repeat with the other pieces of floral and plain fabric.

Pin the fabrics with their right sides facing inwards

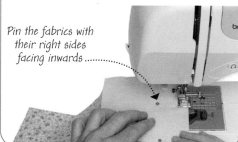

4 Remove all the pins and place each piece of seamed fabric with the right side face down. Iron along the seams, pressing them apart. Iron fusible interfacing onto the back of your two seamed pieces. It's important to get the seams as flat as you can, so that the seamed fabric feels like one continuous piece.

Iron on your interfacing once your seam is flat

5 Choose which piece of fabric is to be the front of your tote and pin the ribbon along the seam joining the floral and plain fabrics. Machine stitch the ribbon in place using a straight stitch and thread in a matching colour. To keep the ribbon flat, sew along one long edge first, then go back and sew along the other.

Sew back along the bottom edge of the ribbon once the top edge is secure

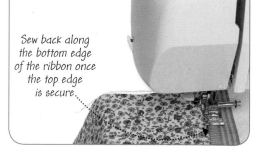

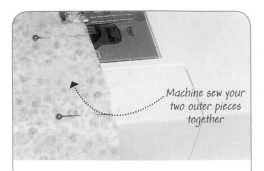

Machine sew your two outer pieces together

6 Lay the interfaced front and back on top of each other, right sides together. Pin around the two long sides and the bottom, leaving the top edge open. Machine around the three pinned sides about 1cm (½in) from the edge of the fabric. Remove the pins. Make sure you form neat right angles as you sew around the corners (see p.56).

7 Using sharp fabric scissors, trim away the excess fabric from the corners at an angle. Leave about 5mm (¼in) between the stitches and the edge of the fabric. This will ensure that your corners are neat when the bag is turned the right way out. If you don't trim the fabric away, the corners will look bulky.

Be careful not to snip through your stitches

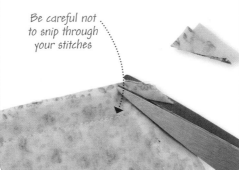

Slide the lining in until the two top edges align

The lining must be turned the right way out

8 Place the two pieces of lining fabric right sides together. Pin along the two long sides and along one short edge, leaving a gap of 13cm (5in) in the middle of this edge – you will use the gap to turn your bag the right way out in Step 11. Machine around the pinned sides as in Step 6. Remember, once the thread is secure, trim the excess fabric from the corners (see Step 7).

9 Turn the lining the right way out. With the outer bag still inside out, slip the lining bag into it until its top edge is in line with the top edge of the outer bag. Pin the open edge of the bag to the open edge of the lining. It's important that the two top edges line up so that the finished seam sits on the very top of the opening when you turn the bag to the right side.

10 Machine stitch the open edge of the bag to the open edge of the lining about 1cm (½in) from the edge of the fabric. Take care not to stitch all the layers together. You will need to manipulate the fabric to get it into the correct position under the presser foot. Sew around the edge of the bag, not through all the layers.

Stitch around the rim of the bag, joining the inner and outer layers

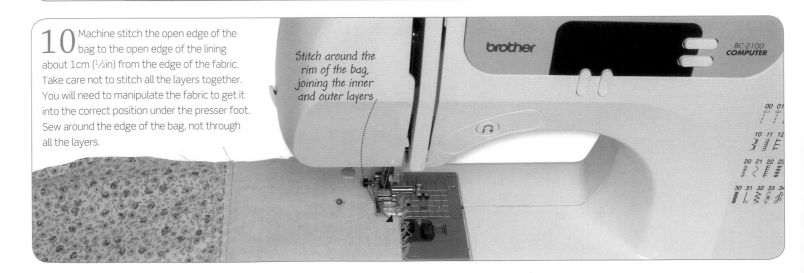

11 Remove all the pins. You now have two bags joined together at the top. Pull the lining out of the bag – the joined pieces will both be inside out. Gently pull the bag through the gap in the stitching that you left when you sewed up the lining in Step 8. The bag will now be the right way out. Use a knitting needle to carefully poke out the corners so they are nice and square. Use slip stitch to close the gap in the lining.

Use slip stitch to neatly sew up the gap

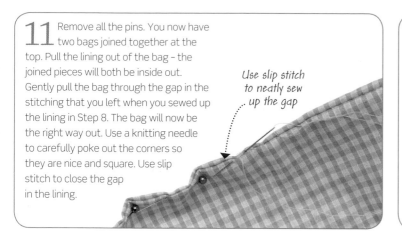

12 Push the lining into place inside the bag and iron around the top of the bag to ensure that the lining lies flat and that you have a sharp seam. Topstitch a row of machine stitches around the top of the bag, about ½cm (¼in) from the edge. This will ensure that the lining stays put. Finally, position the two straps, with the bottom of each end 7cm (3in) from the edge of the bag. Pin in place then machine into position.

Adding handles

These smart leather handles and others like them are available to buy from craft shops and over the internet. Make your tote bag following Steps 1–11 on pp.156–159, then simply machine sew these handles onto the outside of the bag using a size 120 needle and strong machine thread. Alternatively, fabric straps can be sewn in place between the outer bag and the lining. To make, adapt the steps on pp.156–159. At the end of Step 9, slip each end of the straps between the outer bag and the lining, sliding them in so that about 2.5cm (1in) is sandwiched. Pin in place then continue with Step 10, machine-stitching the straps in position. For extra strength, you can machine over the ends of the straps a second time.

Adding pockets

A splash of colour in the form of a useful pocket or two can perk up the appearance of an otherwise run-of-the-mill tote. Pockets are incredibly simple to make. Before you put your tote together, cut rectangles of fabric for your pockets making them about 1cm (½in) larger all round than the size you want them to be. Don't be afraid to mismatch colours and sizes. Fold 1cm (½in) over on the top and bottom of the rectangle and iron in place. Repeat on the other two edges. All you need to do now is position the pocket on the front of your tote – making sure that it isn't wonky – and pin it in place. Machine stitch neatly along the bottom and two sides, then make the tote following Steps 4–12 on pp.156–159.

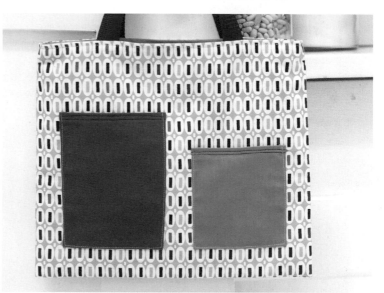

Hessian bag

It's easy to make your own stylish bag. You could replace the hessian used here with denim or heavy cotton. Make the bag to your own measurements, if you would like it to be longer or deeper – just remember to use the template for the lower corners.

❧ how to make

1 Mark the tucks and corners on to piece 1 with chalk. Pin the tucks in place.

2 On both ends, attach the band (piece 2) to the top edge of piece 1 over the tucks, using a 1.5cm (⅝in) seam allowance.

3 Press the seam open and top-stitch.

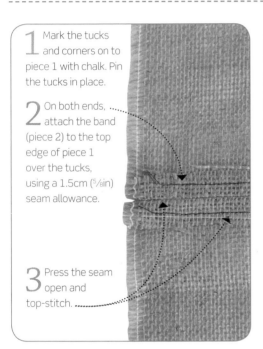

4 Join the side seams from the top, stopping at the dot. Press the seam open.

5 Fold the corners by bringing the stitching lines together.

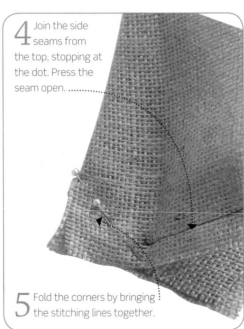

6 Stitch along the diagonal lines. Press the corners up. Turn to the right side.

7 To make the four carrier strips, cut pieces 3 and 4 in half along the fold. Fold the long edges of each piece to the centre, then fold lengthways in half.

8 Machine down the folded edge through all layers to join the halves.

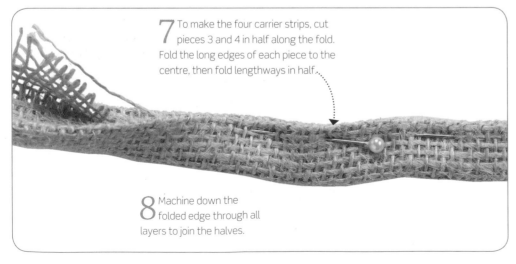

9 Wrap the carriers around the handles and pin in place.

🍂 you will need

- Template p.211
- 1m x 115cm (40 x 46in) hessian
- 1 reel thread
- 1 pair bag handles
- 1m x 115cm (40 x 46in) cotton fabric for lining

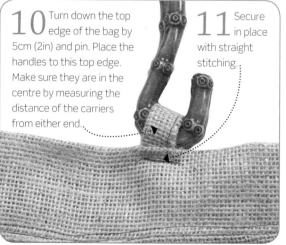

10 Turn down the top edge of the bag by 5cm (2in) and pin. Place the handles to this top edge. Make sure they are in the centre by measuring the distance of the carriers from either end.

11 Secure in place with straight stitching.

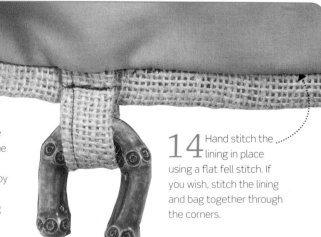

12 Make up the lining to match the bag (steps 1-6).

13 Cut a piece of thick cardboard to fit the bottom of the bag. Insert the card and then the lining (turning its top edge down by about 7cm/2¾in so it does not show at the top), wrong side to wrong side.

14 Hand stitch the lining in place using a flat fell stitch. If you wish, stitch the lining and bag together through the corners.

Door hanging

Store all your clutter in a stylish door hanging like this one. Make it from sturdy cotton so it stays firm when fully laden, add a coat hanger and voilà – it's ready to hang from the back of any door.

❧ how to make

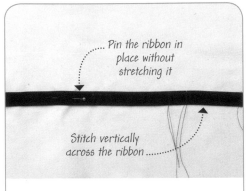

Pin the ribbon in place without stretching it

Stitch vertically across the ribbon

1 Cut out all your fabric pieces using the templates given on p.207. Lay the front piece out in front of you and position the stretch ribbon across it, 10cm (4in) from the top edge. Pin it in place. Machine sew vertical rows of stitches at intervals along it – the spacing will depend on the items you plan to store. Lay out the items before you sew, to ensure that they will fit.

2 Fold both pieces of pocket fabric in half, lengthways with the wrong sides of the fabric facing in. Iron them flat. Pin your decorative braid or trimming along the folded edges and then stitch it carefully into place. Remove the pins. Sew very slowly to ensure that you stitch in a straight line along the centre of the braid. If you don't, the braid will gape.

Pin the braid onto the folded edge

3 Each of the pockets will have three sections divided by a pleat held in place with a line of stitching. Lightly mark with tailor's chalk on the reverse of each piece of pocket fabric 20cm (8in) and 40cm (16in) from the left-hand edge of the pocket. Gather the fabric into a pleat around each mark, pin it, and iron so that it forms the shape shown below. Line up the raw edge of the lower pocket with the bottom edge of the front piece and pin. Machine a vertical line of stitching through the centre of each pleat.

Machine sew the lines that divide up your pockets

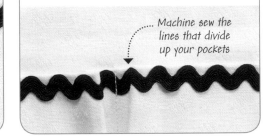

4 Iron the pleats into place, manipulating the fabric to make sure that it comes together at the bottom of each pleat, creating sharp "V" shapes. This will cause the upper edge of each pocket section to tip forwards slightly. With your three sections created and your lower edges pinned in position, machine sew the pocket at either end to secure it. You don't need to sew along the bottom edge, as this will be secured when you sew the hanging together in Step 8.

Press the pleat in place

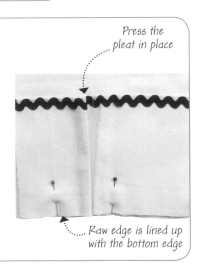

Raw edge is lined up with the bottom edge

5 Measure 27cm (11in) at intervals from the top edge of the front piece and mark these points with pins. Run a row of tacking stitches along the pins at the 27cm (11in) line in a bright thread colour. This is the line for positioning the upper pocket. With right sides together and the decorated edge of the upper pocket hanging down towards the bottom, pin the raw edge of the pleated pocket along the positioning line. Machine sew in place 1cm (½in) from the edge, then remove the pins.

Line of tacking stitches

Machine sew along this line

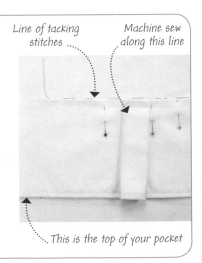

This is the top of your pocket

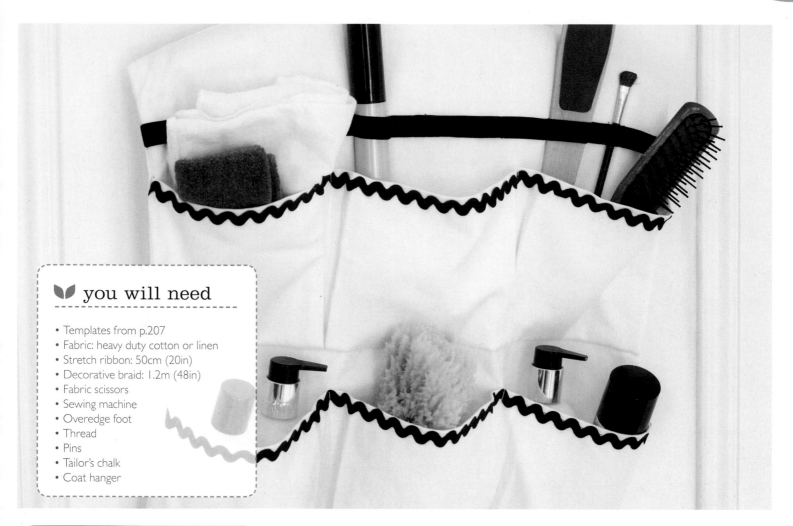

you will need

- Templates from p.207
- Fabric: heavy duty cotton or linen
- Stretch ribbon: 50cm (20in)
- Decorative braid: 1.2m (48in)
- Fabric scissors
- Sewing machine
- Overedge foot
- Thread
- Pins
- Tailor's chalk
- Coat hanger

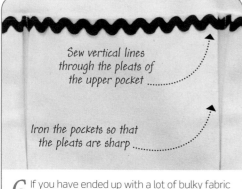

Sew vertical lines through the pleats of the upper pocket ......

Iron the pockets so that the pleats are sharp ......

6 If you have ended up with a lot of bulky fabric in the bottom of your pocket, trim this away carefully, taking care not to snip the stitches or any of your fabric. Flip the pocket up into position and machine sew each end to the sides of the front piece. Machine a vertical line of stitches through the centre of each pleat. Iron the pleats in place.

7 Lay the coat hanger on the wrong side of the back piece and draw around it with chalk. Pin the front and back pieces, right side to right side, all the way around except for a gap of 20cm (8in) along the bottom edge and a gap of about 1cm (³⁄₈in) at the centre top for the coat hanger. The pockets will now be sandwiched between the front and back.

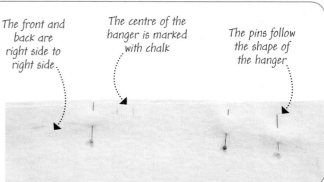

The front and back are right side to right side .

The centre of the hanger is marked with chalk ......

The pins follow the shape of the hanger

8 Sew around all four sides, 1.5cm (½in) from the edge, following the shape of the hanger and leaving the gaps in the top and bottom. Remove the pins and trim away any excess fabric from the seams. Turn the hanging the right way out and iron carefully. Insert the coat hanger and use slip stitch (see p.50) to close up the gap in the bottom edge.

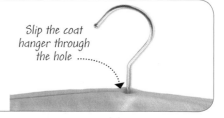

Slip the coat hanger through the hole ......

you will need

- Template p.209
- 60 x 115cm (24 x 46in) silk dupion
- 60 x 115cm (24 x 46in) non-woven fusible interfacing
- 25 x 90cm (10 x 36in) polyester wadding about 6mm (¼in) thick
- 18cm (7in) skirt zip
- 1 reel matching thread
- 1 snap fastener
- 1m (40in) no 3 piping cord
- 1m (40in) ribbon, 5mm (³⁄₁₆in) wide

Jewellery roll

Going away? Where do you put your jewellery? This handy wrap will fit any handbag or weekend holdall, and keep not only earrings but also your rings and chains. It could easily be adjusted to have more than one ring holder and could also have a larger zip pocket or two.

❧ how to make

1 Prior to cutting out, apply the fusible interfacing (p.47) to the wrong side of the silk. Pin wadding securely to the top layer of piece 1 (the top of the jewellery roll) and tack across diagonally to secure.

2 Make a pocket with the zip (p.95). Take piece 3 and press in half, wrong side to wrong side. Place the folded pressed edge to the side of the zip and stitch in place with the zip foot.

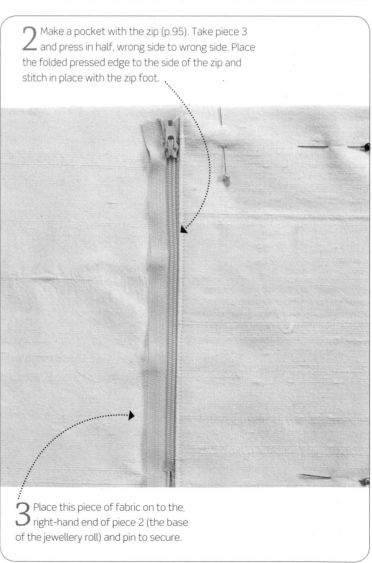

3 Place this piece of fabric on to the right-hand end of piece 2 (the base of the jewellery roll) and pin to secure.

4 Take piece 4 and press under 1.5cm (⅝in) along one short edge. Place the pressed edge along the other side of the zip, and pin in place.

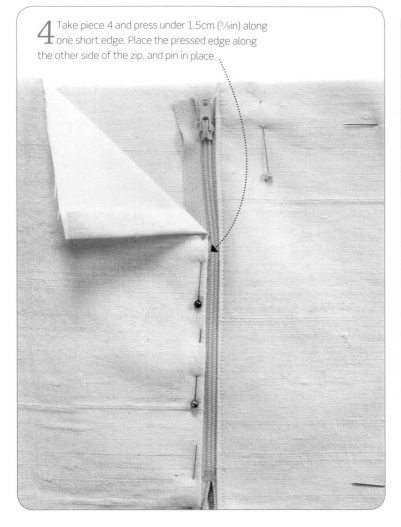

5 Using the zip foot, stitch along the side of the zip through all layers. This makes a pocket on just the right-hand side.

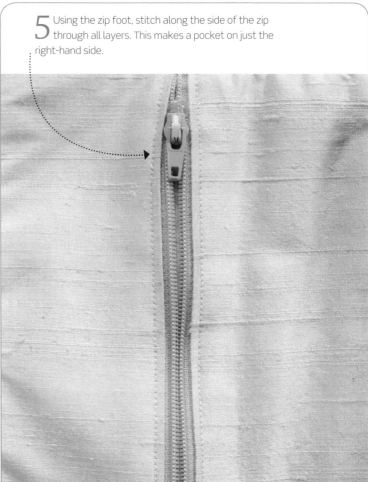

6 To make a pocket at the other end, take piece 5 and press in half, wrong side to wrong side. Edge-stitch along the folded side.

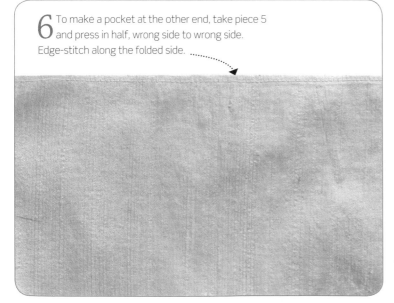

7 Place this piece to the left-hand side of the base and pin around the edges to secure. Stitch along the centre of the piece to make two pockets.

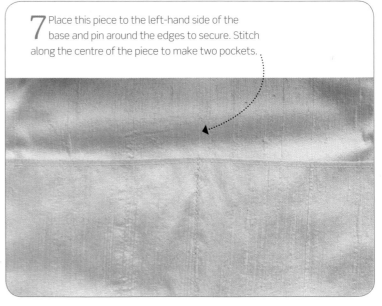

8 To make the ring holder, take piece 6 and a piece of wadding 6 x 22cm (2¼ x 9in). Wrap the silk around the wadding to make a fat tube shape, turning in the raw edge by 1.5cm (⅝in) on one long side and one end. Press if required.

9 Secure by hand with a flat fell stitch.

10 Pin the ring holder to the base of the jewellery roll between the pockets. Sew a snap close to the end of the ring holder.

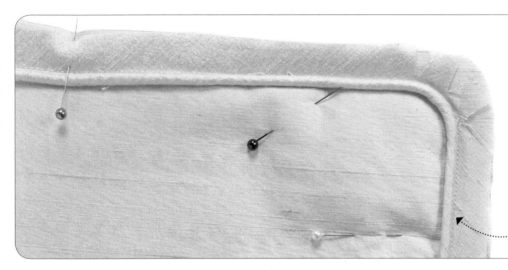

11 Cut 4cm (1½in) wide bias strips from piece 7 for the piping. With the cord, make up enough piping to go all around the edge of the roll.

12 Round off the corners of the base fabric and top fabric. An easy way to make a nice curve is to draw around a large thread spool.

13 Stitch the piping to the base (pp.85–86).

14 Before attaching the top layer, stitch on the ribbon ties. Attach one piece of ribbon at the centre point on the left-hand side and another piece about 15cm (6in) to the right of this piece.

15 Place the top piece to the base, right side to right side. Using the zip foot, stitch the two sections together along the piping. Leave a gap of about 7cm (2¾in) to turn through.

16 Trim and layer the seams. Remove all tacks. Press and turn while still warm. Hand stitch the gap with a flat fell or blind hem stitch.

Baby blanket

This fleece baby blanket can be cut to any size . A soft washable wool or acrylic would also be ideal. The edges of the blanket have been bound with a soft satin polyester to make a contrasting tactile edge for the baby, but they could be bound in cotton if you prefer.

❧ how to make

1 Cut out two pieces of fleece large enough to fit your baby's cot. If you are going to machine embroider the fleece, this is the time to do so, following your machine's instruction manual.

2 Place the two pieces of fleece together, wrong side to wrong side, and lay them on a flat surface so you can avoid wrinkles. Tack around the outside edge.

3 Cut bias banding strips (pp.80-81) 12cm (5in) wide from the satin and join them together to make a strip that is long enough to go all around the blanket (measure around the edge of the blanket and add about 9cm/3¾in for each corner). Apply the banding to the edge of the blanket.

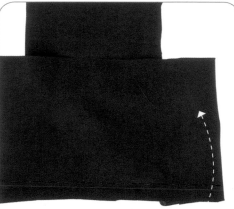

4 As all four corners of the banding need to match, it is a good idea to make a triangular-shaped template from card or paper to give the angle of the point. Machine one point first and make sure it is correct, then trace off the stitching lines to make your template.

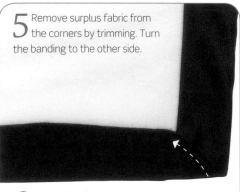

5 Remove surplus fabric from the corners by trimming. Turn the banding to the other side.

6 Turn under the edge of the banding and hand stitch in place with a flat fell stitch.

7 If you are using a fusible appliqué (p.116), apply the appliqué using the iron and a pressing cloth.

8 Fold up your completed teddy blanket ready to present to the lucky baby of your choice!

🍃 you will need

- -

- 1m x 1.5m (40 x 60in) fleece
- Machine embroidery threads or fusible appliqué
- 1 reel matching thread
- About 30 x 115cm (12 x 46in) satin polyester or cotton

Baby towel

A snuggly towel for a baby or toddler is a must-make project. If you cannot find towelling, you can always buy a large bath sheet and cut it up. Choose a contrast or matching binding and towelling for the edges and the ears. You could even embroider on eyes, a mouth, and whiskers!

❧ how to make

1 Attach binding to the lower edge of the hood (piece 2). Use a stitch length of 3.0 as the towelling is bulky.

2 Wrap the binding to the right side and machine in place.

3 Make the ears. Cut out two from the towelling and two from the face towel. Place one of each colour together, right side to right side. Pin together.

4 Hand stitch around the ear, leaving the bottom edge open.

5 Turn the ear to the right side.

6 Hand stitch the ears to the hood section, about 18cm (7½in) from the bias-bound edge.

7 Pin the hood into one corner of the towel wrap (piece 1).

8 Draw around a plate to achieve corner curves and trim to shape. Bind all the outside straight and curved edges as for steps 1 and 2.

❤ you will need

- Template p.210
- 1.2 × 1.5m (48 × 60in) towelling, or one large bath sheet for the wrap and a hand towel for the hood
- 1 contrast colour face towel (flannel) for the inside of the ears
- 1 reel thread
- 5m (16ft) bias binding, 2cm (¾in) wide (same colour as inside of ears)

Child's skirt

This is a simple skirt, cut from a long strip of fabric. The skirt features tucks at the hem edge that have been top-stitched to produce a decorative effect, and then embroidered with a machine stitch. The waist edge of the skirt has an elasticated finish. This pattern could be adapted for a child of any age – or even an adult.

❧ how to make

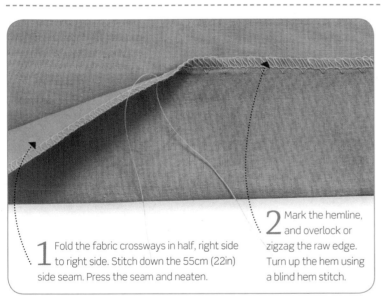

1 Fold the fabric crossways in half, right side to right side. Stitch down the 55cm (22in) side seam. Press the seam and neaten.

2 Mark the hemline, and overlock or zigzag the raw edge. Turn up the hem using a blind hem stitch.

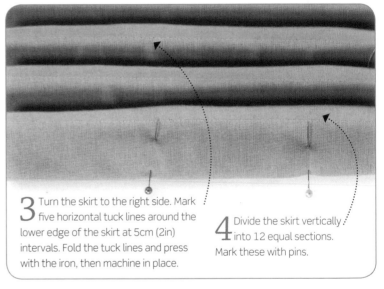

3 Turn the skirt to the right side. Mark five horizontal tuck lines around the lower edge of the skirt at 5cm (2in) intervals. Fold the tuck lines and press with the iron, then machine in place.

4 Divide the skirt vertically into 12 equal sections. Mark these with pins.

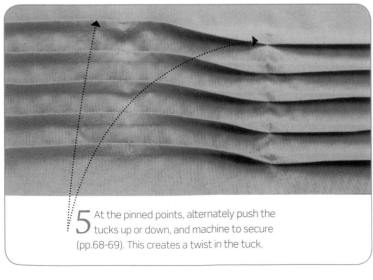

5 At the pinned points, alternately push the tucks up or down, and machine to secure (pp.68-69). This creates a twist in the tuck.

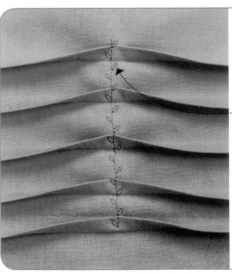

6 On all of the tucks pointing towards the waist, stitch over the machining with a decorative stitch, or do this by hand.

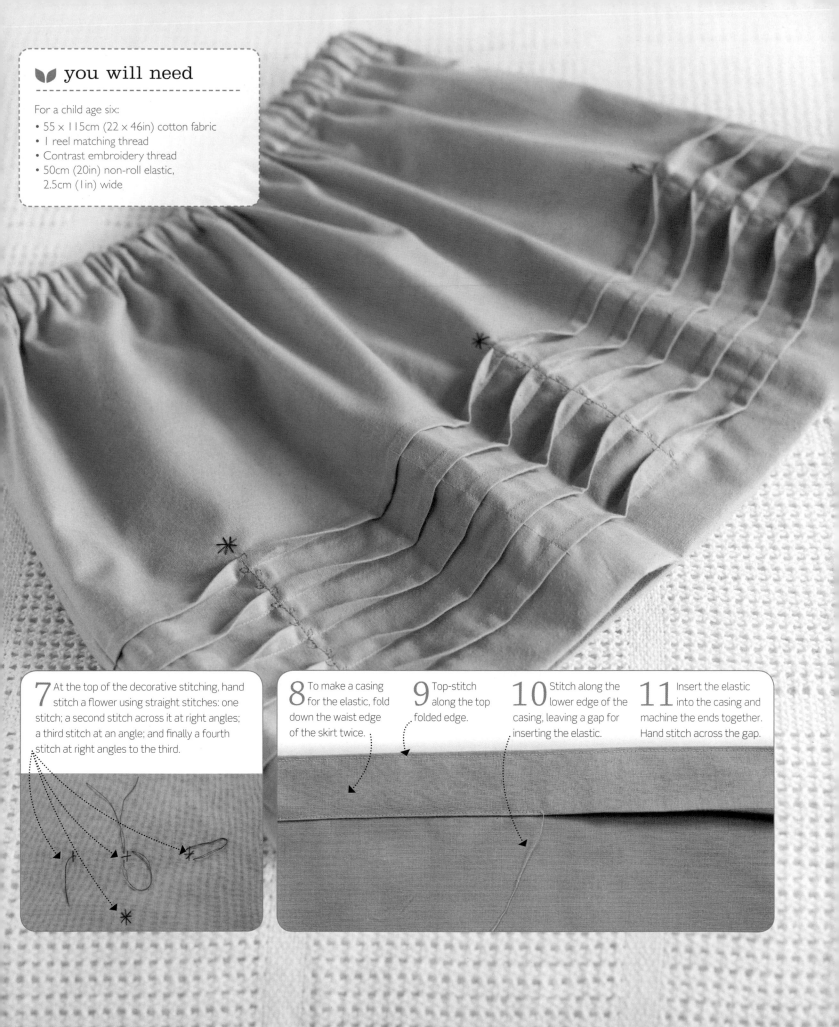

7 At the top of the decorative stitching, hand stitch a flower using straight stitches: one stitch; a second stitch across it at right angles; a third stitch at an angle; and finally a fourth stitch at right angles to the third.

8 To make a casing for the elastic, fold down the waist edge of the skirt twice.

9 Top-stitch along the top folded edge.

10 Stitch along the lower edge of the casing, leaving a gap for inserting the elastic.

11 Insert the elastic into the casing and machine the ends together. Hand stitch across the gap.

Floral cotton skirt

Your little girl will simply love this adorable cotton skirt – and you'll love how easy it is to dress her in it. No fiddly buttons or zips: just a made-to-measure elasticated waistband. If you create an extra long hem you will be able to let the skirt down as she grows..

❧ how to make

1 As an approximate guide, for a two- to three-year-old use a piece of fabric 110 x 35cm (44 x 14in); for a three- to four-year-old use 110 x 38cm (44 x 15in). For the length of the elastic: measure your child's waist and add 2.5cm (1in) to that measurement. Once the elastic is in place with the ends sewn together, it will be a comfortable fit. Cut your fabric. Pin the short edges together with the right sides facing in.

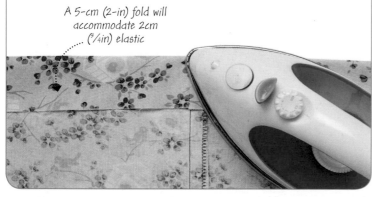

2 Sew along the short edge with a straight machine stitch, leaving a margin of about 1cm (½in). Remove the pins. Neaten the raw edge with an overedge or zigzag stitch (see p.55) to stop it fraying. Iron the seam to one side.It is important to finish the raw edges or they could fray and cause holes in the seam.

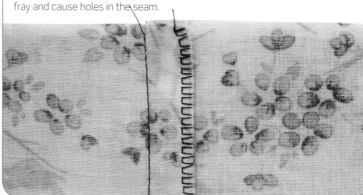

3 If you are using 2cm (¾in) elastic, turn 5cm (2in) of fabric at the waist edge to the wrong side and iron flat. If your elastic is wider than this, make the fold deeper. This fold will create the channel that will hold your elastic, so it is important to get the depth correct.

A 5-cm (2-in) fold will accommodate 2cm (¾in) elastic

4 Tuck the raw edge under and iron it in place. Your channel will now be about 2.5cm (1in) deep. Pin it securely, spacing the pins every 7cm (3in) or so. Position them facing outwards so you can easily sew over them and then remove them afterwards.

Position the pins perpendicular to the fabric

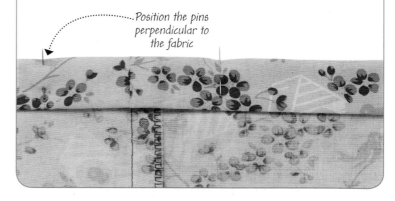

5 Sew around the turnover, a few mm (1/16in) from the fold. Tie off the ends of the thread and remove the pins. When sewing along the bottom edge of this turnover you'll need to leave about a 7-cm (3-in) gap in your stitching, so that the elastic can be fed in and pulled through. Use a pin to mark your finishing point. Start stitching about 7cm (3in) beyond this, and then stop when you get back round to the pin.

Stop when you reach you marker pin...

The two rows of stitches should be just under 2.5cm (1in) apart

6 Attach a safety pin to one end of the elastic and feed it through the channel. It may help to pin the other end to the skirt to stop the elastic being pulled right through (see p.104). When the pin emerges from the end of the channel, check that the elastic hasn't twisted, then pin the ends together so they overlap by about 4cm (1 1/2in).

The safety pin helps you pull the elastic through...

7 Sew over the overlapped ends to form a rectangle with an "X" across it. This will make the join extra-secure. Remove the pin that holds the ends together as soon as you have sewn the first line of stitches: you won't be able to sew over the pin – the first line of stitches will keep everything in place until you have finished. Secure the thread, then work the elastic through the channel so the waistband is evenly gathered.

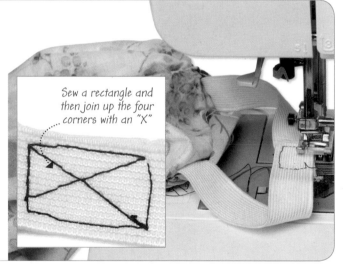

Sew a rectangle and then join up the four corners with an "X"

8 Use slip stitch (see p.50) to sew up the gap, sealing the elastic inside the channel. Make sure that you do not catch the elastic in your stitches as you close up the gap. If you do, it will prevent the elastic from stretching.

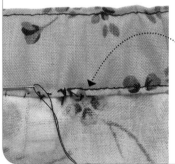

Use the same thread colour as you used in your machine

9 Before you stitch the hem, you'll need to work out how long the skirt should be. Try it on your child and measure the length. Turn the lower edge to the wrong side so the fold is where you want the skirt to end. Here it was turned over by 2.5cm (1in). Iron the fold in place, then tuck the raw edge under, iron again, then pin. Machine carefully along the upper fold using a straight stitch. Remove the pins.

Position the pins so you can easily sew over them

10 Measure round the bottom of the hem and cut your ribbon to this length, plus a little for an overlap. Place one end of the ribbon at the skirt side seam. Pin it round the hemline on top of the stitching, overlapping it slightly at the end. Machine sew in place. If you feel confident, you can attach the ribbon at the same time as you sew the hem. Pin the ribbon to the right side of the folded hem in Step 9, then sew through the ribbon and the hem together.

Your ribbon trim will cover up your hemline stitches

Child's shorts

You might look at a pair of shorts and think that they are far beyond your technical reach, but don't be put off.

❧ how to make

1 Using the template on p.207, cut out your pieces to the size that you need. Mark the front of each piece using a pin – this will prevent you getting the two pieces round the wrong way. Fold each leg piece in half so that the right sides of the fabric face inwards – pin them to create two leg pieces. On each piece, sew a seam from the waistband down to the crotch, and then overedge it to neaten. You will have created two leg tubes. Turn one leg tube the right way out and then slip it inside the leg that is inside out. Ensure that your two marker pins line up – this is crucial. The crotch joins must align.

This edge of the fabric will form the waistband

Slide one leg tube inside the other

2 Match up the edges that run up and down the inside of the leg pieces and pin them together. Machine sew the pieces together, stitching about 1cm (½in) from the edge of the fabric. Trim away any excess fabric to neaten and then overlock the edges.

The seam forms an inverted "U" shape

Neaten the seams between the leg pieces

3 Turn the shorts the right way out. Sew two lines of thread along the central seam – this is the seam that runs from the front of the shorts, between the legs and up the back – to reinforce it. Measure your child to work out how long you want your shorts to be, and create the waistband and leg hems as you did for the child's skirt (see pp.175–176).

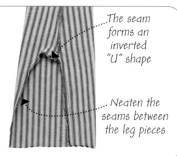

Sew a double line of stitches along the crotch seam to reinforce it

These simple shorts rely on many of the techniques you will have used before, when making a child's skirt (see pp.175–176), so why not give it a go? If you are feeling creative, you could sew on a decorative fly for a professional finish.

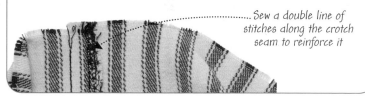

Pillowcase dress

If you have a couple of spare pillowcases that are in good condition, why not upcycle them to make this sweet, summery dress? Adapt the style to suit your child's taste – you could substitute the straps for ribbons or customize it using some felt flowers in a matching colour.

how to make

1 First make the straps. With the fabric face down, fold it lengthways in half and crease a line down the centre. Fold the edges inwards to meet the crease, iron in place, then press the folded edges inwards again. Pin then machine sew along the open edge. You can make ribbon straps if you prefer but you'll need to put a few small stitches in at the arm holes so the ribbon can't slip out.

Place the fabric face down and crease it

Fold to form a 4-ply strap, with the end tucked under, and pin.

Sew with straight stitch close to the open edge.

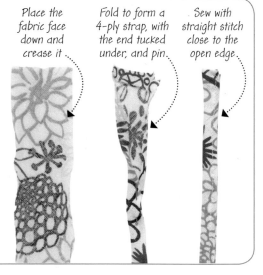

Pin the template to the open edge of the fabric

2 The plain pillowcase forms the main part of the dress. Fold it in half lengthways then cut along the closed short end to remove about 5mm (¼in). You will now have a tube that is open at both ends. Leave it folded. Cut out template "J" on p.202 and pin it to the unfolded edge of the pillowcase in the top corner. Cut around the template to create the arm holes.

3 Decide how long you want the main part of the dress to be, bearing in mind that you will be adding a band of patterned fabric around the bottom and straps to the top. Using a tape measure, measure and mark this length then cut the excess fabric from the bottom. Decide how long you want the patterned band to be then follow Steps 2-3 to cut the patterned pillowcase to form a tube of the correct length.

Bear in mind that you will lose some length when you create your seams

Use pillowcases that are the same width

4 Turn the patterned band inside out then slide it onto the bottom of the plain pillowcase so that the edges line up. What will be the top of the patterned band is now lined up with the bottom of the dress. If the pillowcases are the same size they should match up perfectly with their side seams aligned.

Your plain pillowcase should be the right way out

5 Pin the two pieces together, starting at the side seams and working inwards. This will help to keep the two existing pillowcase seams aligned, and to prevent the fabric gaping apart. Tip Insert the pins every 5cm (2in) to make sure the patterned band is securely attached.

Point the pins downwards to make them easy to sew over

Make sure the edges are flush before you pin

6 Stitch through both layers of fabric using a straight stitch about 1.5cm (½in) from the edge. Remove all the pins. To neaten the raw edge and prevent it from fraying, use a zigzag or overedge stitch (see p.55), or an overlocker.

You'll need an overedge foot when using overedge stitch

7 Turn the dress inside out, fold the seam towards the bottom, and iron it flat. Turn the pillowcase dress the right way out and iron again. If one of your fabrics is much darker than the other, make sure that you iron the light fabric over the dark fabric, and not the other way around, or the dark fabric will show through.

This is the outside of the dress

8 Measure the bias binding carefully to make sure it matches the length of the arm holes and then cut two lengths to fit. Open out one folded edge of the bias binding and pin it round the arm hole, right side to right side, aligning the raw edge of the binding with the edge of the arm hole. Machine stitch the binding to the arm hole, sewing along the crease in the binding with a straight stitch.

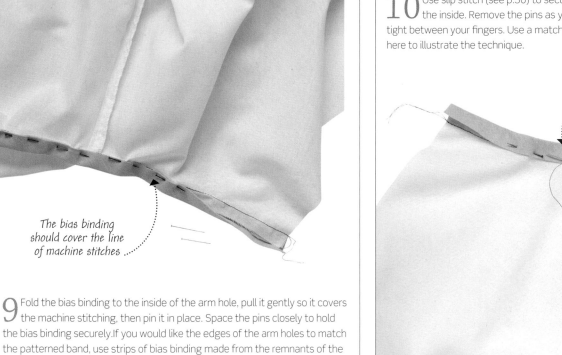

The bias binding should cover the line of machine stitches

9 Fold the bias binding to the inside of the arm hole, pull it gently so it covers the machine stitching, then pin it in place. Space the pins closely to hold the bias binding securely. If you would like the edges of the arm holes to match the patterned band, use strips of bias binding made from the remnants of the patterned pillowcase (see pp.80–81).

10 Use slip stitch (see p.50) to secure the edge of the bias binding on the inside. Remove the pins as you sew but keep the fabric held tight between your fingers. Use a matching thread colour – green was used here to illustrate the technique.

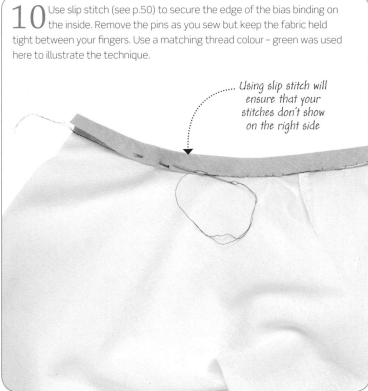

Using slip stitch will ensure that your stitches don't show on the right side

11 The dress should still be inside out. Turn the top over by 5mm (¼in) and iron it flat. Turn it over again by 2.5cm (1in), and iron, to create a channel for the straps to run through. Machine stitch along the bottom edge of this turnover. Repeat this on the back of the dress. If you want wider straps than the ones used here, make this channel deeper to fit them through.

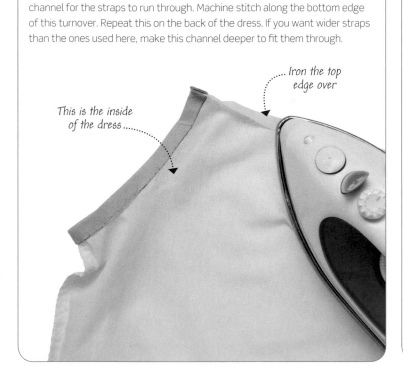

This is the inside of the dress

Iron the top edge over

12 Attach a safety pin to the end of each strap and thread one through the front channel and one through the back channel. Pull the straps to make gathers and tie the ends together with a bow (see opposite). Make a double-turn hem at the bottom of the dress (see p.75): fold up the bottom edge twice to achieve the desired length, pin in place, then machine the hem close to the upper fold. Remove the pins.

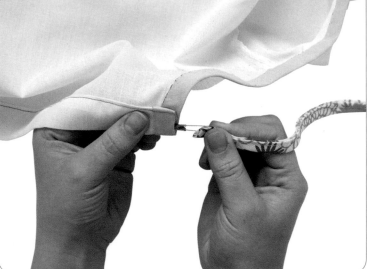

Polar fleece hat and scarf

Suitable for both children and adults, this matching hat-and-scarf set keeps you so warm in the winter months. As polar fleece fabric is available in a wide variety of colours and prints, you can make yourself a whole wardrobe of hats and scarves.

❧ how to make

Hat

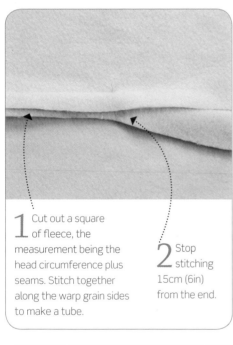

1 Cut out a square of fleece, the measurement being the head circumference plus seams. Stitch together along the warp grain sides to make a tube.

2 Stop stitching 15cm (6in) from the end.

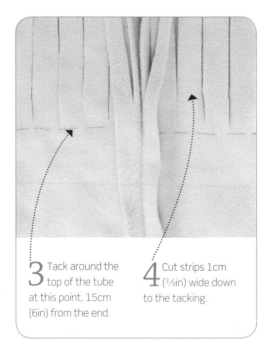

3 Tack around the top of the tube at this point, 15cm (6in) from the end.

4 Cut strips 1cm (⅜in) wide down to the tacking.

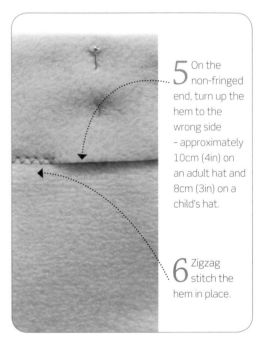

5 On the non-fringed end, turn up the hem to the wrong side – approximately 10cm (4in) on an adult hat and 8cm (3in) on a child's hat.

6 Zigzag stitch the hem in place.

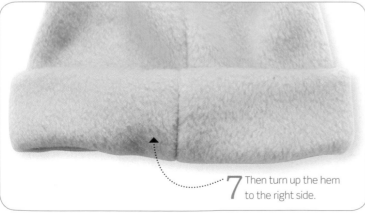

7 Then turn up the hem to the right side.

8 Cut a strip of fleece 1cm (⅜in) wide. Tie it tightly around the base of the fringing (over the tacking stitches), to make a tassel.

9 Decorate the hem with a bow.

Scarf

1 Cut a piece of fleece 30cm x 1.5m (12 x 60in). Cut strips of fringing, 1cm (³⁄₈in) wide and 15cm (6in) deep, at each short end.

4 Thread ribbon through the slots.

5 At one end, fold the ribbon back on itself, and secure by stitching across.

2 At one of the short ends, fold the fabric 10cm (4in) above the fringing, and pin in place.

3 Cut very small slots (just large enough to accommodate the ribbon) vertically into the fold at 2cm (¾in) intervals.

6 Make a large loop from one of the ribbon sections. Cut through, then tie into a bow.

7 Cut and secure the other end of the ribbon to finish.

🌱 you will need

- 90cm x 1.5m (36 x 60in) polar fleece – this will make approximately two hats and one scarf
- 1 reel matching thread
- 1m (40in) ribbon

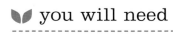

eReader case

There are plenty of eReader cases on the market but it's so much nicer to have a homemade one. Not only is it more unique, but it adds a low-tech touch to your high-tech piece of kit. Well padded with wadding, this case will protect your eReader for years to come.

how to make

1 Cut out all the pieces of fabric and interfacing required for the eReader case and its tab, using the templates on pp.200–201. Use the template to cut the strips of Velcro™. Begin by preparing the eReader tab: apply the fusible interfacing to the wrong side of the tab lining fabric.

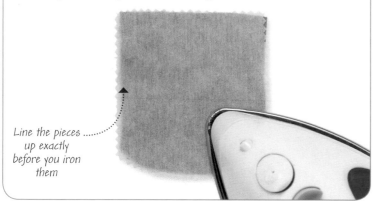

Line the pieces up exactly before you iron them

2 Attach the tab wadding to the interfaced side of the tab and the hooked strip of Velcro™ to the right side of the tab using one pin. Position the Velcro™ about 2cm (¾in) from the top of the tab, centred horizontally. Attach the Velcro™ so that the hooked half is on the tab, and the soft half is attached to the case.

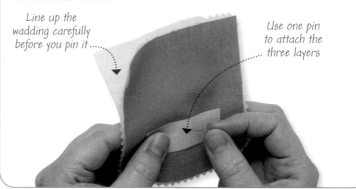

Line up the wadding carefully before you pin it

Use one pin to attach the three layers

3 Machine sew the Velcro™ in place by sewing a line of straight stitches along all four edges. Lay the outer fabric of the tab on top, with the right side facing down – the Velcro™ should be sandwiched in the middle. Pin in place then machine along three sides using a straight stitch. Leave the bottom open. Trim the excess fabric away from the corners then turn the tab right side out and iron flat.

Cut the corners away so that the tab isn't bulky when turned inside out

Sew about ½cm (¾in) from the edge

4 Now make the lining for the case. Iron interfacing to the wrong side of each piece of lining. Place the pieces together, lining inwards, interfacing outwards. Pin together along two of the long sides and across one short side, leaving a gap of 8cm (3in) in the middle of the short side. You will need this gap to turn the case to the right side in Step 11. Machine in place about 1cm (½in) from the edge. Remove the pins as you go.

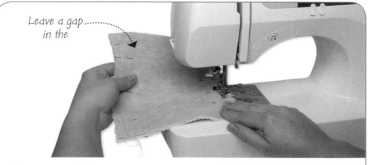

Leave a gap in the

you will need

- Templates from p.200
- Fabric: floral outer and plain lining
- Interfacing
- Sheet wadding
- Fabric scissors
- Velcro™: 6cm (2½in)
- Iron and ironing board
- Pins
- Sewing machine
- Needle
- Thread

5 Pin the hairy looped strip of Velcro™ in place on the front outer piece. Position it 2.5cm (1in) from the top and centre it horizontally. Check it against the tab to make sure the two pieces of Velcro™ will line up. Machine sew it in place, using a straight stitch around its four sides. Ensure that you sew neat right angles at the corners.

Your stitches should form a rectangle on the Velcro™

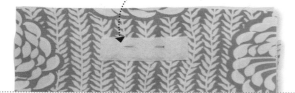

6 Place the two outer pieces of fabric, right sides together. Sandwich these between the two pieces of wadding, and pin all four layers together along the bottom edge and the two sides. Doublecheck which end of the case is the top before pinning the layers in place – you must leave the top unpinned.

Point your pins outwards

Ensure that both layers of fabric are facing inwards

7 Machine the four layers of fabric together along the three pinned sides. Sew about 1cm (½in) from the edge of the fabric. Remove all the pins. Using fabric scissors, trim the two corners by cutting away a small triangle. Trimming the corners will mean that they turn inside out cleanly and won't be bulky.

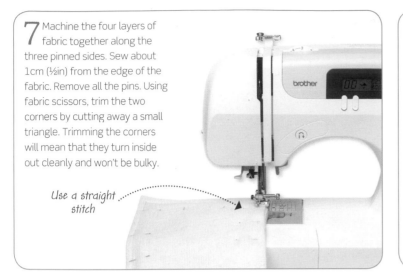

Use a straight stitch

8 Turn the lining the right way out. Place the tab in position, with the Velcro™ facing down. The tab must be centred and straight, with the edge aligned with the top of the case – measure it to make sure it is in the right place, then pin. Slide the lining inside the external layer – which is still inside out. The tab should now be touching the external layer of the case that doesn't have Velcro™ on it.

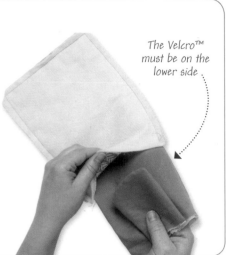

The Velcro™ must be on the lower side

9 Hold the tab in place then remove the pin and reinsert it so that the tab is sandwiched between the two layers – otherwise the pin will become trapped inside the lining. Ensure that the top of the outer and inner layers are lined up then pin them together. It is vital to get these to line up as closely as possible, so that the seam sits on the top edge of the join once the case is the right way out.

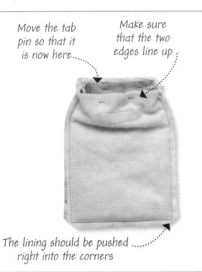

Move the tab pin so that it is now here

Make sure that the two edges line up

The lining should be pushed right into the corners

Sew about 1cm (½in) from the edge of the fabric

10 Machine sew the two layers together, working your way around the rim of the bag, keeping the two layers aligned as closely as possible. You may need to manipulate the fabric to get it into the right position. This is quite fiddly – a little wobble is hard to avoid. If your line looks wonky you can re-sew it.

11 Once you are happy that you have sewn a straight line across the top, remove all the pins and pull the lining fabric back out towards you – the linked pieces will both be inside out. Using the hole you left in the bottom of the lining, gently pull the fabric through to turn the case inside out.

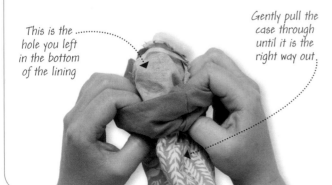

This is the hole you left in the bottom of the lining

Gently pull the case through until it is the right way out

12 Poke the corners out carefully so that they are nice and square – carefully use a knitting needle to get right into the corners. Iron the case flat and then slip stitch up the hole. When you are finished, push the lining into place inside the case, and your eReader case is ready to use.

Use a matching thread colour to disguise the stitches

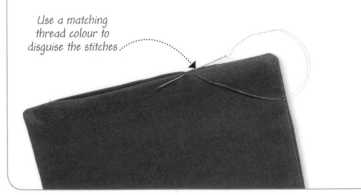

Phone case

As every phone is a different size there is no template supplied for this project. You'll need to measure your phone and add 3cm (1½in) to the width and height. Cut the outer fabric, lining, wadding, and interfacing to this size.

CREATING A PHONE CASE

If you wish to decorate the case with an appliqué heart, such as the one shown here, you must sew it on before you assemble the case. Cut out your heart shape from your chosen fabric, pin it to the case, and then sew around the outside edge using a zigzag stitch. You will make the case in exactly the same way as the eReader, Steps 4–12 (see pp.184–186), but you will need to adapt the instructions in order to create this button fastening. Cut a loop of elastic, about 12cm (5in) long. Do not make and attach a tab but instead, at Step 9, when you pin the case to the lining,

insert the looped elastic between the case and the lining at the back. Centre the loop horizontally, overlapping the ends of the loop by about 2.5cm (1in) to ensure they are secured firmly by the stitching. Pin in place then continue with Step 10. Once you have turned the case the right way out and ironed it flat, sew a button onto the front of the case (see pp.88–91) to align with the elastic. To create the gingham band: measure the width of the case then double this to cover both sides. Cut a strip of fabric 1cm (½in) longer than this and your chosen depth. Fold the edges under on all four sides and iron flat. Pin

Tablet cover

Choose a sturdy fabric if you are likely to be frequently slipping the case in and out of your bag as you travel, and consider investigating different thicknesses of wadding, so that you can ensure that your tablet will be safely cushioned.

CREATING A TABLET COVER

To create a tablet cover, measure your device and add 3cm (1½in) to the width and height. Cut the outer fabric, lining, wadding, and interfacing to this size and cut two lengths of ribbon, 30cm (12in) long. Again, you will make this in the same way as the eReader case, following Steps 4–12 (see pp.184–186). Do not make and attach a tab but instead, at Step 9, slide a length of ribbon between the case and the lining at both the front

and the back. Overlap their ends by about 5cm (2in) to ensure they are secured firmly by the stitching and pin them in place. Ensure they are pinned centrally and that they line up – pinch the top edges of the cover together to check. Continue with Step 10, taking care not to sew over the ribbon pieces or get them tangled. For decoration, sew another piece of ribbon, in a contrasting colour, around the top of the bag – sew along the top and the bottom to secure it.

🌿 you will need

For an A4 notebook:
- 40 x 115cm (16 x 46in) fabric, such as silk dupion or cotton
- 40 x 90cm (16 x 36in) heavy fusible interfacing
- 40 x 90cm (16 x 36in) polyester wadding about 6mm (¼in) thick
- 40 x 115cm (16 x 46in) tear-away embroidery backing
- 40 x 115cm (16 x 46in) contrast lining
- 1 reel machine embroidery thread
- 40 x 115cm (16 x 46in) double-sided fusible web
- Seed beads, to decorate

Book cover

Matching stationery can make office work far more enjoyable, so why not try covering a notebook or diary? A cover will make the book easy to find, as well as protecting the corners. It looks great in a vibrant silk dupion but works just as well with other fabrics, such as cotton. For a finishing touch, decorate the cover with beads or ribbon.

how to make

1 Apply a fusible interfacing to the wrong side of the fabric.

2 Cut out fabric and lining according to the template on page 208. Cut wadding and embroidery backing to fit piece 1.

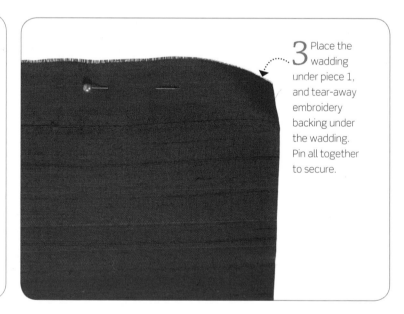

3 Place the wadding under piece 1, and tear-away embroidery backing under the wadding. Pin all together to secure.

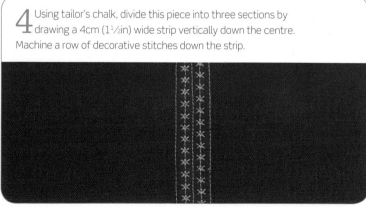

4 Using tailor's chalk, divide this piece into three sections by drawing a 4cm (1½in) wide strip vertically down the centre. Machine a row of decorative stitches down the strip.

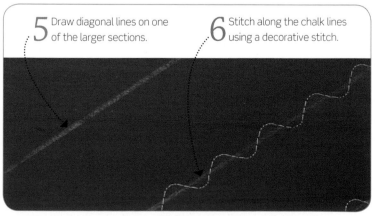

5 Draw diagonal lines on one of the larger sections.

6 Stitch along the chalk lines using a decorative stitch.

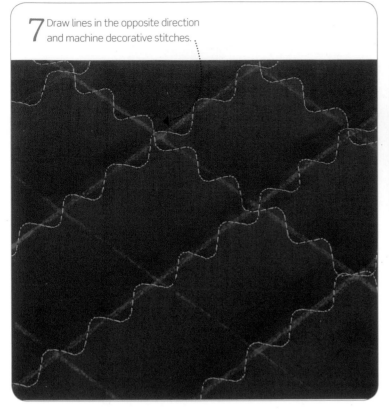

7 Draw lines in the opposite direction and machine decorative stitches.

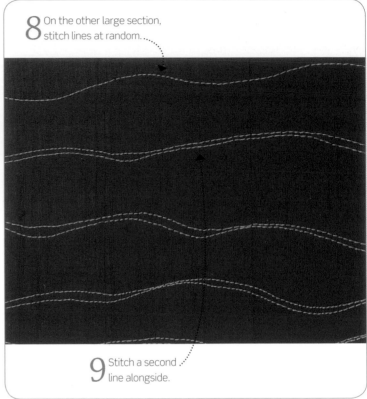

8 On the other large section, stitch lines at random.

9 Stitch a second line alongside.

10 Repeat in the opposite direction.

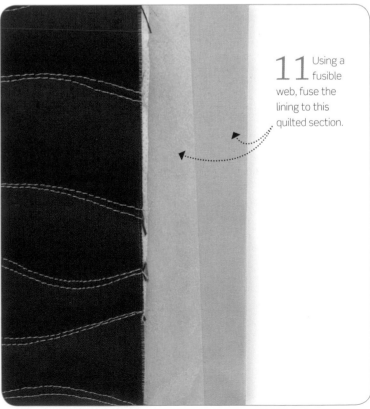

11 Using a fusible web, fuse the lining to this quilted section.

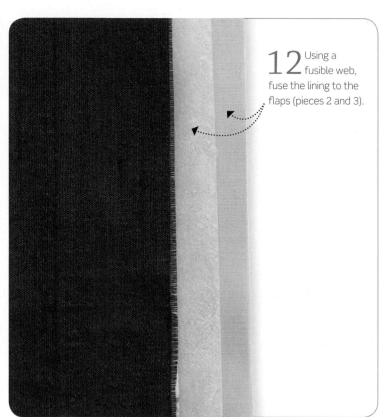

12 Using a fusible web, fuse the lining to the flaps (pieces 2 and 3).

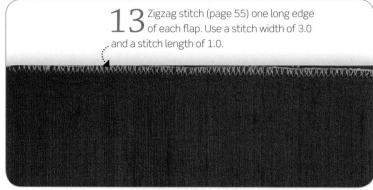

13 Zigzag stitch (page 55) one long edge of each flap. Use a stitch width of 3.0 and a stitch length of 1.0.

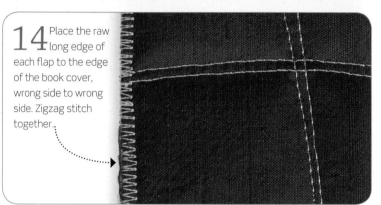

14 Place the raw long edge of each flap to the edge of the book cover, wrong side to wrong side. Zigzag stitch together.

15 Zigzag all around the book cover sides, stitching over the flaps as you do so. Stitch again to reinforce the edges.

16 If you wish, decorate with beads to finish.

you will need

- Fabric: to calculate the amount you need, measure the window's width (at the widest part where the blind will hang), and also the drop (the finished length of the blind). Add 12cm (5in) to the width and 15cm(6in) to the drop for the hems – 5cm (2in) at the top and 10cm(4in) at the bottom
- Curtain lining, of matching size
- 1 reel matching thread
- Decorative trim (optional)
- Sew-and-stick Velcro™
- 2 or more pieces of wooden dowelling to fit
- 4cm (1½in) × finished width slat of wood
- Plastic curtain rings, about 1cm (⅜in) diameter
- Blind cord

Roman blind

A Roman blind is a great way to provide privacy at a window and a splash of colour in the room. Cotton, linen, damask, and brocade are all suitable fabrics. The blind is quick and straightforward to make and will easily fit behind curtains if you so desire. Careful measuring of the window is essential, and a trip to the wood yard will be required to purchase the dowelling and the slat for the bottom edge. You will need a batten fixed to the top of the window frame from which to hang the blind.

how to make

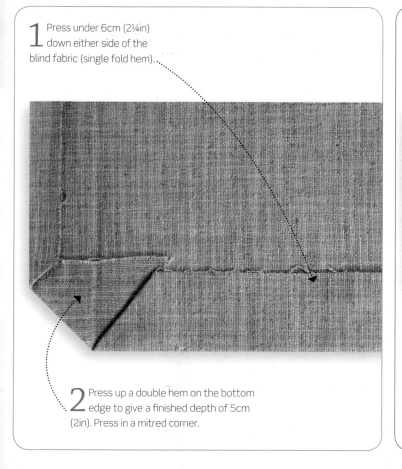

1 Press under 6cm (2¼in) down either side of the blind fabric (single fold hem).

2 Press up a double hem on the bottom edge to give a finished depth of 5cm (2in). Press in a mitred corner.

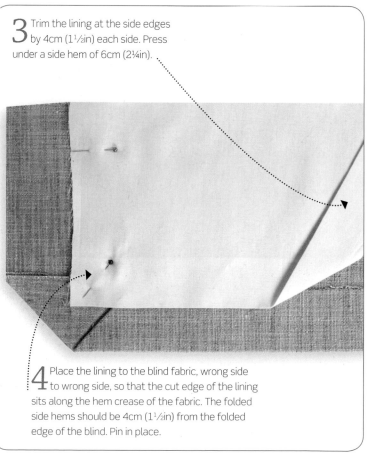

3 Trim the lining at the side edges by 4cm (1½in) each side. Press under a side hem of 6cm (2¼in).

4 Place the lining to the blind fabric, wrong side to wrong side, so that the cut edge of the lining sits along the hem crease of the fabric. The folded side hems should be 4cm (1½in) from the folded edge of the blind. Pin in place.

5 Before securing the lining, make the casings for the wooden dowelling. Measure the lining, and form a pleat at regular intervals. The pleats need to be at regular 30-40cm (12-16in) intervals, starting 40cm (16in) from the hem.

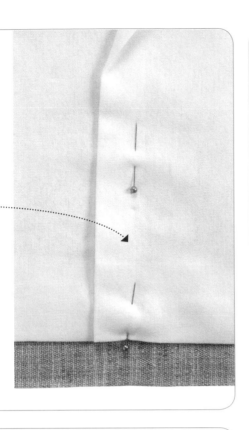

6 Re-position the lining to the blind. Machine across the pleat through both blind and lining to secure. Make sure you leave an opening wide enough to fit the dowelling through.

7 Using a flat fell stitch, hand stitch the lining to the blind down the sides. Leave the ends of the pleats open.

8 Machine the bottom hem in place, over the lining. Leave open at the sides so the wooden slat can be inserted.

9 Place a row of stitching at the lower edge of the hem to keep the hem fold sharp.

10 If you wish to add a trim, you will need a length equal to the finished width of the blind plus 5cm (2in) for turnings. Machine it in place using the zip foot, over either of these rows of stitching.

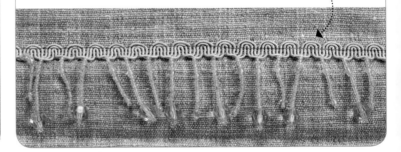

11 Turn down the top edge so that the blind measures the required finished length. Pin in place.

12 Cut a piece of Velcro™ equal to the width of the blind. Sew the soft loop side of the Velcro™ to the blind along the top hem edge.

13 Insert wooden dowelling through the pleats, and the slat through the hem. Hand stitch the ends closed with a flat fell stitch.

14 Using a buttonhole stitch (page 53), sew a curtain ring on to each end of the pleats, and at regular intervals along the dowelling. One, two, or three rings may be required, depending on the width and weight of the blind. Make sure all the rings are in line with each other.

15 Add another row of rings just underneath the Velcro™.

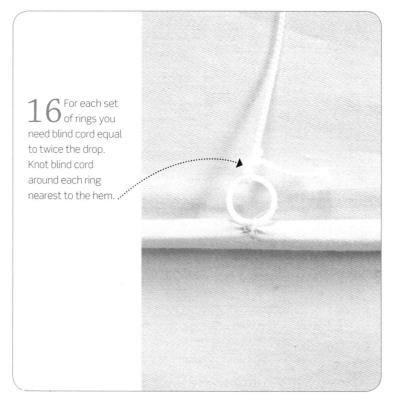

16 For each set of rings you need blind cord equal to twice the drop. Knot blind cord around each ring nearest to the hem.

17 Thread the cord up through each line of rings (see illustration, right). Take all of the cords to one side at the top (see top right). Trim the cords to level, and knot to secure.

18 To finish, stick the other side (the hook side) of the piece of Velcro™ to a batten on the window, and attach the blind.

HOW TO THREAD A ROMAN BLIND

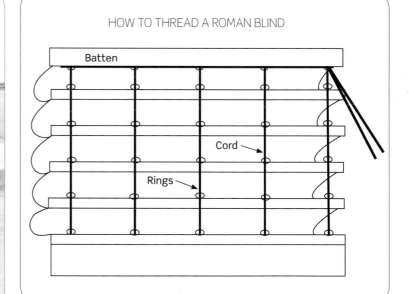

Batten

Cord

Rings

Café curtain

A café curtain is a half curtain that fits the lower part of a window for privacy but allows the light in at the top. It can be made from a curtaining fabric or you could use a semi-sheer voile. It hangs from a simple rod that fits across the window.

🍃 how to make

1 On all sides of the curtain fabric, press 5cm (2in) under to the wrong side once. Fold under 5cm (2in) again and press. Machine in place, close to the upper folded edge.

2 At the hem edge, press a double hem into position 10cm (4in) deep.

3 Unfold and mitre the corner (page 77). Press into place again and machine.

4 Hand stitch across the corner of the mitre.

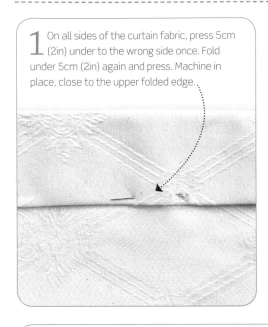

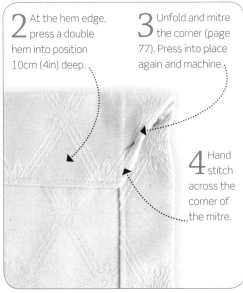

5 To make the tabs, cut straight grain strips 14 x 24cm (5¾ x 10in). Fold in half lengthways, right side to right side, and machine.

6 Fold the fabric so that the seam is in the centre of the strip, and press open.

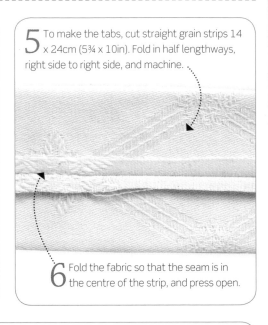

7 Using a template, stitch one end of each tab into a point. Draw around the template with tailor's chalk to make sure all the tabs are the same.

8 Clip, turn through to the right side, and press.

9 Place the tabs to the upper edge of the curtain, seam-side down to the curtain and matching at the raw edge. Place a tab at each side and the rest at equal distances, approximately every 30cm (12in).

10 Pin the tabs into position.

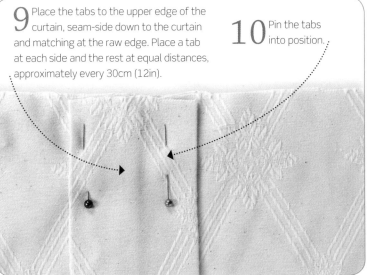

you will need

- Fabric: to calculate the amount you need, measure the window's width, where the track for the curtain will be, and also the drop (the finished length of the curtain). Multiply the width measurement by 2.5 in order to give fullness (you may have to join fabric to obtain this width). Add 20cm (8in) on to the width and 40cm (16in) on to the drop for the hems. You'll also need 30cm (12in) fabric for the facing and tabs
- Materials to make large covered buttons (i.e. buttons and scraps of fabric)
- 1 reel matching thread

13 Press the seam and turn the facing to the wrong side. Top-stitch.

14 Fold under the lower edge of the facing and machine in place.

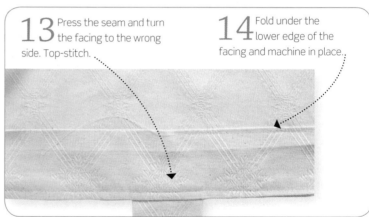

11 For the facing, cut a strip of fabric 10cm (4in) wide and as long as the curtain width.

12 Place the facing over the tabs, right side to right side, and machine in place along the top edge.

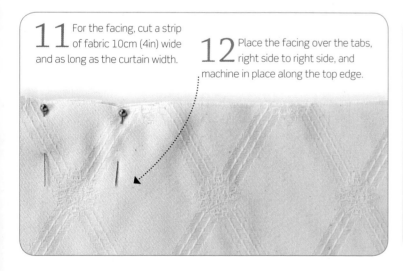

15 Cover a large button for each tab. Fold the tab over to the front of the curtain, to create a loop for the curtain rod. Sew a button on to each tab to secure it to the curtain.

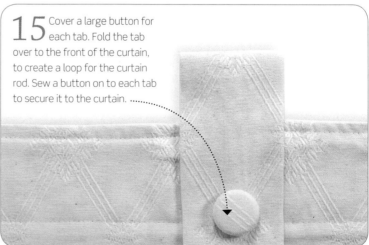

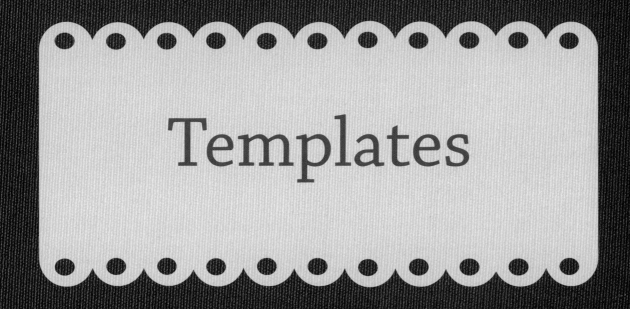

Templates

Templates

Use these templates to ensure that all your project pieces are the correct size. The shapes on pp.200–205 are given at the correct size and can be traced from the book as they are; the templates on pp.206–207 will need enlarging to the correct size. Follow the instructions given.

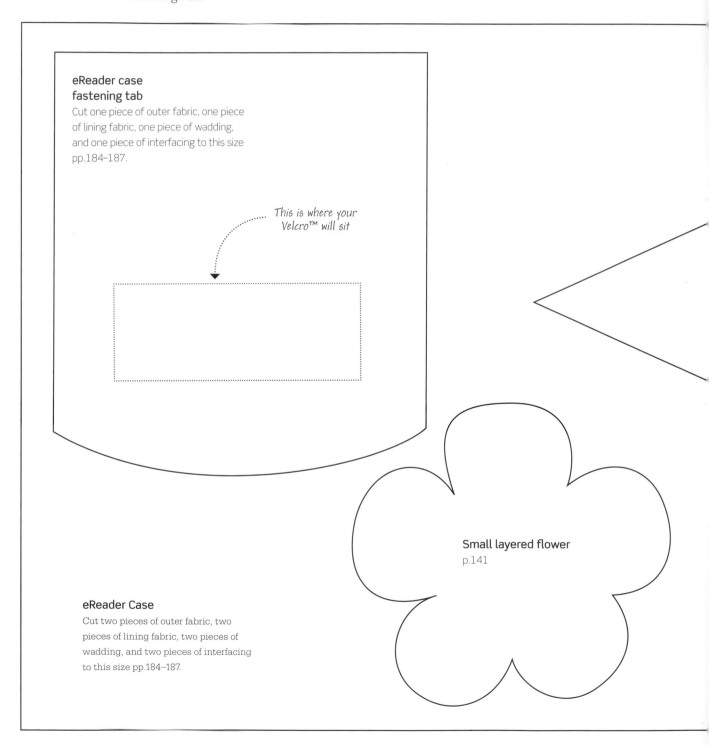

eReader case fastening tab
Cut one piece of outer fabric, one piece of lining fabric, one piece of wadding, and one piece of interfacing to this size pp.184-187.

This is where your Velcro™ will sit

eReader Case
Cut two pieces of outer fabric, two pieces of lining fabric, two pieces of wadding, and two pieces of interfacing to this size pp.184–187.

Small layered flower
p.141

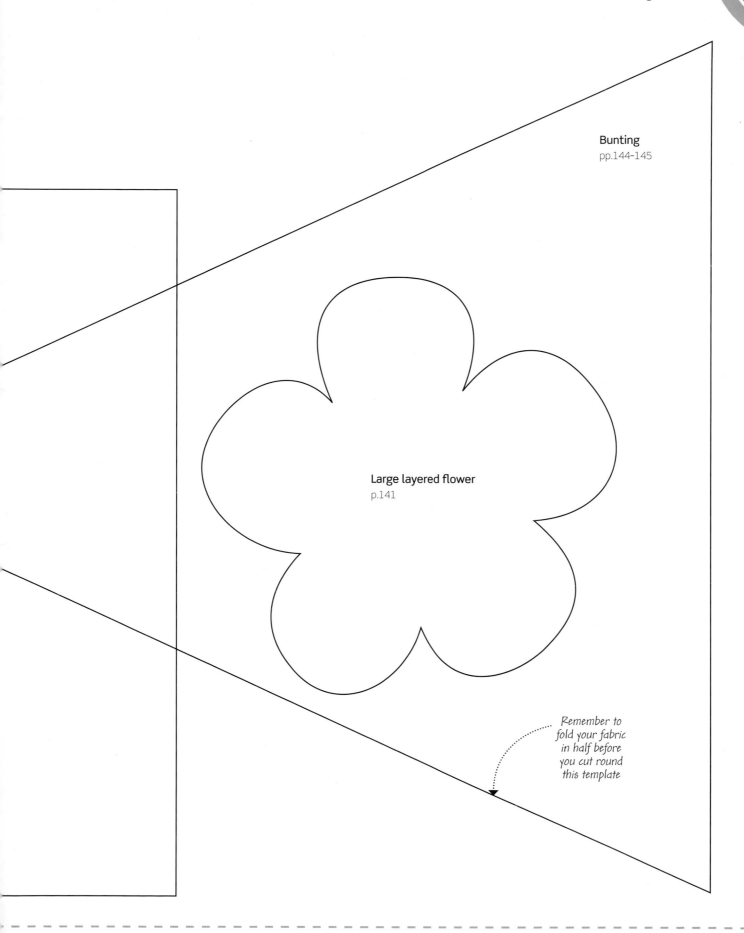

Bunting
pp.144-145

Large layered flower
p.141

Remember to
fold your fabric
in half before
you cut round
this template

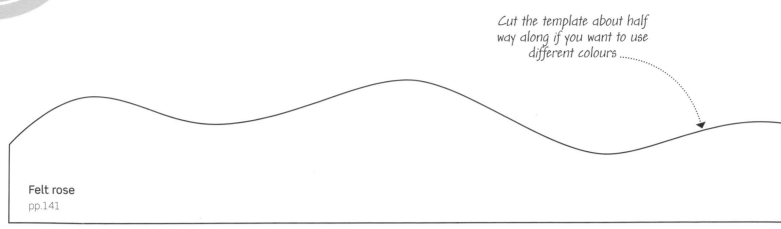

Cut the template about half way along if you want to use different colours ....

Felt rose
pp.141

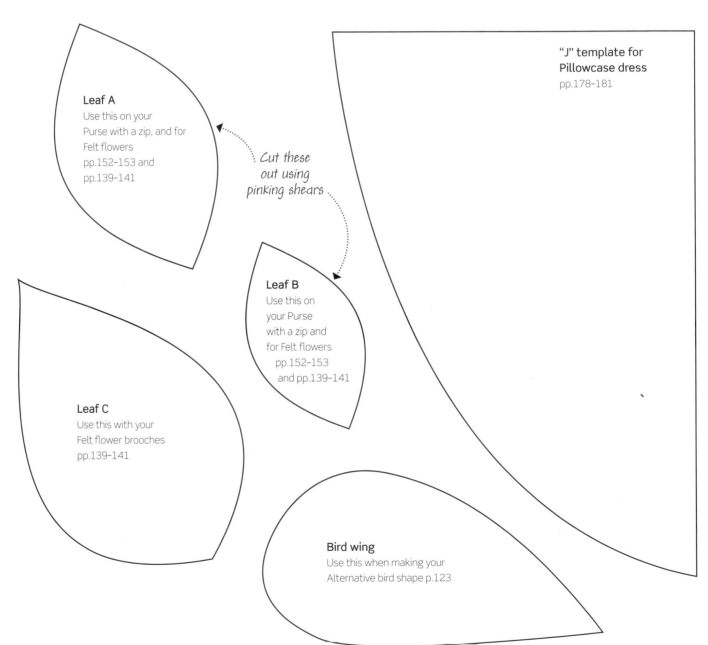

"J" template for Pillowcase dress
pp.178-181

Leaf A
Use this on your Purse with a zip, and for Felt flowers
pp.152-153 and pp.139-141

Cut these out using pinking shears ...

Leaf B
Use this on your Purse with a zip and for Felt flowers
pp.152-153 and pp.139-141

Leaf C
Use this with your Felt flower brooches
pp.139-141

Bird wing
Use this when making your Alternative bird shape p.123

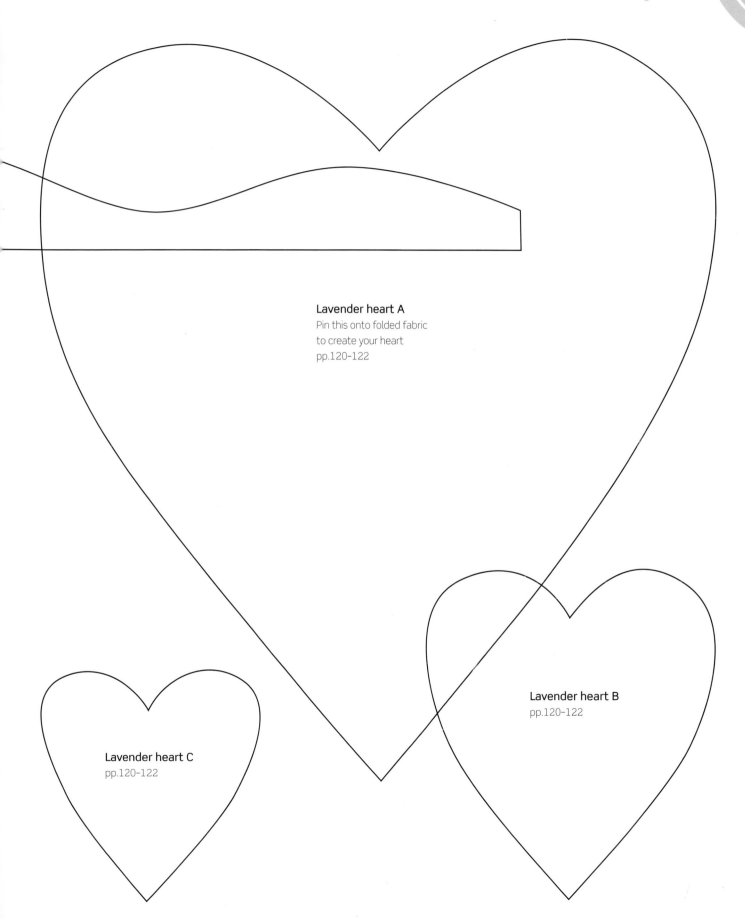

Lavender heart A
Pin this onto folded fabric
to create your heart
pp.120–122

Lavender heart B
pp.120–122

Lavender heart C
pp.120–122

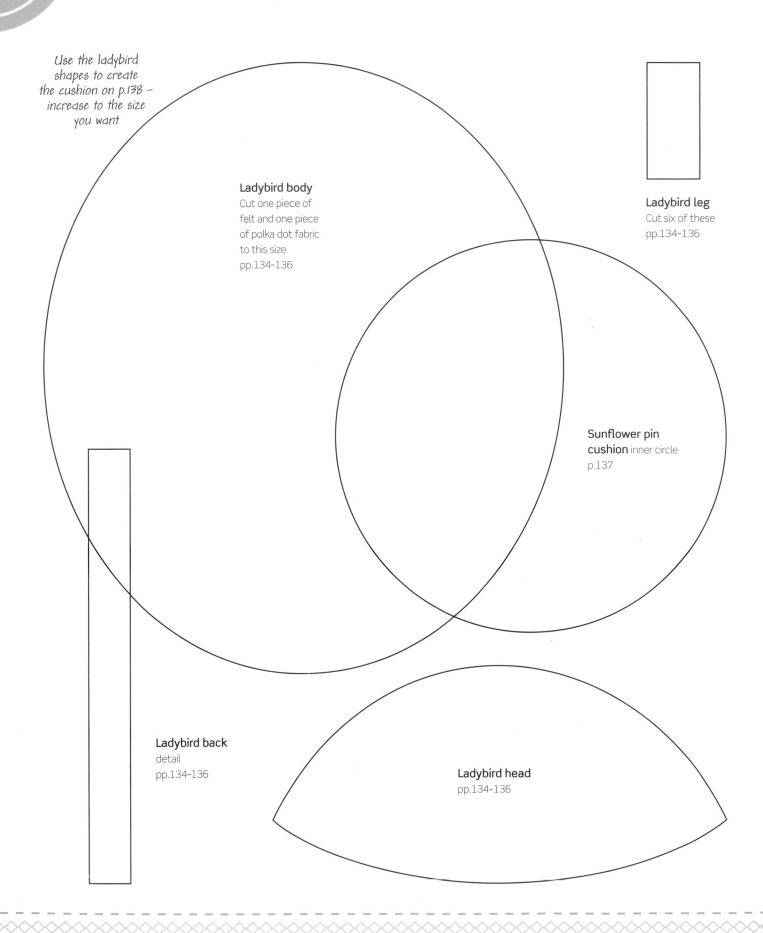

Use the ladybird shapes to create the cushion on p.138 – increase to the size you want

Ladybird body
Cut one piece of felt and one piece of polka dot fabric to this size
pp.134-136

Ladybird leg
Cut six of these
pp.134-136

Sunflower pin cushion inner circle
p.137

Ladybird back
detail
pp.134-136

Ladybird head
pp.134-136

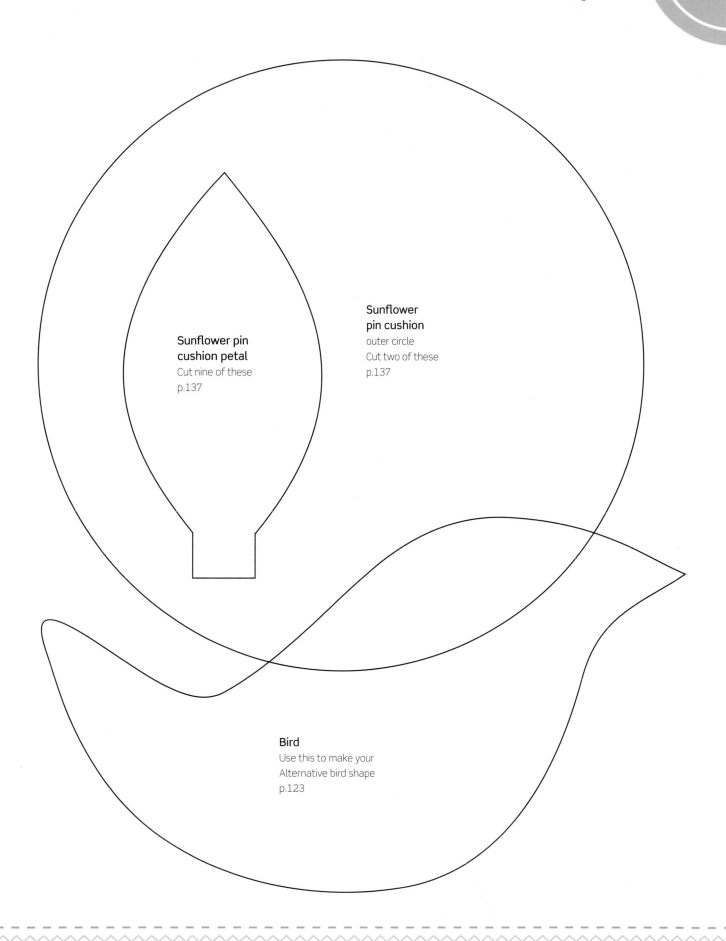

Sunflower pin cushion petal
Cut nine of these
p.137

Sunflower pin cushion
outer circle
Cut two of these
p.137

Bird
Use this to make your
Alternative bird shape
p.123

The templates for these three projects are too large to be shown at full size. The simplest way to create them is to use the dimensions given to carefully measure them out and draw them up on tracing paper. They show the correct positioning on the fabric and give the dimensions you will need.

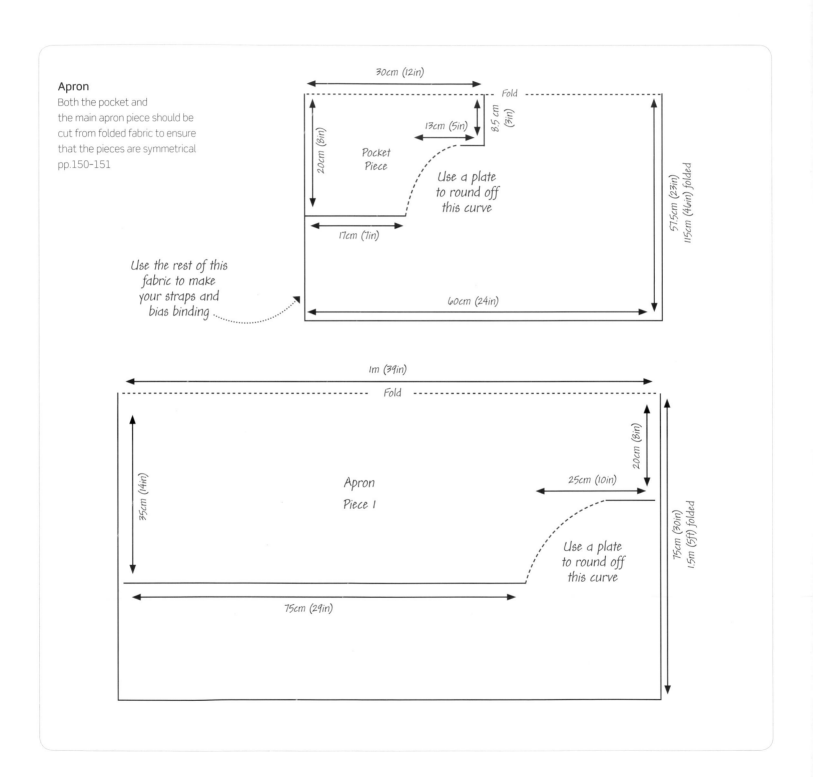

Apron

Both the pocket and the main apron piece should be cut from folded fabric to ensure that the pieces are symmetrical pp.150–151

30cm (12in)

Fold

13cm (5in)

8.5 cm (3in)

20cm (8in)

Pocket Piece

Use a plate to round off this curve

17cm (7in)

57.5cm (23in)
115cm (46in) folded

Use the rest of this fabric to make your straps and bias binding

60cm (24in)

1m (39in)

Fold

35cm (14in)

Apron Piece 1

20cm (8in)

25cm (10in)

Use a plate to round off this curve

75cm (30in)
1.5m (5ft) folded

75cm (29in)

Child's shorts

Use your template to cut out two pieces of fabric, as each will form one leg p.175

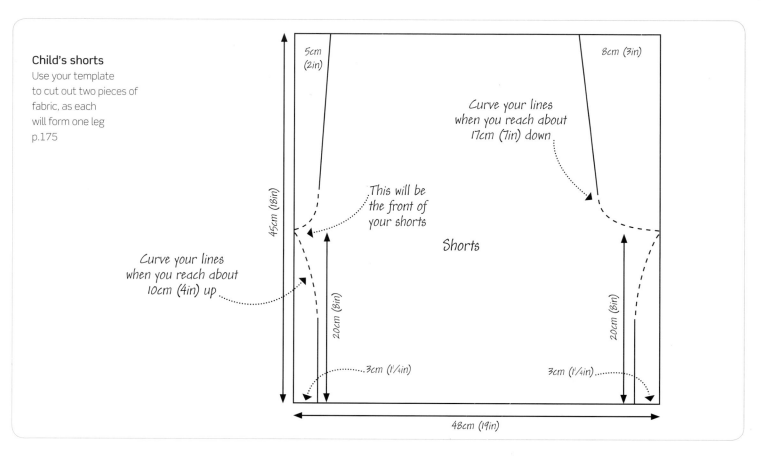

5cm (2in)

8cm (3in)

Curve your lines when you reach about 17cm (7in) down

This will be the front of your shorts

45cm (18in)

Curve your lines when you reach about 10cm (4in) up

Shorts

20cm (8in)

20cm (8in)

3cm (1¼in)

3cm (1¼in)

48cm (19in)

Door hanging

Arrange your pieces like this to avoid wasting any fabric and to ensure that any patterns on the material align pp.162-163

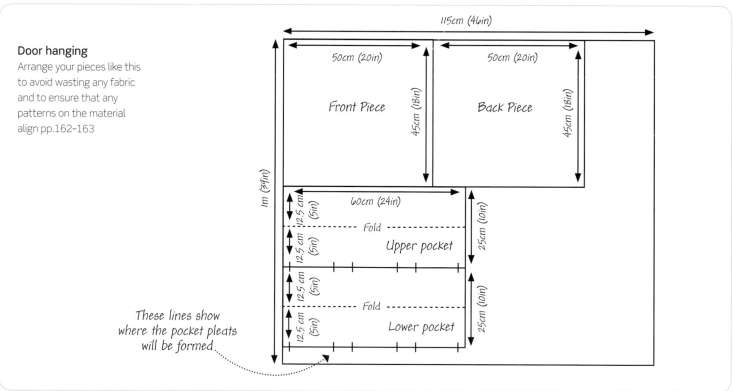

115cm (46in)

50cm (20in)

50cm (20in)

Front Piece

Back Piece

45cm (18in)

45cm (18in)

1m (39in)

12.5 cm (5in)

12.5 cm (5in)

60cm (24in)

Fold

Upper pocket

25cm (10in)

12.5 cm (5in)

12.5 cm (5in)

Fold

Lower pocket

25cm (10in)

These lines show where the pocket pleats will be formed

Sewing aids pp.130–133

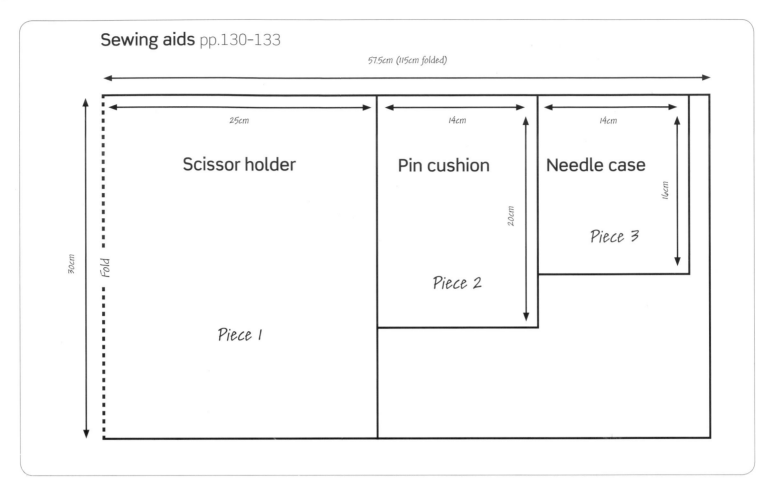

57.5cm (115cm folded)

Fold

30cm

25cm

Scissor holder

Piece 1

14cm

Pin cushion

20cm

Piece 2

14cm

Needle case

16cm

Piece 3

Book cover pp.188–191

115cm

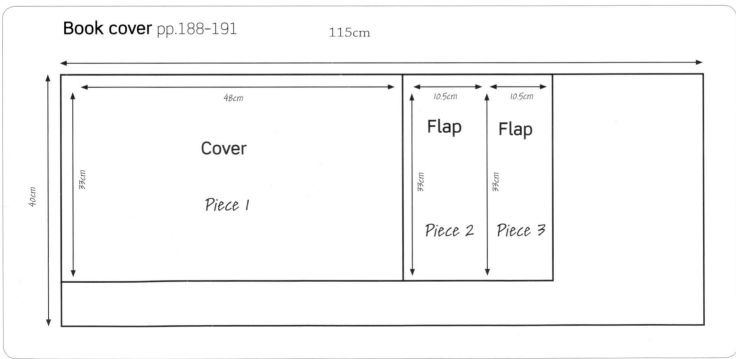

40cm

33cm

48cm

Cover

Piece 1

10.5cm

Flap

33cm

Piece 2

10.5cm

Flap

33cm

Piece 3

Jewellery roll pp.164–167

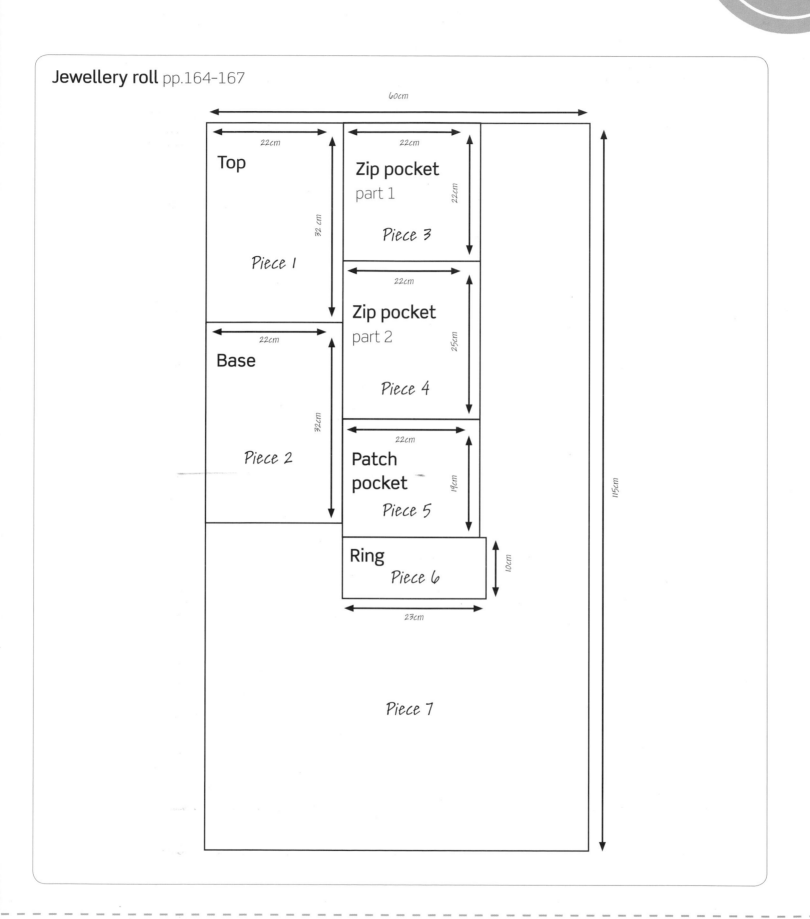

60cm

22cm

Top

Piece 1

32 cm

22cm

Zip pocket
part 1

22cm

Piece 3

22cm

Zip pocket
part 2

25cm

Piece 4

22cm

Base

32cm

Piece 2

22cm

Patch pocket

19cm

Piece 5

Ring
Piece 6

10cm

23cm

115cm

Piece 7

Bolster pillow pp.142-143

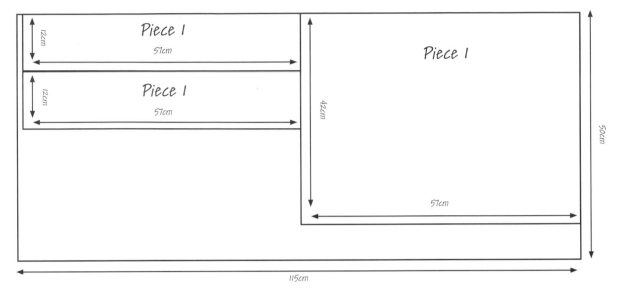

Piece 1
12cm
57cm

Piece 1
12cm
57cm

Piece 1
42cm
57cm

50cm

115cm

Baby towel pp.170-171

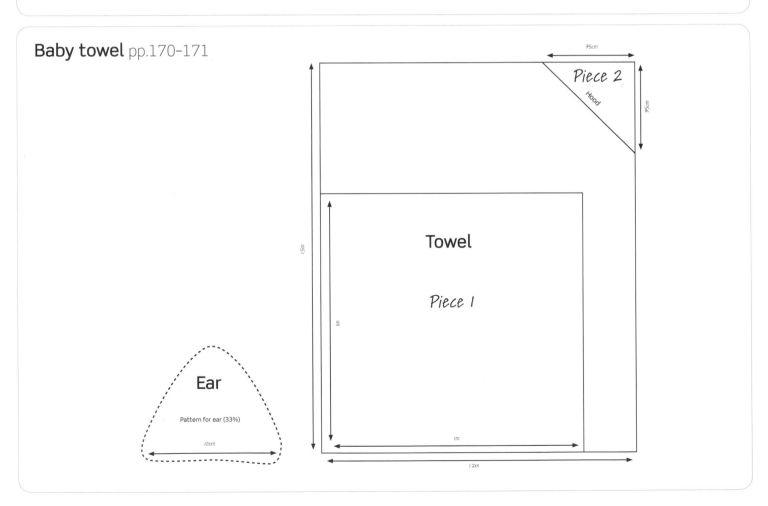

35cm

Piece 2
Hood
35cm

1.5m

Towel

Piece 1

1m

1m

1.2m

Ear

Pattern for ear (33%)

10cm

Hessian bag pp.160–161

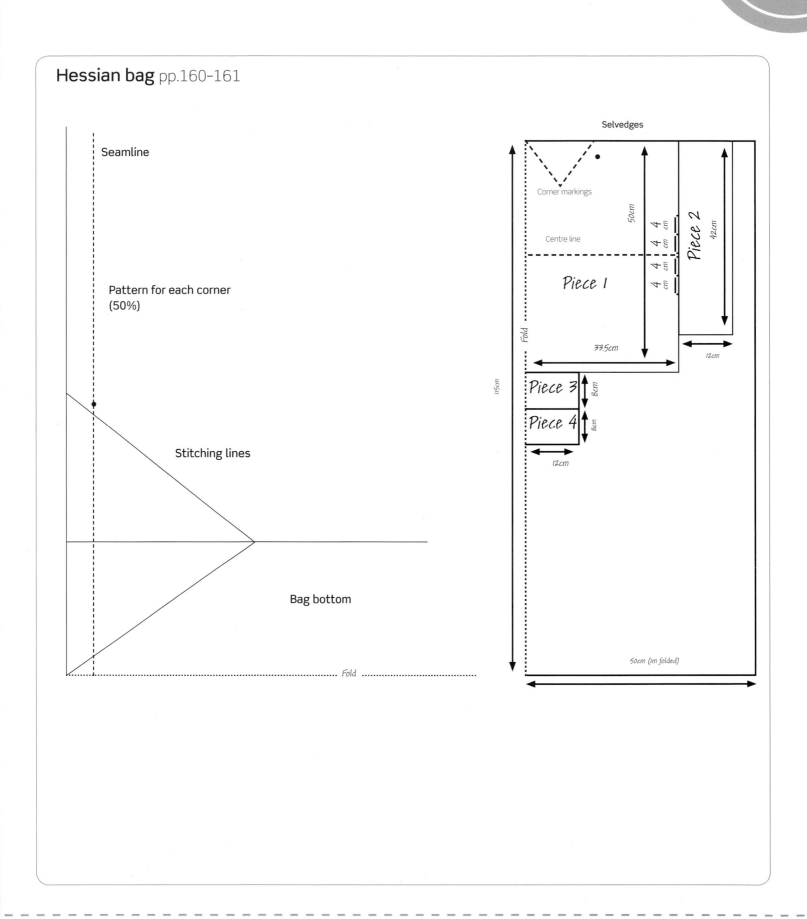

Seamline

Pattern for each corner
(50%)

Stitching lines

Bag bottom

Fold

Selvedges

Corner markings

Centre line

Piece 1

Piece 2

50cm

4 cm   4 cm   4 cm   4 cm

33.5cm

12cm

42cm

Fold

Piece 3

Piece 4

8cm

8cm

12cm

115cm

50cm (1m folded)

Glossary

Appliqué
One piece of fabric being stitched to another in a decorative manner.

Back stitch
A strong hand stitch with a double stitch on the wrong side, used for outlining and seaming.

Bias
45-degree line on fabric that falls between the lengthways and the crossways grain. Fabric cut on the bias drapes well. See also Grain.

Bias binding
Narrow strips of fabric cut on the bias. Used to give a neat finish to hems and seam allowances.

Binding
Method of finishing a raw edge by wrapping it in a strip of bias-cut fabric.

Blanket stitch
Hand stitch worked along the raw or finished edge of fabric to neaten, and for decorative purposes.

Blind hem stitch
Tiny hand stitch used to attach one piece of fabric to another, mainly to secure hems. Also a machine stitch consisting of two or three straight stitches and one wide zigzag stitch.

Blind tuck
A tuck that is stitched so that it touches the adjacent tuck without machine stitches showing. See also Tuck.

Bodice
Upper body section of a garment.

Boning
Narrow nylon, plastic, or metal strip, available in various widths, that is used for stiffening and shaping close-fitting garments, such as bodices.

Box pleat
Pleat formed on the wrong side of the fabric, and fuller than a knife pleat. See also Pleat.

Buttonhole
Opening through which a button is inserted to form a fastening. Buttonholes are usually machine stitched but may also be worked by hand or piped for reinforcement or decorative effect.

Buttonhole stitch
Hand stitch that wraps over the raw edges of a buttonhole to neaten and strengthen them. Machine-stitched buttonholes are worked with a close zigzag stitch.

Button shank
Stem of a button that allows room for the buttonhole to fit under the button when joined.

Casing
Tunnel of fabric created by parallel rows of stitching, through which elastic or a drawstring cord is threaded. Often used at a waist edge. Sometimes extra fabric is required to make a casing; this can be applied to the inside or outside of the garment.

Contour dart
Also known as double-pointed dart, this is used to give shape at the waist of a garment. It is like two darts joined together. See also Dart.

Crease
Line formed in fabric by pressing a fold.

Cross stitch
A temporary hand stitch used to hold pleats in place and to secure linings. It can also be used for decoration.

Cross tuck
Tuck that crosses over another by being stitched in opposite directions. See also Tuck.

Cutting line
Solid line on a pattern piece used as a guide for cutting out fabric.

Dart
Tapered stitched fold of fabric used on a garment to give it shape so that it can fit around the contours of the body. There are different types of dart, but all are used mainly on women's clothing.

Darted tuck
A tuck that can be used to give fullness of fabric at the bust or hip. See also Tuck.

Double-pointed dart
See Contour dart

Double ruffle
Decorative trim made from two plain ruffles where one side is longer than the other. Also a ruffle made from doubled fabric.

Drape
The way a fabric falls into graceful folds; drape varies with each fabric.

Drop
The length of fabric required to make a curtain, the "drop" being the

measurement from top to bottom of the window.

Ease
Distributing fullness in fabric when joining two seams together of slightly different lengths, for example a sleeve to an armhole.

Ease stitch
Long machine stitch, used to ease in fullness where the distance between notches is greater on one seam edge than on the other.

Enclosed edge
Raw fabric edge that is concealed within a seam or binding.

Facing
Layer of fabric placed on the inside of a garment and used to finish off raw edges of an armhole or neck of a garment. Usually a separate piece of fabric, the facing can sometimes be an extension of the garment itself.

Felt
A natural wool fabric can felt when it is stimulated by friction and lubricated by moisture and the fibres bond together to form a cloth. Felting can also be done in a washing machine in a hot cycle.

Flat fell seam
See *Run* and *fell seam*.

Flat fell stitch
A strong, secure stitch used to hold two layers together permanently. Often used to secure linings and bias bindings.

French dart
Curved dart used on the front of a garment. See also Dart.

French seam
A seam traditionally used on sheer and silk fabrics. It is stitched twice, first on the right side of the work and then on the wrong side, enclosing the first seam.

Fusible tape
Straight grain tape used to stabilize edges and also replace stay stitching. The heat of the iron fuses it into position.

Galloon lace
Decorative lace trim shaped on both sides, used to edge a hem.

Gathers
Bunches of fabric created by sewing two parallel rows of loose stitching, then pulling the threads up so that the fabric gathers and reduces in size to fit the required space.

Goblet pleat
Decorative curtain heading in which the fabric is stitched into narrow tubes that are then stuffed with wadding.
See also Pleat.

Grain
Lengthways and crossways direction of threads in a fabric. Fabric grain affects how a fabric hangs and drapes.

Gusset
Small piece of fabric shaped to fit into a slash or seam for added ease of movement.

Hem
The edge of a piece of fabric neatened and stitched to prevent unravelling. There are several methods of doing this, both by hand and by machine.

Hem allowance
Amount of fabric allowed for turning under to make the hem.

Hemline
Crease or foldline along which a hem is marked.

Hemming tape
Fusible tape with adhesive on both sides. Iron in place to fuse and secure hems that are difficult to hand stitch.

Herringbone stitch
Hand stitch used to secure hems and interlinings. This stitch is worked from left to right.

Herringbone weave
A zigzag weave where the weft yarn goes under and over warp yarns in a staggered pattern.

Hong Kong finish
A method of neatening raw edges particularly on wool and linen. Bias-cut strips are wrapped around the raw edge.

Interfacing
A fabric placed between garment and facing to give structure and support. Available in different thicknesses, interfacing can be fusible (bonds to the fabric by applying heat) or non-fusible (needs to be sewn to the fabric).

Interlining
Layer of fabric attached to the main fabric prior to construction, to cover the inside of an entire garment to provide extra warmth or bulk. The two layers are then treated as one. Often used in jackets and coats.

Keyhole buttonhole stitch
A machine buttonhole stitch characterized by having one square end while the other end is shaped like a loop to accommodate the button's shank without distorting the fabric. Often used on jackets.

Kick pleat
Inverted pleat extending upwards from the hemline of a narrow skirt to allow freedom when walking. See also Pleat.

Knife pleat
Pleat formed on the right side of the fabric where all the pleats face the same direction. See also Pleat.

Lapped seam
Used on fabrics that do not fray, such as suede and leather, the seam allowance of one edge is placed over the edge to be joined, then topstitched close to the overlapping edge. Also called an overlaid seam.

Lining
Underlying fabric layer used to give a neat finish to an item, as well as concealing the stitching and seams of a garment.

Locking stitch
A machine stitch where the upper and lower threads in the machine "lock" together at the start or end of a row of stitching.

Mitre
The diagonal line made where two edges of a piece of fabric meet at a corner, produced by folding.

Mock casing
Where there is an effect of a casing, but in fact elastic is attached to the waist, or is used only at the back in a partial casing.

Multi-size pattern
Paper pattern printed with cutting lines for a range of sizes on each pattern piece.

Nap
The raised pile on a fabric made during the weaving process, or a print pointing one way. When cutting out pattern pieces, ensure the nap runs in the same direction.

Notch
V-shaped marking on a pattern piece used for aligning one piece with another. Also V-shaped cut taken to reduce seam bulk.

Notion
An item of haberdashery, other than fabric, needed to complete a project, such as a button, zip, or elastic. Notions are normally listed on the pattern envelope.

Overedge stitch
Machine stitch worked over the edge of a seam allowance and used for neatening the edges of fabric.

Overlaid seam
See Lapped seam.

Pattern markings
Symbols printed on a paper pattern to indicate the fabric grain, foldline, and construction details, such as darts, notches, and tucks. These should be transferred to the fabric using tailor's chalk or tailor's tacks.

Pencil pleat
The most common curtain heading where the fabric forms a row of parallel vertical pleats. See also Pleat.

Pile
Raised loops on the surface of a fabric, for example velvet.

Pill
A small, fuzzy ball formed from tangled fibres which is formed on the surface of a fabric, making it look old and worn; it is often caused by friction. To remove fabric pills, stretch the fabric over a curved surface and carefully cut or shave off the pills.

Pinking
A method of neatening raw edges of fray-resistant fabric using pinking shears. This will leave a zigzag edge.

Pin tuck
Narrow, regularly spaced fold or gather. See also Tuck.

Piped tuck
See Corded tuck.

Piping
Trim made from bias-cut strips of fabric, usually containing a cord. Used to edge garments or soft furnishings.

Pivoting
Technique used to machine stitch a corner. The machine is stopped at the corner with the needle in the fabric, then the foot is raised, the fabric turned following the direction of the corner, and the foot lowered for stitching to continue.

Placket
An opening in a garment that provides

support for fasteners, such as buttons, snaps, or zips.

Plain weave
The simplest of all the weaves; the weft yarn passes under one warp yarn, then over another one.

Pleat
An even fold or series of folds in fabric, often partially stitched down. Commonly found in skirts to shape the waistline, but also in soft furnishings for decoration.

Pocket flap
A piece of fabric that folds down to cover the opening of a pocket.

Raw edge
Cut edge of fabric that requires finishing, for example using zigzag stitch, to prevent fraying.

Rever
The turned-back front edge of a jacket or blouse to which the collar is attached.

Reverse stitch
Machine stitch that simply stitches back over a row of stitches to secure the threads.

Right side
The outer side of a fabric, or the visible part of a garment.

Rouleau loop
Button loop made from a strip of bias binding. It is used with a round ball-type button.

Round-end buttonhole stitch
Machine stitch characterized by one end of the buttonhole being square and the

other being round, to allow for the button shank.

Ruching
Several lines of stitching worked to form a gathered area.

Ruffle
Decorative gathered trim made from one or two layers of fabric.

Run and fell seam
Also known as a flat fell seam, this seam is made on the right side of a garment and is very strong. It uses two lines of stitching and conceals all the raw edges, reducing fraying.

Running stitch
A simple, evenly spaced straight stitch separated by equal-sized spaces, used for seaming and gathering.

Seam
Stitched line where two edges of fabric are joined together.

Seam allowance
The amount of fabric allowed for on a pattern where sections are to be joined together by a seam; usually this is 1.5cm ($\frac{5}{8}$in).

Seam edge
The cut edge of a seam allowance.

Seamline
Line on paper pattern designated for stitching a seam; usually this is 1.5cm ($\frac{5}{8}$in) from the seam edge.

Selvedge
Finished edge on a woven fabric. This runs parallel to the warp (lengthways) threads.

Shell tuck
Decorative fold of fabric stitched in place with a scalloped edge. See also Tuck.

Shirring
Multiple rows of gathers sewn by machine. Often worked with shirring elastic in the bobbin to allow for stretch.

Slip hem stitch
Similar to herringbone stitch but is worked from right to left. It is used mainly for securing hems.

Straight stitch
Plain machine stitch, used for most applications. The length of the stitch can be altered to suit the fabric.

Stretch stitch
Machine stitch used for stretch knits and to help control difficult fabrics. It is worked with two stitches forwards and one backwards so that each stitch is worked three times.

Tacking stitch
A temporary running stitch used to hold pieces of fabric together or for transferring pattern markings to fabric.

Tailor's buttonhole
A buttonhole with one square end and one keyhole-shaped end, used on jackets and coats.

Tailor's tacks
Loose thread markings used to transfer symbols from a pattern to fabric.

Toile
A test or dry run of a paper pattern using calico. The toile helps you analyse the fit of the garment.

Top-stitch
Machine straight stitching worked on the right side of an item, close to the finished edge, for decorative effect. Sometimes stitched in a contrasting colour.

Top-stitched seam
A seam finished with a row of top-stitching for decorative effect. This seam is often used on crafts and soft furnishings as well as garments.

Trace tacking
A method of marking fold and placement lines on fabric. Loose stitches are sewn along the lines on the pattern to the fabric beneath, then the thread loops are cut and the pattern removed.

Tuck
Fold or pleat in fabric that is sewn in place, normally on the straight grain of the fabric. Often used to provide a decorative addition to a garment.

Underlay
Strip of fabric placed under the main fabric to strengthen it, for example under a pleat or buttonhole.

Understitch
Machine straight stitching through facing and seam allowances that is invisible from the right side; this helps the facing to lie flat.

Waistband
Band of fabric attached to the waist edge of a garment to provide a neat finish.

Warp
Lengthways threads or yarns of a woven fabric.

Warp knit
Made on a knitting machine, this knit is formed in a vertical and diagonal direction.

Weft
Threads or yarns that cross the warp of a woven fabric.

Weft knit
Made in the same way as hand knitting, this uses one yarn that runs horizontally.

Welt
Strip of fabric used to make the edges of a pocket.

Whip stitch
Diagonal hand stitch sewn along a raw edge to prevent fraying.

Wrong side
Reverse side of a fabric, the inside of a garment or other item.

Yoke
The top section of a dress or skirt from which the rest of the garment hangs.

Zigzag stitch
Machine stitch used to neaten and secure seam edges and for decorative purposes. The width and length of the zigzag can be altered.

Index

Acknowledgments

About the author

Alison Smith trained as an Art and Fashion Textile teacher, before becoming Head of Textiles at one of the largest schools in Birmingham, where she was able to pursue one of her key interests: the importance of teaching needlecrafts to boys, as well as girls. After successful spells as textiles tutor at the Liberty Sewing School, London, and the Janome Sewing School, Cheshire, Alison set up her own shop, Fabulous Fabric, and sewing school, Alison Victoria School of Sewing, in Ashby-de-la-Zouch, Leicestershire. Her school is the largest independent sewing school in England and offers courses and workshops on all aspects of dressmaking, tailoring, and corsetry.

Alison regularly lectures at specialist sewing shows, is a regular contributor to *Sewing World* magazine, and has appeared on ITV television series *Ladette to Lady* teaching dressmaking skills. She lives with her husband in Leicestershire, and has two grown-up children.

Author's acknowledgments

No book would ever be written without a little help. I would like to thank the following people for their help with the techniques and projects: Jackie Boddy, Nicola Corten, Ruth Cox, Helen Culver, Yvette Emmett, Averil Wing, and especially my husband, Nigel, for his continued encouragement and support, as well as my mother, Doreen Robbins, who is responsible for my learning to sew. The following companies have also provided invaluable help, by supplying the sewing machines, haberdashery, and fabrics: Janome UK Ltd, EQS, Linton, Adjustoform, Guttermann threads, the Button Company, YKK zips, Graham Smith Fabrics, Fabulous Fabric, Simplicity Patterns, and Freudenberg Nonwovens LP.

Dorling Kindersley would like to thank:

Sew Step by Step: Project editors Danielle Di Michiel and Alicia Ingty; Project art editors Neha Ahuja and Jane Ewart. A Little Course in Sewing: Authors Hilary Mandleberg and Caroline Bingham; Illustrator: Debajyoti Datta; Senior editor Alistair Laing; Project editor Becky Shakleton; Project art editors Gemma Fletcher and Ivy Roy; Andy Crawford and Dave King for photography; Susan Van Ha for photographic assistance. The Sewing Book: Project editors Norma MacMillan and Ariane Durkin; Project art editor Caroline de Souza; Designers Viv Brar, Nicola Collings, Mandy Earey, Heather McCarry; Peter Anderson and Kate Whitaker for photography. Also, Vanessa Bird for indexing;